Employee Voice in the Global North

Toyin Ajibade Adisa • Chima Mordi
Emeka Oruh
Editors

Employee Voice in the Global North

Insights from Europe, North America and Australia

palgrave
macmillan

Editors
Toyin Ajibade Adisa
University of East London
London, UK

Chima Mordi
Brunel University London
Uxbridge, UK

Emeka Oruh
Brunel University London
London, UK

ISBN 978-3-031-31125-3 ISBN 978-3-031-31123-9 (eBook)
https://doi.org/10.1007/978-3-031-31123-9

This Palgrave Macmillan imprint is published by the registered company Springer Nature Switzerland AG.
The registered company address is: Gewerbestrasse 11, 6330 Cham, Switzerland

Toyin
To my parents, Oyin, Shasili, and Adam

Chima
To Prof and Dr (Mrs.) Mordi, Tonbara, Nathaniel, and Daniel

Emeka
To Maryam, Elijah, Ciara, and Monique

Contents

Notes on Contributors

Toyin Ajibade Adisa is a senior lecturer at the Royal Docks School of Business and Law, University of East London, UK. He holds master's and PhD degrees in international business management and human resource management from University of East London (UEL) and Brunel University London, respectively. He has taught and researched issues in human resource management, organisational behaviour, employment relations, organisational culture, gender and inequality, flexibility and work-life balance, and reforms in emerging and developing economies. Toyin is a senior fellow of Higher Education Academy, a fellow of Chartered Management Institute (CMI), and a member of Chartered Institute of Personnel and Development (CIPD). Toyin has published articles in journals such as the *British Journal of Management* (BJM); *Work, Employment and Society* (WES); *Gender, Work & Organisation*; *Information Technology & People*; *Personnel Review*; *Employee Relations*; *Gender in Management*; *Journal of Managerial Psychology*; and *Career Development International*, among others. In addition, one of Toyin's articles was awarded the Emerald Literati Network Award: highly commended for best paper award 2017 Emerald Literati Network Awards for excellence. He is passionate about teaching and researching in HRM/OB subject area. Toyin is currently the associate director for Centre of Innovation, Management & Enterprise (CIME) and the course leader for the HRM undergraduate programme at University of East London.

John Burgess is Professor of Human Resource Management in Centre for Organisational Change and Agility, Torrens University Adelaide. Previous Professorial appointments were at the University of Newcastle; Curtin University, Perth; and RMIT University, Melbourne. Current research interests include skills shortages and skills development in the Asia Pacific region, job quality in the gig economy, and psychosocial hazards in the workplace. His most recent co-edited book is *A Field Guide to Managing Diversity, Equity, and Inclusion in Organisations* (Edward Elgar, 2022, editors Subas Dhakal, Roslyn Cameron, and John Burgess).

Laura Carlson is Professor of Private Law at Stockholm University. Carlson specialises in employment and labour law, gender, discrimination, academic freedom, and critical legal theories. She is a Visiting Research Fellow at the Institute of European and Comparative Law, University of Oxford. Carlson is the Editor-in-Chief, Brill Research Perspectives in Comparative Discrimination Law, co-editor of the peer-reviewed *International Journal of Discrimination and the Law*, and a board member of the Berkeley Center on Comparative Equality & Anti-Discrimination Law. Carlson's books include volume editor for *Scandinavian Studies in Law: Vol. 68 Equality* (2022), *The Fundamentals of Swedish Law* (2019), *Workers, Collectivism, and the Law: Grappling with Democracy* (2018), *Comparative Discrimination Law: Historical and Theoretical Frameworks*, Brill (2017), and *Searching for Equality: Sex Discrimination, Parental Leave and the Swedish Model with Comparisons to EU, UK, and US Law* (2007). Carlson has also served as an expert to the Swedish Parliament with respect to wage equality.

Magdalena Gilek is Lecturer in HRM and Organisational Behaviour at the Edinburgh Napier University. She has a PhD in Work and Employment from the University of Strathclyde and an MSc in Psychology from the University of Edinburgh. Her research interests focus on mental health, job quality and particularly on the impact of recent social changes (such as the rise of precarious employment) on young workers and their well-being. Her current research focuses on the effectiveness of well-being interventions in the workplace. She has presented her work at public and policy events in the UK and worldwide.

Nadia K. Kougiannou is Associate Professor of Work and Employment at Nottingham Trent University. Nadia's principal research interests traverse human resource management and work and employment relations. Recent research projects include labour voice and silence in the gig economy, algorithmic management and its effects on the employment relationship and workers' participation in the gig economy. She has written several book chapters, and her work has been published in leading international journals, including *Industrial Relations: A Journal of Economy and Society*, *Human Resource Management Journal*, *British Journal of Management*, *British Journal of Industrial Relations*, *New Technology, Work and Employment* and *Journal of Business Research*.

Pedro Mendonça is Lecturer in Human Resource Management and Organisational Behaviour at Edinburgh Napier University, The Business School. Before joining the School in May 2020, he was a lecturer in Nottingham Trent University, and from 2013 to 2016 he was Marie Curie Early-Stage Researcher for The Changing Employment Network. He is a member of the British Sociological Association and an Editor of the journal *Work, Employment and Society*. His research focuses on trade unions, European employment regulation, and platform work and the changes it produces on labour and the labour process. His work has appeared in *British Journal of Industrial Relation*, *British Journal of Management*, *New Technology, Work and Employment*, *Work, Employment and Society*, etc.

Chima Mordi is Reader in Human Resource Management and Employment Relations. He is Director of Post Graduate Research Brunel Business School, Brunel University London, Uxbridge, UK. He is also Director for Brunel Business School and Ahlia University, Bahrain PhD without residence partnership. He is also a visiting professor at Coal-City University and external examiner to over 15 universities in the UK, Bahrain, Nigeria, Ghana, etc. Chima's research focuses on the social nature of labour problems in Sub-Saharan Africa, Middle East, and Asia and their implications for the variable efficacy of Western management theories and practices. His primary research interests also lie in workload and work-life balance, work-life interface, flexible working arrangements, employee voice, and contemporary employment relations.

Chima has authored over 100 articles in refereed academic journals, practitioner outlets, international conference proceedings, and book chapters. His recent papers have appeared in various outlets, including *Work, Employment & Society* (WES); *Gender, Work & Organization*; *Journal of Managerial Psychology*; *International Journal of Human Resource Management*; *Technological Forecasting and Social Change*; *Thunderbird International Business Review*; *Personnel Review*; *Employee Relations*, and *Career Development International Journal*. In addition, Chima is also a recipient of the Emerald Literati Network awards for excellence.

Kehinde Olowookere is Assistant Professor of Human Resource Management (HRM) at Coventry University, UK. With professional experience in the public sector overseas, her work concentrates on the management and experiences of mental health conditions within the workplace, with particular focus on how difference is constructed within normative organisational contexts. More generally, her interests include the management of diversity and identity construction at work. She teaches a wide range of HRM subjects ranging from performance management and employee relations to basic people management practice. Currently, she is the Course Director for the PGCert Management and Leadership programme.

John Opute is Associate Professor of International HRM and Course Director of MSc International HRM programme in the LSBU Business School at London South Bank University, London. He has over 20 years of industry experience in general management and human resources management. He has a diverse educational and working background from Nigeria, North America (Canada and the USA) and Europe and has held key HR positions in several multinational companies such as Alcan Aluminium Company of Canada (with major responsibilities in Nigeria) and Cincinnati Bell in Ohio State, USA. During this period, he has led several HR initiatives and assignments. He is a senior fellow of the Higher Education Academy of the UK and belongs to various reputable professional associations including membership of the International Labour and Employment Relations Association (ILERA). He is a member of the editorial board of some international journals including *E-Journal of*

International and Comparative Labour Studies. His current research activities are in the areas of comparative international HRM (rewards/compensation management) and employee engagement/participation. His recent book—*HRM in Africa: Understanding New Scenarios and Challenges in an Emerging Economy*—provides the rare opportunity to understand the logic behind the approach of HRM practice in the continent.

Emeka Oruh is Senior Lecturer in Human Resource Management (HRM) and Organisational Behaviour (OB) at Brunel University London, UK, where he obtained a PhD in Employment Relations (ER) and Human Resource Management (HRM). Before now, he lectured at the University of Portsmouth School of Business and Law, UK. His key research examines OB, ER and HRM issues within international business—particularly in emerging and developing markets. Dr Emeka has authored several publications—most of which have appeared in ABS-rated international journals: *International Journal of Human Resource Management*, *International Journal of Contemporary Hospitality Management*, *Journal of Managerial Psychology* and *Employee Relations* journals, among others.

Michael Oyelere is Assistant Professor of International Human Resource Management and Industrial Relations at Coventry University. Previously he was Senior Lecturer of International Human Resource Management at Bedfordshire University, UK. He has authored a book, book chapters, and journal articles. Michael's research interests centre on employment relations and the role of trade unions in emerging economies. Michael's teaching is strongly research-informed and currently teaches on International Human Resource Studies and Industrial Relations at postgraduate level. Michael is a member of several academic and professional bodies including the Chartered Institute of Personnel and Development (CIPD), the Chartered Management Institute, the British Academy of Management (BAM), the British Universities Industrial Relations Association (BUIRA), and a fellow of the Higher Education Academy (HEA). He is currently the SIG Track Chair for the BAM HRM Special Interest Group. Michael is an award-winning scholar, awarded the prestigious Economic and Social Research Council (ESRC) award to undertake his PhD.

Temitope Oyelere is Lecturer of Accounting at Middlesex University. Prior to this, she worked in the financial service industry, including KPMG. Her research interests focus on accounting and accountability in charitable organisations. She is interested in the rule His Majesty Revenue and Customs (HMRC) plays in enforcing compliance. She is a fellow of the Association of Chartered Certified Accountants (ACCA). She is currently a research degree candidate at Middlesex University, United Kingdom. Her research focuses on the issue of accountability in charitable organisations in developing economies. Her teaching also centred around financial management and financial accounting. She has previously published a book chapter in the book: *Financial and Managerial Aspects in Human Resource Management*. Her chapter was titled 'Managing Relocation Costs'.

Sean Edmund Rogers is Spachman Professor of Human Resource and Labor Relations and Professor of Management at the University of Rhode Island College of Business. He also currently serves as Vice President at Chief Diversity Officer at University of Rhode Island (URI). He conducts research on the topics of labor and employment relations, employment discrimination, workforce diversity, and volunteerism, and has published in several leading journals including *ILR Review*, *British Journal of Industrial Relations*, *Academy of Management Discoveries*, *Human Resource Management Review*, and others. Rogers earned a PhD in industrial relations and human resources from Rutgers University, and holds master's degrees from Wake Forest School of Law, University of Illinois Urbana-Champaign and Embry-Riddle Aeronautical University. He holds the Senior Professional in Human Resources (SPHR) certification by the HR Certification Institute and is a Society for Human Resource Management Senior Certified Professional (SHRM-SCP).

Al Rainnie is Research Professor at UniSA, currently working on an ARC project on Troubled Regions (with Sally Weller). Al has researched in the area of labour process analysis, spatiality, work and employment for about 40 years and has published over 100 books, book chapters, journal articles and research reports. Al was the founding Director of the Monash Institute for Regional Studies and Director of Research at both the Centre for Labour Market Studies at the University of Leicester and the Curtin Graduate School of Business. Al's most recent work has been, firstly, on spatiality, Global Production Networks, Global Destruction Networks, waste and labour; and secondly on regions and regional development in Australia.

Arlene Sale is a PhD student at Torrens University, Centre for Organisational Change and Agility. Her research interests include employee voice, organisational change, skills development, and labour regulation in the Philippines and Australia.

Jonathan Sale is Program Director for Human Resource Management and Supply Chain Management and Lecturer in HRM at UniSA Business, University of South Australia. He teaches undergraduate and postgraduate courses on employment relations, industrial relations, and HRM, and conducts research on topics such as employment skills and strategies, labour disputes settlement, labour relations policy, labour and comparative law, labour laws and labour markets, labour regulation and informal work, social security and migrant work, worker voice, decent work, and sustainable development. His study areas include Australia, Malaysia, Philippines, and ASEAN.

List of Tables

1

Introducing Employee Voice in the Global North

Toyin Ajibade Adisa, Chima Mordi, and Emeka Oruh

In today's world of work, workers' interests and their ability to speak up or remain silent about work-related issues remain salient. This position has popularised discussion of the concepts of employee voice and silence in the media, among academics, and among business practitioners. Human resources (employees) remain the backbone of any organisation. Even robotic and artificial intelligence organisations still require human assistance to function very well at various stages. Therefore, humans are involved and cannot be completely set aside in organisation systems.

T. Ajibade Adisa (✉)
University of East London, London, UK
e-mail: t.adisa@uel.ac.uk

C. Mordi
Brunel University London, Uxbridge, UK
e-mail: Chima.Mordi@brunel.ac.uk

E. Oruh
Brunel University London, London, UK
e-mail: emeka.oruh@brunel.ac.uk

T. Ajibade Adisa et al. (eds.), *Employee Voice in the Global North*,
https://doi.org/10.1007/978-3-031-31123-9_1

Thus, the concept of employee voice advocates active rather than passive involvement of employees in work and organisation-related issues. It projects employees as important stakeholders whose ideas, opinions, concerns, complaints, and suggestions must be taken seriously and acted upon, which gives rise to the phenomenon of employee involvement, whose adoption could be direct or indirect. Employee voice entail the various mechanisms by which employees are able to exert their input—formally or informally, collectively or individually—in organisational decision-making processes, with the goal of influencing not just their personal and work-related interests but also those of their superiors and organisations (Barry & Wilkinson, 2016; Wilkinson et al., 2020). The contrast here is employee silence, where employees' means of participating in organisational decision-making process is rendered near impossible or disabled at worse, which also presents numerous implications for the individuals and organisations in question (Dundon & Gollan, 2007; Morrison, 2014). Employee silence is the withholding of genuine expression and information about the organisation from important stakeholders who can make things happen in an organisation. Silence may be acquiescent—a passive withholding of relevant information—or quiescent—an active withholding of relevant information, which is often done because of fear and potential risk (see Pinder & Harlos, 2001).

Since Hirschman's study (1970) on exit, voice, and loyalty, the concept of employee voice has incrementally gained scholarly prominence across many disciplines, including employment relations, human resource management, and organisational behaviour. However, the employment relations and human resource management view of employee voice differs from that of the organisational behaviour view, with the former looking at the efficacy of employees' ability to have a say in the affairs of the organisation in which they work (Freeman et al., 2007; Wilkinson & Fay, 2011) and the latter capturing employee voice in the context of 'extra-role upward communication behaviour', which can enhance organisational operations (Morrison, 2014, p. 174). Based on the works of researchers such as Gollan et al. (2015), the employment relations and human resource management perception of employee voice prescribe that employees exert some degree of their fundamental right to (voice) expression and control over managerial decisions, and without such opportunity, they will be left with a sense of diminished dignity (Wilkinson et al., 2010). However, from the organisational behaviour perspective, Barry and Wilkinson (2016) explain that the employee voice arrangement is initiated to ensure operational efficiency among other strategic concerns of the organisation; hence, the practice relies on managerial discretion as to whether the existing voice arrangement should remain unchanged, strengthened, or eliminated entirely, which often depends on specific factors such as an economic downturn.

The concept of employee voice is often seen as a diluted version of other related constructs, such as employee participation, which does not involve having influence or sharing power, but, as noted by Wilkinson et al. (2010) and Morrison (2014), the enactment of participation can only be possible in circumstances in which employee voice is prevalent. Employment relations and human resource management focus on how the concept is defined and structured as well as the effectiveness of employees' various modes of participation, including the collective and individual process, union or non-union mechanisms, direct and indirect approaches, or formal and informal approaches, among others (Gollan & Patmore, 2013). Although employee voice in this context can be prosocial because of its assumed inclination to benefit organisations, it is also viewed as a means by which employees can individually or collectively counter management's overindulgences. The context can also bring to life self-determining efforts by workers to see themselves in manners that set their interests aside from those of their organisations (Barry & Wilkinson, 2016). Much of the employment relations and human resource management debate has largely explored how (and for what reasons) employee voice systems are put in place (Dundon & Gollan, 2007), how they are implemented, and their outcomes (Marchington, 2007). Importantly, researchers have explored the 'degree', 'level', and 'range' at which employee participation process are being arranged, which is a useful heuristic for investigating employee voice efficacy (Wilkinson et al., 2013). In terms of 'degree', researchers such as Viveros et al. (2018) have questioned the extent to which employees can actually be involved in decision-making processes that relate to organisational affairs or whether the process is simply about informing or consulting by smokescreen, rather than by involving them actively in the whole change process. In the case of 'level', the authors explore whether employees can express their voices regarding issues such as tasks, departments, establishments, and whether this is at the corporate level or not. Finally, the third dimension points to the 'range' of subject matters in which employees are enabled to have an input, ranging from operational concerns, a need to improve the production line, and investment strategies, among other strategic concerns. Appelbaum and Batt (1995) draw on the nature or form by which employee participation can be facilitated to determine the efficacy of employee voice. This position may include employees being involved in daily work-related affairs via online media or employees being encouraged to make contributions in person at the organisational premises—also known as the formal scheme or offline approach. As Gomez et al. (2010) note, such a range of participatory mechanisms explore the pro-social means of advancing the operations of the organisations and serve as a medium for challenging managerial excesses.

While it is often assumed that a formalised structure is the most effective way of implementing employee voice practice, informal voice structures have emerged recently in the context of non-programmed relationships between managers and employees, which appear as a useful mechanism for information sharing and consultation within organisations. This is particularly useful for employees who may desire the opportunity to voice, albeit via a range of other voice channels, as opposed to a single voice choice (Morrison, 2011; Mowbray et al., 2015). It is important to note that the extant literature on employee voice has uncovered crucial findings, but there remain some limitations that necessitate further exploration of the concept, both theoretically and practically. This book examines employee voice in broad but specific contexts, including at macro (societal), meso (organisational), and micro (individual) levels. At the societal level, the regulatory framework shaping organisational policy needs to be scrutinised, while the voice systems adopted and the degree to which they are implemented by organisations at the departmental level should be considered (Kwon et al., 2016). Finally, the individual-level motivator that is responsible for motivating or demotivating employee voice expression also needs more critical examination (Morrison, 2014). To further the exploration of these macro, meso, and micro levels for a more nuanced understanding of the concept of employee voice, this book examines employee voice in the global north. It draws on insights from countries in Europe, North America, and Australia. The book contains seven chapters, each of which examines different topics related to employee voice and is based on conceptual, theoretical, and empirical methods, using qualitative and quantitative methodologies. Following this introductory chapter, Chap. 2 present a synthesis and overview of some of the early conceptualisations of employee voice and unionism in the UK. The chapter highlights the current state and projects the future of employee voice and unionism in the UK. The chapter reveals how the concept of voice has been significantly reinvented by modern-day scholars and further reveals management's unwillingness to implement employees' demands during the current permacrisis. Chapter 3 examines different perspectives on employee voice in the US through a historical and contemporary examination of workers' voice and influence in their workplaces and work experiences. The chapter situates the concept of worker voice within the context of two important theories on employment relationship: the unitarist and pluralist theories of employment relations. This approach helps us understand employees' and employers' interests; the alignment and tension between them; and how this shapes voice activation, actualisation, and efficacy. The chapter also examines various manifestations of employee voice in American workplaces. Chapter 4 examines the state of employee voice and engagement in the Greek organisations by reviewing recent publications on employee voice in the Greek context. The chapter highlights the subtleties of employee voice and engagement in the Greek context, which is characterised by weak institutional foundations such as employment policies, employment protection, industrial relations, and social protection. The chapter highlights potential managerial implications and provides an agenda for future research. Chapter 5 examines established and newly developed voice trajectories and channels in Portugal and the impacts thereof on the representation of workers at macro, meso, and micro levels. As trade union membership and influence decline, Portuguese employees may be in search of innovative and novel ways of expressing dissent and having their interests represented. The chapter uses conceptual and empirical approaches to explore and elaborate on (1) workers' motivations in building new and developing existing voice channels, (2) the content and purpose of different voice channels, and (3) the outcomes in terms of voice effectiveness, employment conditions, and working lives. Chapter 6 examines the legal regulations and balance of collective and individual employee voice within the Swedish labour law model. Employee voice is exercised almost exclusively through the labour unions in Sweden. Employees receive information, are consulted, and are a part of codetermination/joint decision-making only through the unions and employee participation in unions. The Swedish labour unions are tenacious in retaining this power and privilege. The chapter presents the development of the Swedish (and Nordic) labour law model based on single-channel employee voice. It then discusses collective bargaining, industrial action, and codetermination between employers and labour unions. The chapter also discusses the lack of access to justice mechanisms that could enable individual employee voice, particularly with respect to issues of grievances in Sweden. Chapter 7 examines the role of employee voice in addressing mental health issues in Polish workplaces. Employee mental health and wellbeing is a responsibility of every organisation, but in practice, most organisations do not recognise the role of employee voice as a means of promoting wellbeing. The chapter discusses the sharp decline of collective representational forms of voice in Poland and the issues associated with quality of work. Chapter 8 examines the evolution of the employee voice mechanism in Australia and how social media has been used to publicise workplace issues, support employee voice, and support coalitions of employee and non-governmental organisation activism in terms of improving working conditions. The chapter highlights the diversity of and the relationship between different voice mechanisms and evaluates the role of social media in providing workers with voice in terms of publicising and securing action to settle grievances that extend beyond the workplace. These chapters expand the scope of debate on the topic of employee voice and thereby broaden our knowledge and understanding of it. Issues discussed in each chapter are not absolute. Rather, they are intended to stimulate further thinking and open frontiers for further research on employee voice in the global north. This book thus calls for further country-specific research on employee voice across the globe to better understand the topic in different contexts.

References

Appelbaum, E., & Batt, R. (1995). Worker participation in diverse settings: Does the form affect the outcome, and if so, who benefits? *British Journal of Industrial Relations, 33*(3), 353–378.

Barry, M., & Wilkinson, A. (2016). Pro-Social or Pro-Management? A Critique of the Conception of Employee Voice as a Pro-Social Behaviour within Organizational Behaviour. *British Journal of Industrial Relations, 54*(2), 261–284.

Dundon, T., & Gollan, P. J. (2007). Re-conceptualising voice in the non-union workplace. *International Journal of Human Resource Management, 18*(7), 1182–1198.

Freeman, R., Boxall, P., & Haynes, P. (2007). *What workers say: Employee voice in the Anglo-American workplace.* Cornell University Press.

Gollan, P. J., Kaufman, B. E., Taras, D., & Wilkinson, A. (Eds.). (2015). *Voice and involvement at work: Experience with non-union representation.* Routledge.

Gollan, P. J., & Patmore, G. (2013). Theoretical perspectives of legal regulation and industrial relations at the workplace: Limits and challenges of interdisciplinary employee voice. *Journal of Industrial Relations, 55*(4), 488–506.

Gomez, R., Bryson, A., & Willman, P. (2010). Voice in the wilderness? The shift from union to non-union voice in Britain. In A. Wilkinson, P. J. Gollan, M. Marchington, & D. Lewin (Eds.), *The Oxford handbook of participation in organizations* (pp. 383–406). Oxford University Press.

Hirschman, A. (1970). *Exit, voice and loyalty: Response to decline in firms, organisations and states.* Harvard University Press.

Kwon, B., Farndale, E., & Park, J. G. (2016). Employee voice and work engagement: Macro, meso, and micro-level drivers of convergence? *Human Resource Management Review, 26*(4), 327–337.

Marchington, M. (2007). Employee voice systems. In P. Boxall, J. Purcell, & P. Wright (Eds.), *The Oxford handbook of human resource management* (pp. 231–250). Oxford University Press.

Morrison, E. W. (2011). Voice and silence within organizations: Literature review and directions for future research. *The Academy of Management Annals, 5*(1), 373–412.

Morrison, E. W. (2014). Employee voice and silence. *Annual Review of Organizational Psychology and Organizational Behaviour, 1*, 173–197.

Mowbray, P. K., Wilkinson, A., & Tse, H. H. M. (2015). An integrative review of employee voice: Identifying a common conceptualization and research agenda. *International Journal of Management Reviews, 17*(3), 382–400.

Pinder, C. C., & Harlos, K. P. (2001). Employee silence: Quiescence and acquiescence as responses to perceived injustice. In K. M. Rowland & G. R. Ferris (Eds.), *Research in personnel and human resources management* (Vol. 20, pp. 331–369). JAI Press.

Viveros, H., Kalfa, S., & Gollan, P. J. (2018). Voice as empowerment practice: The case of an Australian manufacturing company. In P. J. Gollan & D. Lewin (Eds.), *Advances in industrial and labor relations* (Vol. 24, pp. 93–114). Emerald Group Publishing.

Wilkinson, A., Dundon, T., Donaghey, J., & Freeman, R. (Eds.). (2020). Employee voice: Charting new terrain. In *The handbook of research on employee voice* (2nd ed.). Edward Elgar Press.

Wilkinson, A., Dundon, T., & Marchington, M. (2013). Employee involvement and voice. In S. Bach & M. Edwards (Eds.), *Managing human resources* (pp. 268–288). Blackwell.

Wilkinson, A., & Fay, C. (2011). New times for employee voice? *Human Resource Management, 50*(1), 65–74.

Wilkinson, A., Gollan, P., Lewin, D., & Marchington, M. (2010). Conceputualising participation in organisations. In A. Wilkinson, P. J. Gollan, M. Marchington, & D. Lewin (Eds.), *The Oxford handbook of participation in organisations* (pp. 3–25). Oxford University Press.

2

The Conceptualisation of Employee Voice in Permacrisis: A UK Perspective

Michael Oyelere, Kehinde Olowookere, Temitope Oyelere, John Opute, and Toyin Ajibade Adisa

Introduction

The use of the term 'voice' has increased in recent years, and both academic and practitioner literature are more frequently deploying the term (Wilkinson, Donaghey et al., 2020). Research on employment relations

M. Oyelere (✉) • K. Olowookere
Coventry University, Coventry, UK
e-mail: ad1753@coventry.ac.uk

T. Oyelere
Middlesex University, London, UK

J. Opute
London South Bank University, London, UK

T. Ajibade Adisa
University of East London, London, UK
e-mail: t.adisa@uel.ac.uk

T. Ajibade Adisa et al. (eds.), *Employee Voice in the Global North*,
https://doi.org/10.1007/978-3-031-31123-9_2

often adopts analytical frameworks primarily related to the concept of 'voice'. While the term 'voice' was originally defined as the effort to effect change by Hirschman (1970), its meanings and conceptualisations have since evolved. Later writers, such as Freeman and Medoff (2016), have described the concept from the viewpoint of union monopoly of representation, that is union articulation of workers' concerns. This chapter is a synthesis and overview of some of the early conceptualisations of employee voice in the UK. Its goal extends beyond a simplistic sketch, catalogue, or historical analysis of voice and uses such analysis as an instrument for understanding the current state and trajectory of employee voice and unionism in the UK. The chapter has been conceived in light of current social, political, and economic developments that have led to a state of permacrisis. The chapter reveals that the concept of voice has been significantly reinvented by modern-day scholars and practitioners.

The research of Marchington and Kynighou (2012, p. 1) revealed that the global financial crisis has had a significant impact on the practice of human resource management and has thus shaped issues concerning employee voice, employee involvement, and employee participation in their organisation. Similarly, there is a consensus among researchers that the voice, participation, and involvement of employees are used by employers as a tool for high commitment among employees at times when the world seems to experience a level of steady economic development (Wood, 2010; Boxall & Purcell, 2011; Marchington & Kynighou, 2012; Marchington, 2015). Although, the techniques used by organisations and in different industries vary. However, the consensus that employees are involved in their organisation's decision-making process at some level remains constant. This supposition immediately gives rise to one important question: What is the state of employee involvement and participation during this period of permacrisis? Alternatively, how is employee voice construed during years that are characterised by economic, political, financial, and environmental crises?

Interestingly, in the UK, the literature on employee voice has increased in volume, but not many works have focused on understanding voice during permacrisis. Although the term 'permacrisis' was Collins Dictionary's word of the year for 2022, it has always been part of our lexicon. The concept is a combination of two words 'permanent' and 'crisis', and succinctly describes the political and economic state of the UK (Turnbull, 2022). Inevitably, both the political and economic state of a nation determines the situations in organisations. Hence, the question of how employee voice is perceived today is highly relevant. To answer this question, we juxtapose two approaches: industrial and labour process theory (employment relations approach) with work psychology (organisational behaviour approach). Although there are several other relevant approaches, this chapter focuses on these two, given their similarities and some sharp contrasts. Labour process theory is a sociological approach according to which voice rationale is about power and control through the process of collective bargaining, work council, and partnership (Chillas & Marks, 2021). The approach is based on a radical-pluralist (power-sharing) philosophy. On the other hand, the organisational behaviour approach, a psychological approach, explains the rationale for voice through job design improvement. Its philosophical basis is mainly unitarist, articulated through the engagement and commitment of employees (Barry et al., 2018). The structure of the chapter is as follows: first, we consider the different conceptualisations of voice and theoretical perceptions of the concept. Next, we consider voice in the context of the permacrisis in the UK and then explore the future of employee voice. We conclude with a discussion of the implications of the systematic review.

Organisational Behaviour and Industrial Relations Conceptualisation of Voice

The term 'voice' has increasingly gained prominence in both practitioner and academic literature on industrial/employee relations, human resource management and organisational behaviour. When referring to the term 'voice', academics from other disciplines often use terms such as engagement, involvement, participation, and empowerment interchangeably. This approach, however, does not capture the true essence of the word from the perspective of employees and their unions. Employee voice has often taken centre stage in the works of Sydney and Beatrice Webb, Karl

Max, and Adam Smith. More recently, the use of the term has eclipsed other managerial prerogatives (Wilkinson et al., 2021), which again failed to define the word precisely. From the early days of conceptualisation of the term 'employee and union voice', it has experienced significant changes in meaning and usage. Academics and practitioners in different fields frequently give specific meanings to relevant terms in line with how they are perceived in their field. According to Wilkinson and Fay (2011), this difference in meaning arises because academics do not understand the conceptual and philosophical views of other academics in different fields.

One element of voice is considered from the organisational behaviour and managerial standpoint. This element articulates voice as an informal type of vocal communication aimed at providing constructive suggestions to a management team by an employee. This approach often focuses on the individual employee's suggestions and feedback for the management team (Wilkinson & Barry, 2016). This is one of the reasons why much literature on voice within the field of management often takes the organisational behaviour perspective (Dibben et al., 2022). For example, the economic approach, whose roots can be traced to transactional cost economics, perceives voice as a form of 'batter', with implications in costs and benefits for both the management and employees (Willman et al., 2021). In this instance, employees are seen as 'customers' who exit the patronage of the business if their voice is not heard. Meanwhile, the management may choose the most cost-effective option from the various options available to them. This is a utilitarian (transaction-efficacy) model. The work of Dibben et al. (2022, p. 4) seems to advance this position in that it suggests that studies of advanced economies often describe voice from a unitarist philosophical standpoint that emphasises job design and organisational improvement. A clear understanding of this individualistic utilitarian approach is essential for a thorough grasp of the approach to voice in a period of permacrisis.

Another theoretical approach that we consider in this chapter is the human resource management/high-performance work systems approach. Voice from this theoretical standpoint is thought to be the response of an organisation to customers' attitudes towards their product or services (Hirschman, 1970). The rationale for voice according to this approach mainly concerns organisational performance (Allen, 2021). According to Hirschman (1970), voice is 'any attempt at all to change rather than to escape from an objectionable state of affairs' (p. 30). The most important point about voice here is how to ensure that improvement is made and that customers are kept happy. In terms of attempting to satisfy external customers, Dundon et al. (2004) reiterate that those internal customers (employees) who are dissatisfied with the work systems may be forced to act because of a lack of alternative employment. Hirschman's (1970) position is that voiced concerns or voicing are likely to lead management to make decisions (Wilkinson et al., 2021).

There are several studies that examine the factors surrounding the concept of voice. Examining voice from the organisational behaviour or psychological perspective is likely to give a clear picture of why employees want or do not want to voice their concerns with management. According to Dibben et al. (2022), such examinations often serve the interests of management. Employees tend to voice their concerns in cases in which employee voicing has previously led to a favourable outcome for employees. Detert and Burris (2007) note that employees are only active in advancing their voice if they perceive their manager to be 'open': 'that their boss listens to them, is interested in their ideas, gives fair consideration to the ideas presented, and at least sometimes takes action to address the matter raised' (p. 871). Openness in this case is seen as reducing the inequality (especially of power) between employees and the management. Additionally, the study of Detert and Treviño (2010), which examines the influence of leaders on employees' perceptions, concludes that the expectations of employees concerning their use of their voice depend on whether the voice will be accepted or rejected by their managers rather than on their views about the framework or mechanism of voice employed. Research has shown that it is possible for management to collate employee voice in such a manner that is beneficial to the organisation and the employees (Cox et al., 2006; Dietz et al., 2011; Townsend et al., 2013).

Conversely, however, there are also situations in which managers are seen as discouraging employee voice. Instances, in which employee voice is met with negative outcomes, such as stigmatisation and villainization can result in employees avoiding exercising their voice (Robinson & Shuck, 2019; McNulty et al., 2018). Donaghey et al. (2011)

acknowledge that there has been an increase in the number of organisational behaviour studies reporting employee silence. The key observation of their study relates to management uses of agenda-setting and organisational structure to encourage silence concerning certain issues in the organisation. While employees may consider not exercising their voice as an option, this may also have some negative consequences for them. Their management is likely to construe employee silence as disloyalty and misbehaviour. Furthermore, the study of Wæraas and Dahle (2020, p. 1), which examines the relationship between human resource management, organisation reputation management, and employee voice, finds that organisations often follow a path of chosen reputation through their official voice and discourage prohibitive employee voice with coercive human resource management practices. Hence, there is a tendency for management to use their prerogative in their management of employees' use of voice (Donaghey et al., 2011).

It is noteworthy that examining voice solely from the organisational behaviour perspective does not result in sufficient understanding of the concept. In fact, according to Dibben et al. (2022), the growing 'psychologisation of voice' has been criticised because of the increasing focus on management prerogative and interests; the individualistic rather than collective approach; contextual factors; and the downplaying of the power wielded by institutions over its employees and the role of external stakeholders (Barry & Wilkinson, 2022; Burris et al., 2017). Moreover, academics within the organisational behaviour field criticise the approach as it is employed in the field for being too narrow. They argue that there is a tendency among organisational behaviour scholars to focus on voice that advances the prerogative nature and interests of management and to overlook the extent to which informal voice behaviour is influenced by formal collective voice mechanisms (Morrison, 2023). Conversely, however, the industrial relations or labour process theory considers voice as the inherent right and capacity of employees to demand and protect their interests. According to this approach, voice is considered in the formal, informal, and structured settings that allow collective action and divergence between management and employees' desires. The industrial relations approach to voice addresses some of the concerns that arise when following the organisational behaviour approach because it enunciates the bases of the relationship between employees and management and it focuses on broader social, political, economic, and environmental factors that have direct and indirect impacts on employment relationships (Chillas & Marks, 2021), including legal enactments, labour laws, and the practice of human resource management (Edwards, 2011).

Employee voice refers to both the formal and informal techniques or mechanisms employed by workers and their unions to influence decision-making in their organisation. Due to the relevance of the term in the life of working people, it has consistently evolved and has now masked other organisational processes, such as involvement, participation, engagement, and empowerment (Chillas & Marks, 2021, p. 85). As earlier mentioned, some of these terms are used interchangeably to refer to voice, while in other situations, they signify a completely different meaning. The choice and meaning of a specific term are based on the relevant theoretical strand and the philosophical meaning employed within that theoretical strand. For example, as pointed out above, the human resource management/high-power work system approach defines voice as a process that involves employees in making decisions about their wellbeing and working conditions while ensuring that management can carry out the necessary improvement in the workplace (Chillas & Marks, 2021; Mowbray et al., 2015). The industrial relations or labour process theory/approach is more critical of how employees' and employers' interests can be harmonised. It is this level of criticality that made this theoretical strand more acceptable as an approach that mitigates managerial prerogative and the misuse of employee voice simply for managerial gain. There has, however, been some criticism of this approach. Ramsay (1977) warned against the use of participation mechanisms as tools for furthering management interests. Ramsay (1985) further argued that a lack of state involvement is likely to leave the process at the whims of management. Due to the decline in trade unionism and individualisation projects by management, the power of collectivism and trade unions can be considered to have been eroded.

Regardless of the relevant conceptualisation, theoretical strand, and philosophical standpoint that is being considered, employee voice is centrally about the management of workplace relationships (Dundon et al., 2004). While management is doing all it can to control employees, the process of wrestling back some of the control and ensuring that workers' interests are at the fore has become increasingly important both to management and academics. Labour process theory captures the core of the processes and mechanisms that demonstrate the functionality of a system within organisations and especially between management and employees or employee representatives. Although the establishment of a single definition of the term 'employee voice' may be difficult given the divergent philosophical approaches employed in different fields, for the purpose of this chapter, we provide an articulate meaning of the term 'employee voice' as expressed in Table 2.1: 'Employee voice' refers to the formal or informal methods used by employees—either individually or collectively—to articulate their concerns, seek a better working environment

Table 2.1 Multiple meanings of employee voice

Voice as:	Purpose and articulation of voice	Mechanism and practices for voice	Range of outcomes
Articulation of individual dissatisfaction	To rectify a problem with management or prevent deterioration in relations	Complain to line manager grievance procedure	Exist-loyalty
Expression of collective organisation	To provide a countervailing source of power to management	Union recognition collective bargaining industrial action	Partnership-derecognition
Contribution to management decision-making	To seek improvements in work organisation quality and productivity	Upward problem-solving groups. Quality circles. Suggestions scheme attitude surveys. Self-managed teams	Identity and commitment. Disillusionment and apathy. Improved performance
Demonstration of mutuality and cooperative relations	To achieve long-term viability for organisation and its employees	Partnership agreement. Joint consultative committees. Work councils	Significant influence over management decisions-marginalisation and sweetheart deals

Source: Wilkinson et al. (2021, p. 6)

for themselves, and foster the interests of management and other stakeholders.

Contextualising Voice During a Permacrisis

While recent developments are important, we consider the long-term picture, including developments in relations to gig economy. We attempt to understand the new realism of what employee voice stands for and what it can achieve. Uber drivers spent about five years in court before they could be heard, and today, teachers, lecturers, nurses, and train drivers (to mention but a few) are all preparing for 'battles' with their employers. Can we conclude that employees' attempts to speak out are making their issues worse? Should employees accept this position and remain permanently silent? Where exactly is the voice of employees in the UK during this permacrisis? Historically, the UK is known for passing laws that support the rights of workers. Employment law emanates from parliament through the legislative process and in the courts through judicial decisions. All these laws and processes consider the rights of employees, especially voice. However, since late 1970, there have been laws introduced that tend to curtail some of these rights or give prerogative to management (Kaufman, 2020). The frequent argument given by successive governments is that there is a need to ensure that businesses develop and grow. However, some scholars have observed that surrendering the rights of employees to employers does not necessarily develop and grow businesses (Ioannou & Dukes, 2021).

Nevertheless, there now appears to be a continuous problem in the global economy. We therefore ask how employee voice is considered in today's Britain. There are indications that employee voice is increasingly being stiffened by employers and by the government during this situation of permacrisis. According to the CIPD (2022), 'the ability of employees to express their views, opinions, concerns and suggestions, and for these to influence decisions at work' is constantly under attack. In some organisations, employees can no longer have their say through individual and collective channels, and it is becoming increasingly difficult for employees to speak directly to management or indirectly through employee representatives and trade unions. Although formal and informal voice techniques such as employee surveys, consultation groups, team meetings, and business intranets are still open to employees, there is evidence that the voice expressed is hardly implemented, except in cases in which it aligns with the management's interests (Prouska et al., 2022). In an extensive study that examines large multinational, national, and regional organisations in airline logistics, fast food, education, health, and construction, King et al. (2021) reveal the current dilemma facing employee voice. Their study suggests that even in cases in which the channels of employee voice are open, they are only open for issues that align with management interests. The study identifies the forms of voice experienced in the workplace and presents an overview of the study participants' responses (see Fig. 2.1).

Given the current economic climate, exacerbated by the backdrop of the coronavirus pandemic, political instability, Brexit, inflation, and recession, UK employers and the government are turning a deaf ear to employees' voice. While the research of King et al. (2021, p. 31) shows that the channels of employee voice are open, it concludes that these

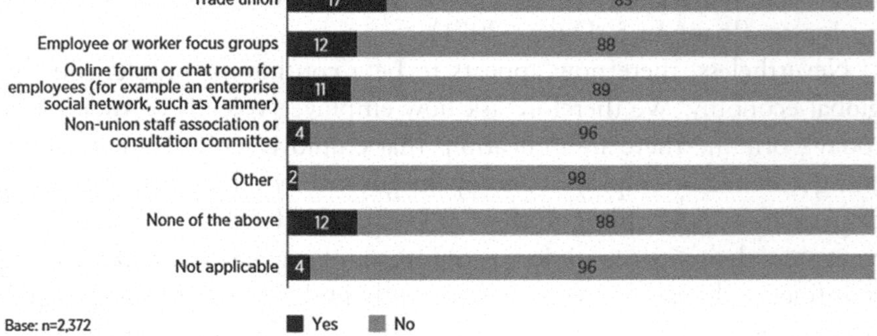

Fig. 2.1 Forms of voice experienced in the workplace (%). (Source: Shipton et al. (2019))

channels alone cannot guarantee successful exercise of employee voice. For example, the study shows that only 17% of its respondents experienced the use of voice through the trade union relevant to their organisation (Fig. 2.1). Additionally, 96% were found to have had no experience at all with non-union staff associations or consultation committees in their organisation. It is therefore imperative that we re-examine the nature and application of voice in this period of permacrisis. It is insufficient to assume that employee voice has always been part of the industrial relations system and that employees are aware of the channels without considering the level of awareness and access to the channels or without transforming the expectations among employees (King et al., 2021).

The Future of Employee Voice in the UK

The concept of employee voice in the UK has evolved over the years and is continuing to develop. Initially, it was needed primarily in the collective format—through unions—for securing basic employee rights. From the 1960s, it was promoted for organisations as a means of incorporating workers' opinions and gaining a competitive advantage in the market. Voice has become even more prominent since the 1980s, with increased attention being paid to how managerial concepts such as total quality, teamwork, and empowerment contribute to business performance (Wilkinson et al., 2021). The concept has, however, experienced changes as the employment relations environment continues to adapt to a dynamic labour market, shaped by major developments, such as Brexit (Prouska et al., 2022), and the resulting effects on businesses and increased globalisation. We consider two developments that have contributed to the evolution of voice: digitalisation and the growth of non-standard employment. First, discussions of the future of voice in the UK must acknowledge that the context of voice in the UK is the outcome of several considerations, including the social, economic, legislative, and cultural contexts within which businesses and employees operate. Legislation plays a key role, as different countries have different amounts and levels of employment legislation and voice opportunities. The more organised the regulatory structure is, the more likely it is that employee relations measures are in place and that employees are protected (Oyetunde et al., 2021). The UK is typically classified as a liberal market economy, characterised by the devolution of wage negotiations, defensive union tactics, constrained employment policies by the government, easy recourse to flexible working arrangements, extensive external labour markets, and restricted employment protection. This supports the managerial tendency to regulate employee voice and silent opposing views (Gegenhuber et al., 2021). Yet, while voice is challenged, it remains prevalent in the country (Prouska et al., 2022), particularly in large organisations.

Non-standard Employment

Recent years have seen the advent of new sectors, business models, and employment arrangements. There has been a growth in non-standard employment opportunities (Wilkinson et al., 2021); freelance or gig-economy jobs; self-employment; seasonal work; outsourced contracting; agency and part-time jobs; disguised employment; multiparty employment; on-call/zero-hour contracts; temporary employment; and precarious working arrangements, which are all characterised by insecurity, instability, and temporal flexibility. It has been projected that the number of employees taking up such jobs will continue to rise (ILO, 2016), and indeed, it has risen because of the effects of the coronavirus pandemic on work designs and the increase in non-traditional and remote jobs (Oyetunde et al., 2021). Traditional jobs typically have income protection, long-term career prospects, continuous work, required working hours, and contract longevity. Conversely, employees working in non-standard jobs have a high level of flexibility in their working location and hours; regulate their work processes and scheduling; have a reduced level of employer control; and have restricted administrative, physical, and temporal attachments to their employer. These jobs are often flexible with more influence on working arrangements (Haapakorpi, 2021). The term 'disguised work' refers to employees with concealed legal standing due to the nature of the role in which they are engaged (gig employees and freelancers). Zero-hour employment typically involves a high degree of irregularity in working hours. Multiparty roles have multiple parties involved in the employment process (temporary agencies). Part-time employment involves condensed working hours, accompanied by some level of perpetuity compared with other temporary employees (Zeytinoglu & Cooke, 2008). Fixed-term contracts run for a set amount of time and are terminated at a set date, either based upon the completion of a task or event. Temporary work arrangements include fixed-term roles, project-based contracts, casual work, and seasonal work (Oyetunde et al., 2021).

Much of the extant literature on voice has focused on the outcomes, inhibitors/determinants, and dimensions of voice for traditional employees, and less attention has been given to non-traditional employees' voice—the voice of those who occupy the aforementioned atypical job positions. Existing literature also assumes the uniformity of employees, and less attention has been given to the particularities of atypical employees. Therefore, there is an opportunity to develop the theoretical models of diversity in voice literature (Syed, 2014). The absence of theorisation for these employees has resulted in a limited understanding of employee voice. As more and more people are undertaking informal employment, it has become important that these employees have a voice and can express their perspectives. Research suggests that non-standard employment arrangements can facilitate the exploitation of employees, without consequence. According to Wilkinson et al. (2021), the growth of informal jobs and the accompanying precarity poses unresolved challenges regarding voice, as the employees have reduced voice opportunities. It has been found that 25% of gig employees are not aware of the voice channels through which they can voice their concerns about their work (CIPD, 2017). It is also more likely that the companies that offer informal or temporary jobs take advantage of employees or disregard and subdue voice. Hence, there is a need for indirect representation and unions (Woodruff, 2016).

However, traditional roles do not necessarily offer better opportunities than non-traditional ones. Some employees in the gig economy or informal sector are highly skilled and have skills that are valued and in demand, so they have some level of influence in the labour market (Wilkinson et al., 2021). Non-standard employment is an alternate option to standard work, adopted by some by choice (Katz & Krueger, 2019). Furthermore, the qualities ascribed to standard or non-standard jobs can permeate or intersect with employees in standard employment increasingly working remotely and having flexibility in their working arrangements. Research shows that attempting to classify jobs as standard or non-standard is no longer sufficient, as the characteristics credited to each type are interconnected and overlap. This is even truer considering the effects of the coronavirus pandemic on work designs and the increase in non-traditional and remote jobs. Nevertheless, the voice experiences of non-standard and standard employees vary, and there seem to be many complexities and many voice techniques involved based on the type of employment. Recent literature points to the disparity in perspectives and standpoints in theorising employment arrangements (Liu et al., 2022). While disparate, the majority view non-standard employment as having different qualities and traditions to standard employment. Exploring the means through which employees in non-standard jobs experience participation, representation, and voice in the workplace is significant for understanding the psychological structure of their employment relationships (Mowbray, 2022). Voice for these employees can exist in different forms and at various levels.

Employees in standard jobs are typically protected by employment legislation, have long-term career prospects, are economically reliant on their employer, have mutual employment relations, and have a great degree of individual subservience, with employers taking control of the employment relationship (Prouska et al., 2022). In contrast, the degree to which the stated characteristics are present or absent for non-standard employees differs. For example, zero-hour, part-time, and temporary employees typically share similar experiences to standard employees with regard to having mutual employment relations and individual subordination (Mowbray, 2022). They, however, have little or no protection through employment legislation, defined work periods, short-term career intervals, and economic liberation. In particular, employees working in disguised employment and with temporary agency services have more varied employment experiences compared to employees who have standard jobs (Mowbray, 2022), such as reduced protection; indeterminate and irregular work locations; on-demand work arrangements; secondary compensation; and a lack of mutual commitment with employers or individual subordination.

The direct form of employee voice is more frequently used among atypical employees (Goñi-Legaz & Ollo-López, 2017). Indirect mechanisms such as grievance procedures and trade unions are found to be less common. Some of the more common collective voice systems are virtual networks, professional networks, short-term task forces, joint consultative committees, quality circles, and workgroups (Borghi et al., 2021). In cases in which such employees have joined a union, the effect on voice has been found to be nominal (Oyetunde et al., 2021). Agency and temporary employees have more reasons to collectively bargain, and they have limited access to voice prospects due to the precarious and transitory nature of their jobs (Dundon et al., 2020). Freelancers and temporary workers often experience precarity, an absence of social relationships, and employment insecurity—and a resultant absence of voice privilege (Sluiter et al., 2020). Many such jobs are temporary or short term, which contributes to disadvantaged voice prospects. It is therefore less likely for freelancers to be involved in direct consultations. There is an increased interest in using professional networks for achieving collective representation for this group due to the perception that unionism can inhibit their career prospects. The professional networks are usually separate from trade unions (Oyetunde et al., 2021).

It is therefore evident that informal and gig-economy roles are usually associated with reduced union involvement (Sluiter et al., 2020) and not much connected with organised voice prospects, with employers demonstrating hostility to unionism. The nature of this type of work and its associated restricted access to conventional voice prospects have resulted in new systems of mobilisation and collective action as a means of mitigating the absence of rights and voicing of grievances (Wilkinson et al., 2021). There is increasing research on the alternative voice mechanisms available to atypical employees, the types of concerns they have, and the outcomes and determinants of their voice. It is noteworthy that the types of voicing available to atypical employees will impact the degree of their influence on managerial decisions and the concerns they convey. Consequently, in the next section, we examine the issues associated with digitalisation, that is the use of artificial intelligence (AI) and social media as well as their impact on employee voice.

Digitalisation: Artificial Intelligence, Social Media, and E-voice

Since the beginning of the coronavirus pandemic, the workforce has adopted new models of remote and hybrid work. This has been accompanied by an increase in workload and an increase in the variety of roles performed by employees. New technologies have been introduced in order to manage the increased complexities of work. The workplace has become more digitalised, and this is reflected in human resource management discourse (Dutta et al., 2022). Digitalisation in this context signifies the alteration of organisations and cultures through the application of digital technologies (Hanelt et al., 2020). There has also been an increase in the use of voice channels through electronic tools such as social media, resulting in the concept of 'e-voice', which refers to how workers contribute to decision-making and raise their concerns through electronic communication devices (Bernauer & Kornau, 2022). This has been accompanied by an increase in the use of emerging technologies, such as biometrics, speech recognition, virtual reality, geo-tagging, the Internet of things, mobile technology, machine learning, big data, and AI for managing work and employees (Hughes et al., 2019). The term AI is used in this chapter to refer to a wide category of technologies that enable computers to execute roles that typically require human cognition (Budhwar et al., 2022).

The use of these sophisticated technologies has transformed the ways in which organisations operate globally and locally. They have had a substantial effect on how work is designed and how voice is expressed. Research has shown that technology can have a limiting effect on direct voice, which is significant for employees who already have restricted voice prospects, and even more so for those in the platform and gig economy. Employees were also more silent during the coronavirus pandemic than they were before, as the pandemic created a prosocial silence culture. As

Woodfield (2022) notes, voice is more difficult to hear and process in online environments. However, while voice may be adversely affected by the increased reliance on technology-facilitated communications, digitalisation equally offers new patterns, such as reduced hierarchy, and more channels for communicating (including social media) that may enable voice. Social media offers employees the opportunity to voice their concerns and is also an avenue for them to communicate and connect with union members and build solidarity. Additionally, while the Internet can enable solidarity and activism (Frangi et al., 2018), it can also produce counter-mobilisation, as was done by Amazon to avoid collective bargaining (Wilkinson et al., 2021).

Digitalisation offers opportunities to surmount geographical boundaries and has been utilised by gig employees for organising collective action, strikes, and union influence. For example, the Independent Workers Union of Great Britain is a bottom-up trade union formed specifically for Deliveroo riders to challenge the absence of collective employment rights (Wilkinson et al., 2021). The interactional and communicative elements of AI products allow for a tailored and customised approach to employee management and the enhancement of voice (Dutta et al., 2022). Within the context of human resources, applications aided by AI are being used for essential tasks such as coaching, training and development, performance management, and recruitment and selection. It is utilised during recruitment for the initial screening of candidates. Data may be sorted to identify which candidates' characteristics are linked with enhanced job performance and to select the most suitable candidate for the advertised positions. The application can therefore contribute towards the acquisition of talent (Rani, 2019).

Furthermore, AI software also offers new types of learning and development programmes. Algorithms can be used to inform employees of appropriate training. IBM, for example, utilises algorithms to advise workers on suitable training programmes based on the experiences of workers in similar roles (Cappelli et al., 2018). It is also used for monitoring employee engagement during training programmes and for assessing the efficiency of development opportunities. Additionally, AI has been used for managing performance and conducting appraisals. It can deliver information regarding employee turnover rates and contribute to employee retention. More importantly, AI-enabled chatbots have been found useful for building engagement among employees, as they offer a method of direct voice. Chatbots are used by human resources for facilitating openness to voice (Dutta et al., 2022). The interactive nature of these chatbots allows for a more individualised experience for workers, generating feelings of influence and control in the workplace. Dutta et al. (2022) relate these findings to AI-facilitated exchange theory, which suggests that having workers interact with or use AI-aided chatbots helps generate favourable outcomes, such as improved engagement.

Besides the effects on direct (and indirect) voice, digitisation offers increased spatial and temporal flexibility in working arrangements (Spreitzer et al., 2017). As Wilkinson et al. (2021) note, digitalisation has reduced the limiting elements of time and space and has obscured the boundaries between work and home. Technology, including social media, can therefore be valuable for creating new voice systems. However, workers in the low-skilled, low-paid sectors may not have access to these technologies or Internet-aided devices as part of their job roles (Woodruff, 2016). Technologies also tend to focus on direct voice, which facilitate individual participation and involvement, with less emphasis on the indirect means such as collective representation through unions and non-union organisations (works councils or advisory boards) (Bernauer & Kornau, 2022). Employees in informal jobs may have restricted prospects for direct voice and therefore need the indirect systems of voice to enhance their voice prospects and outcomes.

Hence, while the digitalisation of the labour market may not necessarily constrain voice in the future, it may also not enable it, which can result in overlooked voices in the labour market. It has, for instance, been argued that AI could have an adverse effect on civilisation's very core and essence (Budhwar et al., 2022). Indeed, the use of AI in human resource management comes with many conceptual and practical challenges. The nature of data science analysis itself, when used in relation to people, can conflict with the standards typically seen as essential by society for making significant decisions regarding people (Cappelli et al., 2018). Yet, there is evidence that AI and related intellect-based applications can generate prospects for businesses to attain optimum strategic organisational outcomes. These developments can have both positive and negative effects on employee voice. Thus, a reassessment of the existing voice procedures must be undertaken in order to identify new trajectories. It has become evident that there may still be voices in the modern workplace that are not being heard (Wilkinson et al., 2018). As the labour market continues to change, there will be more challenges related to employee voice. It is imperative to consider the future of voice for the rising number of people working in non-standard employment. There is also a need for more research relating to digitalisation and the effects of technologies, such as AI-enabled chatbots on employee outcomes, including voice (Dutta et al., 2022). While the interface between human resource management and AI is popular among human resource specialists and academics, research on this topic remains at an emergent stage. Understanding how workers experience employment relations and how voice is mediated through AI applications, alongside the impact thereof on employee outcomes, would contribute to this field of interest.

Voice in all its forms will remain significant in the UK. The indirect (representative, collective) and direct (face-to-face, individual) forms will continue to exist in uneven ripples dependent on the strength of collective bargaining, labour market pressures, and regulatory systems (Donaghey et al., 2022). The future of the concept in both forms, however, remains unclear. Examining voice on multiple levels, ranging from the micro (individual), to meso (organisational), and macro (societal) levels, would be useful. As Wilkinson et al. (2018) note, the micro level would examine individual-level enhancers and restrictions to voice, including employee perceptions and attitudes. The meso level would take into consideration the voice procedures used by companies and the degree to which these are used in practice, while consideration at the macro level relates to the regulatory frameworks that determine organisational policies. There is an imminent need for research on the concept of voice in all these forms.

Conclusions and Implications

In this chapter, we have provided a review and illustration of the term 'employee voice' within a particular context. We examined the historical approach to and current developments in the use of and factors affecting the term 'employee voice'. Additionally, we focused on recent developments, especially the permacrisis in the UK. We considered extant literature with a specific focus on literature addressing employee voice issues in the UK as well as other literature that does not directly address the UK's issues', but that has an impact on or has addressed theoretical issues. Our study revealed how employers now neglect acting on employee voice when such voice does not directly support management's views. Although employees (acting individually or collectively) can use any of the voice channels available to them, it is, however, the prerogative of the management to implement the desired action. In addition, we highlighted that there are many channels of voice open to employees of an organisation, and most of these channels are open in a standard work setting, while they are almost non-existent in some non-standard work environments. In our juxtaposition of two of the main existing theories, industrial and labour process theory (employment relations approach) with work psychology (organisational behaviour approach), we realise that although these theories are relevant to our understanding and the processes of employee voice, it is clear that the current developments in different fields of study have resulted in different meanings being given to the term in different fields and professions. For instance, labour process theory acknowledges the complexities that exist in a capitalist production system and that there is room for differing views within the system (Smith, 2015). Like the pluralist approach, labour process theory attempts to challenge the monolithic view. Hence, this approach presents the best narrative of employee voice in a permacrisis.

Thus, while employee voice remains an integral part of and a channel for addressing employee concerns and achieving organisational objectives, the term has taken on different meanings and dimensions in different fields. Philosophically, different theoretical strands have different outlooks. For example, human resource management or high-performance work systems assume a managerial/unitarist philosophy that engenders loyalty and enhances corporate performance. Similarly, organisational behaviour also assumes a humanist/unitarist philosophy that supports engagement and commitment. On the other hand, the labour process theory is a radical-pluralist philosophy that propagates power-sharing and countervailing power in an organisation (Wilkinson et al., 2021).

References

Allen, M. M. C. (2021). Hirschman and voice. In A. Wilkinson, J. Donaghey, T. Dundon, & R. B. Freeman (Eds.), *Handbook of research on employee voice* (pp. 38–53). Edward Elgar Publishing.

Barry, M., & Wilkinson, A. (2022). Employee voice, psychologisation and human resource management (HRM). *Human Resource Management Journal, 32*(3), 631–646.

Barry, M., Dundon, T., & Wilkinson, A. (2018). Employee voice: Conceptualisations, meanings, limitations and possible integration. In M. Barry & A. Wilkinson (Eds.), *The Routledge companion to employment relations* (pp. 251–265). Routledge.

Bernauer, V., & Kornau, A. (2022). E-voice in the digitalised workplace. Insights from an alternative organisation. *Human Resource Management Journal.* https://doi.org/10.1111/1748-8583.12460

Borghi, P., Murgia, A., Mondon-Navazo, M., & Mezihorak, P. (2021). Mind the gap between discourses and practices: Platform workers' representation in France and Italy. *European Journal of Industrial Relations, 27*, 1–19.

Boxall, P., & Purcell, J. (2011). *Strategy and Human Resource Management*, 3rd edn. Basingstoke: Palgrave Macmillan.

Budhwar, P., Malik, A., De Silva, M., & Thevisuthan, P. (2022). Artificial intelligence—Challenges and opportunities for international HRM: A review and research agenda. *The International Journal of Human Resource Management, 33*(6), 1065–1097.

Burris, E., Rockmann, K. W., & Kimmons, Y. S. (2017). The value of voice to managers: Employee identification and the content of voice. *Academy of Management Journal, 60*(6), 2099–2125.

Cappelli, P., Tambe, P., & Yakubovich, V. (2018). Artificial intelligence in human resources management: Challenges and a path forward. *SSRN Electronic Journal*, 1–29.

Chillas, S., & Marks, A. (2021). Labour process perspective on employee voice. In A. Wilkinson, J. Donaghey, T. Dundon, & R. B. Freeman (Eds.), *Handbook of research on employee voice* (pp. 85–102). Edward Elgar Publishing.

CIPD. (2017). New research explores the future of employee voice. https://www.cipd.co.uk/news-views/news-articles/future-employee-voice

Cox, A., Marchington, M., & Suter, J. (2006). Employee involvement and participation: Developing the concept of institutional embeddedness using WERS2004. *International Journal of Human Resource Management, 20*(10), 2150–2168.

Detert, J. R., & Burris, E. R. (2007). Leadership behavior and employee voice: Is the door really open?. *Academy of Management Journal, 50*(4), 869–884.

Detert, J. R., & Treviño, L. K. (2010). Speaking up to higher-ups: How supervisors and skip-level leaders influence employee voice. *Organization Science, 21*(1), 249–270.

Dibben, P., Cunningham, I., Bakalov, N., & Xian, H. (2022). Conceptualising employee voice in the majority world: Using multiple intellectual traditions inspired by the work of Mick Marchington. *Human Resource Management Journal.* https://doi.org/10.1111/1748-8583.12473

Dietz, G., Martins, A., & Searle, R. (2011). Trust, HRM and the employment relationship. In A. Wilkinson & K. Townsend (Eds.), *The future of employment relations: New paradigms, new perspectives* (pp. 141–162). Palgrave Macmillan.

Donaghey, J., Cullinane, N., Dundon, T., Dobbins, T., & Hickland, E. (2022). Employee choice of voice and non-union worker representation. *Industrial Relations Journal, 53*(6), 503–522.

Donaghey, J., Cullinane, N., Dundon, T., & Wilkinson, A. (2011). Reconceptualising employee silence: Problems and prognosis. *Work, Employment & Society, 25*(1), 51–67.

Dundon, T., Lucio, M. M., Hughes, E., Howcroft, D., Keizer, A., & Walden, R. (2020). *Power, politics and influence at work.* Manchester University Press.

Dundon, T., Wilkinson, A., Marchington, M., & Ackers, P. (2004). The meanings and purpose of employee voice. *International Journal of Human Resource Management, 15*(6), 1149–1170.

Dutta, D., Mishra, S., & Tyagi, D. (2022). Augmented employee voice and employee engagement using artificial intelligence-enabled chatbots: A field study. *The International Journal of Human Resource Management, 33*, 1–30.

Edwards, R. (2011). *Rights at work: Employment relations in the post-union era.* Brookings Institution Press.

Frangi, L., Noh, S., & Hebdon, R. (2018). A pacified labor? The transformation of labor conflict. In A. Wilkinson, T. Dundon, J. Donaghey, & A. Colvin (Eds.), *The Routledge companion to employment relations* (pp. 285–304). Routledge.

Freeman, R., & Medoff, J. (2016). What do unions do? *Industrial and Labour Relations Review, 38*(2), 244–260.

Gegenhuber, T., Ellmer, M., & Schüßler, E. (2021). Microphones, not megaphones: Functional crowd worker voice regimes on digital work platforms. *Human Relations, 74*(9), 1473–1503.

Goñi-Legaz, S., & Ollo-López, A. (2017). Temporary contracts, participation in decision making and job satisfaction in European workers: Is there a buffering effect? *International Journal of Manpower, 38*(6), 875–892.

Haapakorpi, A. (2021). Freedom but insecurity: The business consulting profession in the post-industrial service society. *Nordic Journal of Working Life Studies, 11*(1), 45–62.

Hanelt, A., Bohnsack, R., Marz, D., & Antunes, C. (2020). A systematic review of the literature on digital transformation: Insights and implications for strategy and organizational change. *Journal of Management Studies, 58*(5), 1159–1197.

Hirschman, A. O. (1970). *Exit, voice and loyalty: Response to decline in firms, organisations and states*. Harvard University Press.

Hughes, C., Robert, L., Frady, K., & Arroyos, A. (2019). Artificial intelligence, employee engagement, fairness, and job outcomes. In C. Hughes, L. Robert, K. Frady, & A. Arroyos (Eds.), *Managing technology and middle- and low-skilled employees* (pp. 61–68). Emerald Publishing Limited.

ILO. (2016). *Non-standard employment around the world: Understanding challenges, shaping prospects*. International Labour Office.

Ioannou, G., & Dukes, R. (2021). Anything goes? Exploring the limits of employment law in UK hospitality and catering. *Industrial Relations Journal, 52*(3), 255–269.

Katz, L., & Krueger, A. (2019). The rise and nature of alternative work arrangements in the United States, 1995–2015. *ILR Review, 72*(2), 382–416.

Kaufman, B. E. (2020). Employee voice before Hirschman: Its early history, conceptualization and practice. In *Handbook of research on employee voice* (pp. 19–37). Edward Elgar Publishing.

King, D., Shipton, H., Smith, S., Rendall, J., & Renkema, M. (2021). *Talking about voice: Insights from case studies*. London: Chartered Institute of Personnel and Development.

Liu, X., van Jaarsveld, D. D., & Yanadori, Y. (2022). Customer aggression, employee voice and quit rates: Evidence from the frontline service workforce. *British Journal of Industrial Relations, 60*(2), 348–370.

Marchington, M. (2015). Analysing the forces shaping employee involvement and participation (EIP) at organisation level in liberal market economies (LME s). *Human Resource Management Journal, 25*(1), 1–18.

Marchington, M., & Kynighou, A. (2012). The dynamics of employee involvement and participation during turbulent times. *The International Journal of Human Resource Management, 23*(16), 3336–3354.

McNulty, Y., McPhail, R., Inversi, C., Dundon, T., & Nechanska, E. (2018). Employee voice mechanisms for lesbian, gay, bisexual and transgender expatriation: the role of Employee-Resource Groups (ERGs) and allies. *The International Journal of Human Resource Management, 29*(5), 829–856.

Morrison, E. W. (2023). Employee voice and silence: Taking stock a decade later. *Annual Review of Organizational Psychology and Organizational Behavior, 10*, 79–107.

Mowbray, P. K. (2022). Is anybody there? An examination of the voice experiences of Uber ride-share drivers. In *Missing voice?* (pp. 175–193). Edward Elgar Publishing.

Mowbray, P. K., Wilkinson, A., & Tse, H. H. (2015). An integrative review of employee voice: Identifying a common conceptualization and research agenda. *International Journal of Management Reviews, 17*(3), 382–400.

Oyetunde, K., Prouska, R., & McKearney, A. (2021). Voice in non-traditional employment relationships: A review and future research directions. *The International Journal of Human Resource Management, 33*(1), 142–167.

Prouska, R., McKearney, A., Opute, J., Tungtakanpoung, M., & Brewster, C. (2022). Voice in context: An international comparative study of employee experience with voice in small and medium enterprises. *The International Journal of Human Resource Management, 33*(15), 3149–3174.

Ramsay, H. (1977). Cycles of control: worker participation in sociological and historical perspective. *Sociology, 11*(3), 481–506.

Ramsay, H. (1985). What is participation for? A critical evaluation of "labour process" analyses of job reform. Job Redesign: critical perspectives on the labour process. Aldershot: Gower, 52–80.

Rani, S. (2019). Human resource management and artificial intelligence. *International Research Journal of Management, 10*(7), 17–25.

Robinson, R., & Shuck, B. (2019). A penny for your thoughts: Exploring experiences of engagement, voice, and silence. *Journal of Organizational Psychology, 19*(4), 121–135.

Shipton, H., King, D., Pautz, N., & Baczor, L. (2019). Talking about voice: Employees' experiences. London: Chartered Institute of Personnel and Development.

Sluiter, R., Manevska, K., & Akkerman, A. (2020). Atypical work, worker voice and supervisor responses. *Socio-Economic Review, 20*(3), 1–21.

Smith, C. (2015). Continuity and change in labor process analysis forty years after labor and monopoly capital. *Labor Studies Journal, 40*(3), 222–242.

Spreitzer, G., Cameron, L., & Garrett, L. (2017). Alternative work arrangements: Two images of the new world of work. *Annual Review of Organizational Psychology and Organizational Behavior, 4*, 473–499.

Syed, J. (2014). Diversity management and missing voices. In A. Wilkinson, J. Donaghey, T. Dundon, & R. Freeman (Eds.), *The handbook of research on employee voice: Participation and involvement in the workplace* (pp. 421–428). Edward Elgar Publishing Ltd.

Townsend, K., Wilkinson, A., & Burgess, J. (2013). Filling the gaps: Patterns of formal and informal participation. *Economic and Industrial Democracy, 34*(2), 337–354.

Turnbull, N. (2022). Permacrisis: What it means and why it's word of the year for 2022. https://theconversation.com/

Wæraas, A., & Dahle, D. Y. (2020). When reputation management is people management: Implications for employee voice. *European Management Journal, 38*(2), 277–287.

Wilkinson, A., & Barry, M. (2016). Voices from across the divide: An industrial relations perspective on employee voice. *German Journal of Human Resource Management, 30*(3–4), 338–344.

Wilkinson, A., Donaghey, J., Dundon, T., & Freeman, R. B. (Eds.). (2020). *Handbook of research on employee voice*. Edward Elgar Publishing.

Wilkinson, A., Dundon, T., Donaghey, J., & Freeman, R. B. (2021). Employee voice: Bridging new terrains and disciplinary boundaries. In A. Wilkinson, J. Donaghey, T. Dundon, & R. B. Freeman (Eds.), *Handbook of research on employee voice* (pp. 38–53). Edward Elgar Publishing.

Wilkinson, A., & Fay, C. (2011). New times for employee voice?. *Human Resource Management, 50*(1), 65–74.

Wilkinson, A., Gollan, J., Kalfa, S., & Xu, Y. (2018). Voices unheard: Employee voice in the new century. *The International Journal of Human Resource Management, 29*(5), 711–724.

Wilkinson, A., Knoll, M., Mowbray, P., & Dundon, T. (2021). New trajectories in worker voice: Integrating and applying contemporary challenges in the organization of work. *British Journal of Management, 32*(3), 693–707.

Willman, P., Bryson, A., Gomez, R., & Kretschmer, T. (2021). Employee voice and the transaction cost economics project. In A. Wilkinson, J. Donaghey, T. Dundon, & R. B. Freeman (Eds.), *Handbook of research on employee voice* (pp. 54–67). Edward Elgar Publishing.

Wood, S. (2010). High involvement management and performance. In A. Wilkinson, P. Gollan, M. Marchington, & D. Lewin (Eds.), *The Oxford handbook of participation in organisations*. Oxford University Press.

Woodfield, R. (2022). Maximising employee voice in a hybrid working world. University of St Andrews. https://peopleprofession.cipd.org/insights/articles/employee-voice

Woodruff, L. (2016). What does 'voice' mean for the millions of UK employees who live in poverty? https://community.cipd.co.uk/cipd-blogs/

Zeytinoglu, I., & Cooke, G. (2008). Non-standard employment and promotions: A within genders analysis. *Journal of Industrial Relations, 50*(2), 319–337.

3

Worker Voice in the U.S.: Unitarist and Pluralist Perspectives

Sean Edmund Rogers

Introduction

Worker voice in the U.S. has been dynamic over the past several decades. Many scholars and casual observers argue that voice—or the extent to which workers have say and influence over the nature and conditions of their workplace and work experiences—has declined over time, leaving employees in an increasingly precarious predicament. Others argue that what has really changed is the nature of the employment relationship and how workers and employers interact and exchange with one another, resulting in voice taking on different and multifaceted forms in modern work environments. In this chapter, I engage with these and other perspectives on worker voice in the U.S. through a historical and contemporary examination of workers' say and influence in their workplaces and work experiences. First, I situate the concept of worker voice within the context of two important theories of the employment relationship,

S. E. Rogers (✉)
University of Rhode Island, Kingston, RI, USA
e-mail: rogers@uri.edu

T. Ajibade Adisa et al. (eds.), *Employee Voice in the Global North*,
https://doi.org/10.1007/978-3-031-31123-9_3

namely unitarist and pluralist theories of employment relations. Doing so sets the stage for understanding workers' and employers' interests, any alignment or tension between the two, and how this shapes voice activation, actualisation, and efficacy. Then, for the remainder of the chapter, I review various manifestations of worker voice in American workplaces. Given the first section's examination of unitarist and pluralist employment relations, I delve into this examination of voice among American workers along two tracks—individualistic (unitarist) and collectivist (pluralistic) expressions of voice. As part of this discussion, I consider the ways in which various academic traditions (such as industrial relations [IR], human resource [HR] management, and organisational behaviour) have influenced the scholarly study of worker voice, as well as how voice operates within workplace environments. Where applicable, I also consider how U.S. labour law and government policies influence the employment relationship, interact with the interests of workers and employers, and facilitate or inhibit worker voice.

Worker Voice in the Context of Employment Relations Theory

At its core, worker voice is about individuals having meaningful input into how they experience the world of work. This might include input on proximal issues like rates of pay or promotion, the design of jobs and what tasks will be performed and how, or workplace safety considerations. But it can also extend to input on more distal aspects of the employment experience, such as an employing organisation's strategic plan or investment decisions (think of recent calls for firms to divest from fossil fuel and other industries, for example), the hiring or compensation of managers and senior leaders, or political involvement by an organisation or its executives. The ways in which individuals choose to exert say and influence in their workplaces, and the stances employers take and how they respond to worker voice, are undoubtedly influenced by how each party conceives the employment relationship and expectations about one another's positionality and performance. Employment relations theory, then, proves useful for contextualising, and providing a "frame of reference" (Budd & Bhave, 2008; Fox, 1974) for, worker voice. Two theories that describe varying depictions of the interaction between individuals and employing organisations, and that present different implications for worker voice, are the unitarist theory of industrial relations (also referred to as unitarism) and the pluralist theory of industrial relations (also referred to as pluralism). These two theories, along with others from industrial relations literature (such as egoist, critical, or radical perspectives, which are not covered in this chapter), revolve around the interests of, and nature of conflict between, workers, employers, and other actors (such as the state, demographic groups, and societal institutions).

Unitarism

One way to think about the employment relationship and interactions between individual workers and employing organisations is that both have a singular vested interest in the success of the organisation. Employers benefit from positive employment relations via maximised profits or through achieving other important organisational objectives (such as effectively serving clients or beneficiaries, as in the case of a non-profit). And workers enjoy access to desirable, fulfilling, well paying, and upwardly mobile jobs that might result from positive employment relations and sustained organisational achievement and goal attainment. Unitarism, or the unitary frame of reference, presumes alignment between the interests of workers and employers (Barry & Wilkinson, 2016; Budd & Bhave, 2008). Because of this presumed congruence, human resource management policies and practices are the preferred method for maintaining interest alignment and managing the employment relationship (Bacon, 2003).

Indeed, the unitarist view undergirds much of the historical voice scholarship in organisational behaviour and industrial-organisational (I-O) psychology and arguably gave rise to modern-day employer approaches to human resource management. Sayings like "happy employees don't need unions" emerge out of a unitarist world view. Among those who espouse this unitary frame of reference, conflict between workers and organisations is not perceived to be a natural or welcomed aspect of the employment relationship. Any presence of employment relations conflict, particularly in the form of worker voice aimed at improving suboptimal working conditions, reflects poorly designed or not-well-executed human resource management policies and practices. Such shortcomings might include, for example, compensation that does not appropriately reflect individual contributions or internal or external equity, abusive supervision, unhealthy imbalances between work and life activities, lack of professional development or career growth opportunities, inadequate job security or safety, and so on. Optimal human resource management, unitarism posits, will effectively align the interests of workers and employers (Lewin, 2001) and enable both parties to maximise outcomes and fulfilment (Ulrich & Brockbank, 2005).

Pluralism

In contrast to the unitarist perspective, pluralism posits that employers have both shared and conflicting interests (Kochan et al., 2019). As a result, conflict is seen as a natural aspect of all employment relationships between individuals and organisations. Heery and colleagues (2008) outline five core beliefs about employment relations that grow out of the pluralist frame of reference. First and primary is the reality, mentioned above, that employers and workers have their own sets of interest and that some of these interests align while others conflict. Importantly, some measure of this conflict is irreducible and must be managed as part of the employment relationship (or else it will grow out of control and lead to dysfunction). Also, both sets of interests—those of employer organisations and those of workers—are equally legitimate despite being in conflict. A second belief, and one that directly relates to worker voice, is that "the expression of conflict is not … pathological" (Heery et al., 2008, p. 15). If individuals naturally have some interests that diverge from the interests of organisations (e.g., workers wanting to obtain the highest wages possible vs. firms wanting to control or minimise labour expenses), and if conflict is thus an inevitable aspect of the employment relationship, then it is not problematic or necessarily pathological when workers raise concerns about perceived workplace shortcomings.

The next three beliefs speak specifically to how workers experience the employment relationship, how they can enhance their outcomes at work, and how positive worker outcomes and healthy employment relations systems can more widely benefit the general public and society. A third belief is that "there is an imbalance of power within the employment relationship and that the dependence of workers on employers for a means of subsistence places [workers] in a vulnerable position" (Heery et al., 2008, p. 15). This is a key point of distinction between pluralism and unitarism. The unitary frame of reference often conceptualises workers and their employers as a team, even a team of equals, and downplays any imbalance between the two. Sometimes, unitary employment relations even take on familial rhetoric. When US Airways attempted a hostile takeover of Delta Air Lines in 2006, Delta employees launched a campaign called "Keep Delta My Delta" (Isodore, 2007) and touted their direct, family like relationship with the airline as a primary reason for not wanting it to be bought out. Conversely, pluralism accepts that employers are in a position to have the upper hand in an employment relationship. This leads to the fourth belief: that workers can only counterbalance this lopsided power structure by combining themselves into collectives that enable them to accumulate power, influence, and voice. Historically, and from an industrial relations perspective, the medium for this rebalancing is trade unionism and collective bargaining. The fifth and final belief is that a healthy employment relations system marked by effective regulation of conflict, legal structures that facilitate (rather than hinder) collective organisation, and trade unionism and collective bargaining can contribute to positive societal functioning and industrial democracy. In sum, the pluralist theory of employment relations acknowledges that workers and employers both have legitimate interests that sometimes align and sometimes do not, accepts conflict as a natural aspect of the employment relationship, and advocates for a means for workers to collectively address workplace concerns.

Comparing the Two: Unitarist and Pluralist Employment Relations

Considering these quite different ways of thinking about the employment relationship and the experiences and plight of American workers (and all workers more generally), it becomes clear that the concept of worker voice—what it is, why it arises, its forms, and how organisations might react to expressions of it—will vary depending on which frame of reference one espouses. As might be expected based on the individualistic versus collective nature of these competing employment relations theories, worker voice under the unitary frame is most concerned with individual involvement in organisational life. From this perspective, voice tends to be a function of a person's personality or an organisation's culture, and voice activation often reflects support for organisational objectives or interests (such as the performance of organisational citizenship behaviours or OCBs). For several decades now, this individualistic, organisation-enhancing approach has increasingly influenced the study and practice of workplace relations in America.

On the other hand, voice from a pluralist frame more often reflects expressions of employee dissatisfaction and grassroot and institutional responses to the tensions that arise from a natural divergence between worker and employer interests. Collective action, labour unionism, and the institutionalisation of laws and regulatory guidelines are legitimate and desired vehicles for voice within a pluralist employment relations system. Whereas unitarist perspectives increasingly occupy U.S. workplaces as of late, pluralist indications of worker voice have declined. Union membership in the U.S., for example, decreased from 28% of workers in 1977 to a mere 11% in 2017 (Kochan et al., 2019). In the section that follows, I discuss the complexities of worker voice in America along these two lines—unitarism and pluralism. Throughout the discussion, I consider various academic perspectives on voice and, where applicable, how laws and the regulatory environment influence the employment relationship and worker voice.

Employment Relations as Team Sport: Individual Worker Voice and Organisational Beneficence

A leading voice in the study of employee voice in work organisations, Morrison (2011, 2014, 2023) has conducted several systematic reviews of the academic literature on employee voice from a primarily unitarist perspective. Each of her reviews ties together several strands of organisational behaviour scholarship in an attempt to integrate existing research on voice and also set directions for future exploration. She proffers a definition of voice that has since been cited hundreds of times by subsequent researchers: voice is the "discretionary communication of ideas, suggestions, concerns, or opinions about work-related issues with the intent to improve organisational or unit functioning" (Morrison, 2011, p. 375). This definition builds on foundational ideas advanced by Van Dyne and LePine (1998) and LePine and Van Dyne (1998), namely that voice is *constructive* in nature, reflects *voluntary and prosocial behaviour*, and *goes beyond mere criticism* of one's work environment. It is also grounded in the belief that voice is a behaviour which emerges from generally satisfied workers and that individuals engage in voice behaviour not in response to workplace dissatisfaction but to be helpful to their co-workers and the organisation. Even if the spark for voice is a negative affective state (dissatisfaction), employees regulate their emotions and transform them into productive, organisation-enhancing feedback (Grant, 2013). Such a position contrasts with much of the research from industrial relations (IR), human resources (HR), and other academic disciplines, which perceives worker voice to be one of several options for responding to deteriorating or unsatisfactory employment conditions (Barry & Wilkinson, 2022; Hirschman, 1970; Mowbray et al., 2015) with the primary aim of improving the lot for workers.

Morrison's (2011) early integrative model, along with subsequent reviews by her in 2014 and 2023, captures the full spectrum of the employee voice concept, from a person's motives for engaging in voice on one end of the continuum, to the individual and organisational outcomes of voice on the other end. In between these endpoints are several contextual factors affecting the decision to voice (such as an organisation's structure and culture, or management's openness to receiving employee voice), individual-level factors (such as job attitudes, personality, and experience and tenure), the perceived cost that someone associates with expressing voice, how safe employees feel to engage in voice behaviour and perceptions of the efficacy of those behaviours, and employee voice tactics. As this book takes a comparative look at worker voice, the next several paragraphs spend time examining multiple of these aspects from a U.S. lens, either via elements of national culture or country-level variables, or from studies that utilise samples of American workers or employers.

Predictors of Employee Voice in the U.S.

In a study of 640 nurses and their managers in a midwestern U.S. hospital system, Tangirala and Ramanujam (2012) found that managerial consultation, or the extent to which managers were seen to solicit and listen to suggestions from workers, enhanced employee voice. This happened because consultation activated an important motivational state among employees, namely, perceived influence in the workplace. Using a cross-cultural lens, Botero and Van Dyne (2009) conducted multiple studies and uncovered that leader-member exchange (LMX) dynamics and individual power distance (PD) orientation predicted employee voice behaviour among a sample of private, public, and non-profit sector employees in the U.S. LMX refers to the quality of supervisor-subordinate relationships, and high LMX is a condition marked by mutual respect and liking, loyalty, trust, and reciprocity. PD orientation speaks to an employees' beliefs about supervision, the privilege and status of their leaders, and the distance between themselves and supervisors. People with high PD orientations perceive wider gulfs between managers and employees and accept supervisor authority and decision-making with little question. Conversely, individuals with low PD orientations deemphasise status differentials between managers and subordinates. Botero and Van Dyne (2009) found that LMX was positively related to employee voice behaviours, while PD was negatively related to voice, among their sample of American healthcare industry employees. This latter finding comports with those of Park and Nawakitphaitoon (2018) who, after surveying American automobile industry workers, found no direct effect of conflict avoidance on employee voice behaviour. That is, American workers in their sample did not appear dissuaded from expressing voice even in the face of potential conflict that might arise from speaking up.

The decision to speak up and engage in voice behaviour is not only influenced by one's immediate boss. In a qualitative analysis of employees in four R&D and manufacturing divisions of a Fortune 500 company—three divisions of which were based in the U.S. and a fourth that was situated in a "highly westernised culture"—Detert and Treviño (2010) found that the influence of "skip level leaders" on whether or not employees expressed voice was mentioned as frequently as a reason as was immediate supervisors. Skip-level leaders, they define, are those two to five levels above the focal employee. Theoretically, such leaders are not readily accessible to employees and likely do not directly interact with them. However, the fact that these upper echelons were seen to have "power to handle strategic contingencies and to resolve key uncertainties" (p. 249) in the workplace tempered employees' willingness to bring suggestions to their organisation, even constructive suggestions aimed at improving effectiveness or performance.

Individual traits and attitudes also shape employee voice behaviour. Using a sample of 894 financial employees and their immediate supervisors at a major U.S. financial institution, Walumbwa and Schaubroeck (2009) found that leader personality traits of conscientiousness and agreeableness were positively related to ethical leadership behaviours, which in turn enhanced employee voice behaviour among subordinates. Worker perception of psychological safety was a key driver in decisions to express voice. Taiyi Yan et al. (2022) argued that voice efficacy—or one's confidence in their ability to formulate and articulate work-related suggestions—also influences employee voice behaviour, and they tested their hypotheses in a sample of 546 American workers, as well as 368 more employees from India. They specifically predicted that there would be gender differences in voice efficacy, likely due to gender role socialisation, with women having lower voice efficacy than men. The authors found gender differences, though U.S. respondents developed greater voice efficacy when they had opportunities to see higher up women leaders engage in voice behaviour. Thus, Taiyi Yan et al. (2022) suggest that having more women in leadership can enhance voice efficacy and behaviour among women. Howell et al. (2015) found ethnicity and working time status (part-time vs. full-time) to affect employee voice behaviour and how expressions of voice are received. In an empirical study of 693 employees across 89 different credit union locations in the U.S., the authors found that supervisors were more prone to recognise voice expressed by majority race (in this case, White) and full-time workers. Howell et al. (2015) ascribe this phenomenon to status differences, with majority-race membership and full-time employment signalling higher status within the organisation. Finally, highlighting the role of exchange relationships, King et al. (2019) demonstrate that employee-organisational alignment is a key driver of employee voice. Across two studies involving more than 300 adult U.S. workers and 532 participants in a university human subjects pool, the authors find that the way leaders react to employee voice builds worker voice resilience and leads to subsequent expressions of voice.

Outcomes of Employee Voice

Whereas prior research has uncovered that both positive and negative reactions occur as a result of employee voice, recent research also paints a dynamic picture where reactions can change over time or due to circumstance. Using field data of 143 auditors and their 42 supervisors at two public accounting firms, as well as experimental data, Nelson and Proell (2018) show a situation where employee voice might cause irritation in the moment (such as when it is expressed during auditing activities) but is valued and rewarded later during performance evaluations. As such, organisation-enhancing voice generates benefits for the employer and (eventually) the individual. It can also generate benefits for teams of employees. Using novel observational and survey data from 118 surgical teams across five U.S. hospitals within a large healthcare system, Farh and Chen (2018) found that voice contributed to effective team functioning and performance. They specifically noted that three leader behaviours—directing, coaching, and supporting employees—enable a functional environment that promotes voice behaviour during critical tasks.

Through two studies involving several hundreds of working adults in the U.S., Weiss and Morrison (2019) discovered that employee voice behaviour resulted in those employees being perceived as having relatively high status. This was due to the voicing workers being viewed as more agentic and communal. Advancing understanding of voice effects across gender as well as on leader emergence, McClean et al. (2018) examined participant teams during a field competition at the United States Military Academy at West Point. They found that men who engaged in voice behaviour were more highly rated by peers than women on social status and were also more likely to be ascribed as emergent leaders. As they note, "talking a lot or participating at a high level in a group may not be enough to emerge as a leader—it also depends how you do it and who you are" (p. 1869). There are many more U.S.-specific findings related to employee voice behaviour rooted in the unitarist perspective of employment relations; the paragraphs above only provide a glimpse into the research conducted by organizational behavior (OB) scholars. A more comprehensive review is available from several recent publications, including Morrison's (2023) latest review published in the *Annual Review of Organizational Psychology and Organizational Behaviour.*

Critiques of Worker Voice as Voluntary, Prosocial Behaviour

Morrison's work on employee voice behaviour has been criticised by some scholars from industrial relations (IR) and other academic traditions for being overly narrow and not encompassing historical and broader discourses on worker voice. For example, Barry and Wilkinson (2022) summarise John Godard's (2014) critique of the Morrison (2011) review, describing that the purported "integrative review" actually takes a singular disciplinary perspective (that of OB), that "there is no identification of trade unions as a source of voice," that the "concept of voice … appears to be entirely an individualistic one," and that the lone motive behind worker voice is "to help the organization or work unit" and that "apparently, neither interest conflicts nor injustice matter" (p. 632). More generally, scholars from outside the OB tradition have critiqued OB's siloed approach to thinking about and studying worker voice (e.g., Donaghey et al., 2011; Kaufman, 2015; and Mowbray et al., 2015).

While myself, as an IR and HR scholar, can agree with Godard's (2014), Barry and Wilkinson's (2022), and others' lamentations over important missing elements from Morrison's 2011 and 2014 reviews and other OB treatments of worker voice, I also recognise that the approach taken by OB scholars increasingly reflects modern-day conceptualisations of voice among American workers and how it is expressed and managed in U.S. workplaces. Morrison (2011) herself acknowledges that "there is … a rich literature using the term voice within the industrial labour relations (ILR) and human resource management (HRM) literatures," and highlights "a wide range of formal mechanisms for individual and collective employee input, such as grievance procedures, suggestion systems, ombudsman services, employee-management meetings, non-management task forces, quality circles, work councils, and participative management" (p. 381). In later work, Morrison (2014) expressly recognises formal and institutional mechanisms for employee voice. Nevertheless, in that paper she concluded that "these various literature streams define voice in a way that does not closely match current conceptualisations" (Morrison, 2011, p. 381).

Many might debate the definitiveness of such a point. But the precipitous decline of trade union membership (the primary pluralist voice mechanism) in the U.S. since the 1950s, and the corresponding rise in talk about and interest in workplace empowerment (e.g., Laschinger et al., 2004), workforce engagement (e.g., Schneider et al., 2018), and worker involvement (e.g., Marchington & Kynighou, 2012; Rothenberg, 2003) seem to suggest that a good number of American workers and employers, as well as many scholars who study voice, have directed their attention to individualistic, person-centered, organisation enhancement-focused, non-adversarial manifestations of worker voice. Specifically, and as it relates to scholarship on voice, Barry and Wilkinson (2022) observed that "the central tendency in HRM in the USA" is away from IR traditions and "systems and structures for voice," and more towards "informal and individual identifying attitudes and perceptions and micro-level contextual (e.g., supervisor behaviour, team climate) enablers and inhibitors" of worker voice (p. 635). Thus, while narrow and potentially limiting, unitarism-rooted perspectives remain relevant to any contemporary discussion of worker voice in the U.S.

As a final point, in her latest review of employee voice research, Morrison (2023) tackles head on the criticisms of the OB voice perspective by IR scholars. She characterises many of the criticisms by IR as "exaggerated" and "reflecting deep epistemological differences between the two fields" (p. 83), but acknowledges that "it does seem appropriate to critique the empirical research on voice within OB for insufficient attention to situations where employees are voicing to advance interests at odds with the interests of management, and for largely ignoring the impact of formal and collective voice mechanisms on informal voice behaviour" (p. 83). She then goes on to prescribe recommendations for bridging the gap between the two disciplinary perspectives, including OB scholars "moving away from focusing so heavily on pro-organisational voice," "considering how informal voice behaviour … is affected by the presence or absence of formal voice channels," and "recognising that voice is sometimes a collective-level behaviour and, in fact, may sometimes need to be collective in order to be effective" (p. 99). We now turn to discussion of these collective approaches to worker voice.

Liberty and Justice for All: Worker Voice as Industrial Democracy

Voice mechanisms rooted in a pluralist conceptualisation of employment relations stress collective and workforce-focused, rather than individualistic and organisation-focused, interventions for change and improvement. Historically in the U.S., labour unionisation (or, at least, attempting to unionise) has been the dominant mode for expressing collective voice. This makes sense considering Heery and colleagues' (2008) core pluralist beliefs about the employment relationship, discussed above, which include that conflicting interests between workers and employers is inevitable and (to some extent) irreducible, the balance of power between firms and workers naturally tilts towards the former, collective and cumulative action is required to shift power back to workers and their interests, and a healthy employment relations system (which includes the right of workers to organise and collectively bargaining for their interests) is critical to industrial democracy and a well-functioning society.

However, unionisation rates have been steadily declining among American workers. Union density peaked in the U.S. at 35% during the 1940s. By the 1970s, it had declined to 28%, and in 2022 reached 11.0% according to the Bureau of Labor Statistics (2022). These low percentages are propped up by higher union density among public sector workers in the U.S.; by September 2022, private sector workforce unionisation was just over 6% (Council of Economic Advisers, 2022). There are several possible reasons for this decline, not the least of which has been a deteriorating U.S. labour law system that has made it increasingly harder for workers to organise, and that empowers and emboldens (already disproportionately powerful) employers to oppose initial organising efforts or, once a union becomes legally certified, stall contract negotiations and the successful establishment of a collective bargaining agreement. In a Roosevelt Institute report, Andrias and Rogers (2018) squarely blame the decline of American unionisation on an "outdated and dysfunctional labour law system" (p. 4) and suggest four ways to reform the system, including protecting all workers in all economic segments, making it easier for workers to obtain representation, enabling sectoral-level bargaining, and better protecting worker concerted action such as striking and picketing.

Despite the steady decline in union density and frustrating legal challenges to worker organising, the COVID-19 pandemic appears to have reignited American workers' interest in labour unions. A 2022 Gallup study reported that U.S. public approval of labour unions is at its highest level since the 1960s, with 71% of Americans approving of labour unions in August 2022 (McCarthy, 2022). That report also highlights several other recent trends, including a 57% increase in union election petitions in 2021 and a spike in union election victories in 2021 and 2022 including at firms like Amazon, Starbucks, Apple, and REI. The desire for collective worker voice appears to have been on the rise in the U.S. even prior to the pandemic. Kochan et al. (2019) describe results from a 2017 nationally representative sample of nearly 4000 American workers. They found that 49% of non-union, non-managerial respondents would vote to unionise their workplace if they had the opportunity to do so. Given the chance, half of American workers would choose to exercise collective voice! In this same survey, 83% of respondents who were already union members indicated that they would vote for a union again, which Kochan et al. (2019) characterise as strong union interest given the increased political and policy hurdles associated with union organising.

Benefits of Collective Voice in the U.S.

The benefits of unionisation and collective bargaining for American workers have been well documented. And not only do the workers who unionise benefit; non-union workers, industries, communities, and the entire country also benefit when workers exercise pluralistic, collective voice. According to the Bureau of Labour Statistics, American workers who unionise realise a wage premium compared to non-union employees, with the latter earning only 83% per week the pay of a union represented worker (Bureau of Labor Statistics, 2021). Marginal differences in pay premia are even greater when one drills down into demographics, including gender or race and ethnicity, suggesting that unionisation is an especially effective voice mechanism for groups who have historically faced labour market disparities.

For example, based on Current Population Survey data from 2004 to 2019, the U.S. Department of Labor reported that non-union White women workers earned 80% the weekly wages of non-union White men, whereas unionised White women's weekly earnings were on par with non-union White men. For Black and Hispanic women workers in the U.S., the way in which collective voice closes this gap is even more pronounced. Non-union Black and Hispanic women make 73% and 75% the weekly earnings of non-union White men, respectively. But when compared with this same group of non-union White men workers, Black and Hispanic women, when unionised, earned weekly pay that was 99% and 103%, respectively.

The collective voice of unionisation yields many other benefits highly valued by all American workers and by those who would be union members (Hertel-Fernandez et al., 2022), such as health benefits, retirement security, access to paid leaves and fair scheduling, and occupational safety and health. Through advocacy and representation, unions have enabled American workers to realise significantly improved outcomes compared to non-union employees. For example, according to reports by the U.S. Department of Labor and the Economic Policy Institute (Banerjee et al., 2021):

- More than nine out of ten private industry unionised workers have access to employer-sponsored retirement, compared to two-thirds of non-unionised private workers. Plan participation rates for each group, while lower overall, are higher among unionised workers (84%) than non-unionised workers (49%).
- Ninety-four per cent of unionised workers in the U.S. have access to employer-sponsored health insurance, compared to just two-thirds of non-union employees. Such coverage comes at lower costs, on average, for unionised Americans.
- Whereas 25% of all non-union workers have zero access to paid sick leave, 93% of unionised Americans have access to paid sick days via their collective bargaining agreement. Additionally, 53% of unionised workers report knowing their work schedule four or more weeks in advance. Conversely, 41% of non-unionised workers learn of their work schedule one week in advance or less.
- Workplace safety and the enforcement of Occupational Safety and Health Act (OSHA) laws is stronger at unionised workplaces, so much so that former Administrator of the U.S. Department of Labor's Wage and Hour Division David Weil (1991) argued that "Implementation of OSHA … seems highly dependent upon the presence of a union" (p. 20). Recent data by Sojourner and Yang (2015) suggest specifically how this might occur. Their research reveals a positive effect of union certification on OSHA inspection rates, violations, and penalty assessments. And during COVID-19, unionised essential workers in the U.S. experienced safer work environments than non-union workers. Thirty-nine per cent reported regular COVID-19 testing (compared

to 9% of non-union workers) and 68% regularly used PPE in the workplace (compared to 53% of non-union workers).

Challenges to Collective Voice in the U.S.

Given all the potential benefits of unionising and exercising pluralistic voice, one might wonder why union density in America has been on a constant slide since the 1950s. In examining a potential voice gap—the difference between the amount and type of say workers claim they desire to have at work, compared with their actual or perceived level of influence—in American workplaces, Kochan et al. (2019) hypothesise several reasons for why a voice gap may not be as evident present day. One explanation is that American workers might have become adjusted to new workplace norms and economic expectations and have conceded that how things are must be the way they will be. In a sense, workers have espoused learned helplessness (Peterson et al., 1993) and have little faith that things can change.

Another explanation is that workers have fully embraced the idea of meritocracy in the workplace, viewing themselves and others as "free agents" (p. 6) who can go out and get what they want and need from employers, whether that be their current employer or a prospective one. A by-product of this changing conceptualisation has been that workers demand less and less long-term loyalty and job security from their employers. A third possible explanation points to generational differences and a younger workforce. Here, Kochan et al. (2019) note that early career workers have only been exposed to current ideologies about workplace voice and expectations for employees, and thus might be less likely to expect or demand more influence over their employers or conditions of employment.

Human resource management holds another potential explanation for the decline in collective voice among American workers. As Kochan et al. (2019) remark, "[An] argument for why there may no longer be a sizable voice gap is that employers and workers have reached a satisfactory set of arrangements; that is, with the development of new human resource policies and systems, a gap no longer exists between what workers believe is appropriate regarding their say at work and what they experience on their jobs" (p. 6). Some of these arrangements include alternative dispute resolution and non-union grievance procedures, ombuds offices, employee resource groups, workplace committees, and more direct communication between workers and supervisors. Two other possible explanations Kochan and his co-authors (2019) proffer include: (1) alternative forms of collective voice, including alt-labour organisations, are increasingly replacing unions as a medium for collective voice, and (2) U.S. labour law makes it prohibitively difficult to engage in workplace labour activism and unionism. Alt-labour is a term used to describe organisations and coalitions that advance workers' rights using new strategies that often break with traditional collective bargaining and other union activities, such as publicity campaigning or boycotts up or down the supply chain (Walsh, 2018). I will discuss alt-labour's role in the future of collective voice in the U.S. later in this chapter. But first, I consider the legal environment's role in union density decline among American workers.

Labour Law and Union Decline in the U.S.

Andrias and Rogers (2018), writing for the Roosevelt Institute, contend that "[u]nions' decline can be explained in part by the steady erosion of the [National Labor Relations Act's] worker protections over the years" (p. 10). They chronicle three decades, from the 1930s to the 1960s, where U.S. labour law "did a reasonably good job protecting worker voice" in the workplace, within the economy, and in government (p. 9). After the late 1960s, however, they argue that a perfect storm of business-friendly rulings and interpretations of labour law, corporate restructuring and offshoring, and the proliferation of non-traditional contracting and franchising left workers increasingly limited when it came to organising and collectively exercising voice.

Additionally, they provide four reasons why modern-day labour law in the U.S. inhibits unionisation and collective voice. First, they argue, the law has not kept pace with changes in the status of workers or excludes too many workers and sectors of the economy. For example, it fails to extend protections to "gig economy" workers and independent contractors, and even more longstanding groups of employees such as domestic and farm workers. Second is the fact that employment-at-will is the default mode for American workers and, as such, forming a union has become especially onerous. Employers have countless tools at their disposal to dissuade union organising activities, while workers have few resources and often encounter strong pressures when trying to organise. The Protecting the Right to Organise, or PRO, Act—which is currently working its way through the U.S. Congress—is a legislative attempt to rebalance these scales and give workers more rights when exercising their collective voice. Third is the National Labor Relations Act (NLRA)'s focus on firm-level bargaining rather than sectoral of industry-level negotiations. Andrias and Rogers (2018) note that this limitation is especially troublesome currently given production shifts from large, behemoth factories to smaller, "atomized" worksites. Finally, they cite the law's increasingly tightening restraints on worker strikes and concerted action as a reason behind the decline of unionisation in America.

In a report published by the Economic Policy Institute, Lafer and Loustaunau (2020) provide even more specifics on how "the broken National Labor Relations Board's union election system" emboldens employers to suppress collective voice. They provide information from a first-hand, insider account of "union busting" activities—tactics designed to intimidate, harass, and otherwise dissuade workers from supporting and voting for a union—by two companies in Georgia and Texas. The activities witnessed, which they point out are all currently legal under the NLRA, included:

- Forcing employees to attend daily anti-union meetings where pro-union workers have no right to present alternative views and can be fired on the spot if they ask a question.
- Plastering the workforce with anti-union posters, banners, and looping video ads—and denying pro-union employees' access to any of these media.
- Instructing managers to tell employees that there's a good chance they will lose their jobs if they vote to unionise.

- Having supervisors hold multiple one-on-one talks with each of their employees, stressing why it would be a bad idea for them to vote in a union.
- Having managers tell employees that pro-union workers are 'the enemy within.'
- Telling supervisors to grill subordinates about their views on unionisation, effectively destroying the principle of a secret ballot.

Broader Visions of Collective Voice—Alt-Labour

Despite the legal environment challenges to workers banding together to organise and wield collective influence, and notwithstanding multiple hypotheses concerning the decline of unionisation, American workers seem to desire collective voice now more than they have for many decades. If given the opportunity, nearly half of American workers would join a labour union (Kochan et al., 2019). However, legal, intergenerational, and perceptual barriers to unionisation necessitate the development of alternative forms of collective representation, in addition to more traditional labour unionism, if workers are to maintain and grow collective voice and influence.

In a recently published article in the journal *Industrial and Labor Relations Review*, Hertel-Fernandez et al. (2022) asked the question "what forms of representation do American workers want?" (p. 267). "Overall," they note, "our results make clear that the primary function of the traditional American union, collective bargaining, continues to be highly valued by potential members," and that provisions such as "health insurance, retirement benefits, unemployment benefits, and labour market training" are important for American workers (p. 289). This speaks to a continuing place for traditional labour unionism in the U.S. But they also note that workers "would be even more willing to join and financially support organisations currently unavailable under US law and practice" (p. 267). These might include, for example, collectives that provide labour market services (such as benefits or training) that follow workers across worksites and different jobs (as opposed to single firm-based representation), enable sectoral or industrial bargaining, foster participation and influence in operational and strategic workplace decision-making, facilitate representation on corporate boards, or even coalesce political mobilisation and social movement activity.

Walsh (2018) describes alt-labour as "the informal coalitions of organizations … pushing to advance workers' rights in the wake of decreased union membership," and Catherine Fisk (2020) of UC Berkeley Law writes that it includes "new forms of labour organisation and protest, and … labour market intervention and intermediation." MIT professor Thomas Kochan, in Walsh (2018), provides the example of the Coalition of Immokalee Workers in Florida to illustrate how alt-labour organisations effectively engage in collective action that is currently prohibited by U.S. labour law. The Coalition sustained a four-year boycott, which included highly publicised campaigning, against Taco Bell in an attempt to secure wage increases and better working conditions for tomato pickers. The workers were also lobbying for protections against sexual harassment, brutally long workdays, and a lack of benefits (McKenna, 2015). Eventually, Taco Bell's parent company agreed to the workers' demands. Such concerted actions "up or down the supply chain," Kochan notes, "are impermissible" under the National Labor Relations Act. Further, he adds, "the agricultural sector is exempt from coverage under the act," pointing to the potential for alt-labour organisations like the Coalition to obtain enhanced employment outcomes for American workers. Combined with traditional labour relations and collective bargaining, alternative forms of representation and influence present a promising path for collective voice among American workers.

Conclusion

As in other parts of the world, worker voice in the U.S. is a dynamic and complex topic. This particular chapter has taken a unique approach to examining voice by considering how two foundational employment relations theories—unitarism and pluralism—shape worker and employer thinking and behaviours around voice in the workplace. Unitarist or individual-focused worker voice, with its rooting in the academic tradition of organisational behaviour and its focus on human resource management policies and practices, increasingly dominates the American employment relations landscape. A proliferation of scholarship and business press on topics such as workplace empowerment and engagement reflects this reality. Concurrently, the traditional form of pluralistic and collective voice—labour unionism—has been on a steady decline in the U.S. and is under constant attack by many employers, politicians, and lawmakers. Nevertheless, recently research suggests a resurgence of interest among American workers for collective vehicles of voice, be they traditional labour unions and collective bargaining, newer alternative forms of representation such as those under the alt-labour umbrella, or a combination of the two. Given the ever-changing nature of work, innovations that address both the individual and the collective interests of workers will be required for effective and prosperous employment relations to thrive.

References

Andrias, K., & Rogers, B. (2018). *Rebuilding worker voice in today's economy.* Roosevelt Institute.

Bacon, N. (2003). Human resource management and industrial relations. In P. Ackers & A. Wilkinson (Eds.), *Understanding work and employment: Industrial relations in transition* (pp. 71–88). Oxford University Press.

Banerjee, A., Poydock, M., McNicholas, C., Mangundayao, I., & Sait, A. (2021). *Unions are not only good for workers, they're good for communities and for democracy.* Economic Policy Institute. https://files.epi.org/uploads/236748.pdf

Barry, M., & Wilkinson, A. (2016). Pro-social or pro-management? A critique of the conception of employee voice as a pro-social behaviour within organisational behaviour. *British Journal of Industrial Relations, 54*(2), 261–284.

Barry, M., & Wilkinson, A. (2022). Employee voice, psychologisation and human resource management (HRM). *Human Resource Management Journal, 32*(3), 631–646.

Botero, I. C., & Van Dyne, L. (2009). Employee voice behavior: Interactive effects of LMX and power distance in the United States and Colombia. *Management Communication Quarterly, 23*(1), 84–104.

Budd, J. W., & Bhave, D. (2008). Values, ideologies, and frames of reference in industrial relations. In P. Blyton, N. Bacon, J. Fiorito, & E. Heery (Eds.), *The Sage handbook of industrial relations* (pp. 92–112). Sage Publications.

Bureau of Labor Statistics. (2021). *Union Members—2021*. https://www.bls.gov/news.release/pdf/union2.pdf

Bureau of Labor Statistics. (2022). *Union Members Summary—2022*. https://www.bls.gov/news.release/union2.nr0.htm

Council of Economic Advisers. (2022, September 5). *The state of our unions*. https://www.whitehouse.gov/cea/written-materials/2022/09/05/the-state-of-our-unions/

Detert, J. R., & Treviño, L. K. (2010). Speaking up to higher-ups: How supervisors and skip-level leaders influence employee voice. *Organisation Science, 21*(1), 249–270.

Donaghey, J., Cullinane, N., Dundon, T., & Wilkinson, A. (2011). Reconceptualising employee silence: Problems and prognosis. *Work, Employment and Society, 25*(1), 51–67.

Farh, C. I., & Chen, G. (2018). Leadership and member voice in action teams: Test of a dynamic phase model. *Journal of Applied Psychology, 103*(1), 97.

Fisk, C. (2020). Sustainable alt-labor. *Chicago-Kent Law Review, 94*(1), 9.

Fox, A. (1974). *Beyond contract: Work, power, and trust relations*. Faber & Faber.

Godard, J. (2014). The psychologisation of employment relations?. *Human Resource Management Journal, 24*(1), 1–18.

Grant, A. M. (2013). Rocking the boat but keeping it steady: The role of emotion regulation in employee voice. *Academy of Management Journal, 56*(6), 1703–1723.

Heery, E. J., Bacon, N., Blyton, P. R., & Fiorito, J. (2008). Introduction: The field of industrial relations. In P. Blyton, N. Bacon, J. Fiorito, & E. Heery (Eds.), *The Sage handbook of industrial relations* (pp. 1–32). Sage Publications.

Hertel-Fernandez, A., Kimball, W., & Kochan, T. (2022). What forms of representation do American workers want? Implications for theory, policy, and practice. *ILR Review, 75*(2), 267–294.

Hirschman, A. O. (1970). *Exit, voice, and loyalty: Responses to decline in firms, organizations, and states*. Harvard University Press.

Howell, T. M., Harrison, D. A., Burris, E. R., & Detert, J. R. (2015). Who gets credit for input? Demographic and structural status cues in voice recognition. *Journal of Applied Psychology, 100*(6), 1765–1784.

Isodore, C. (2007). *US Air ends $10B bid for Delta*. https://money.cnn.com/2007/01/31/news/companies/usair_delta/index.htm

Kaufman, B. E. (2015). Theorising determinants of employee voice: An integrative model across disciplines and levels of analysis. *Human Resource Management Journal, 25*(1), 19–40.

King, D. D., Ryan, A. M., & Van Dyne, L. (2019). Voice resilience: Fostering future voice after non-endorsement of suggestions. *Journal of Occupational and Organisational Psychology, 92*(3), 535–565.

Kochan, T. A., Yang, D., Kimball, W. T., & Kelly, E. L. (2019). Worker voice in America: Is there a gap between what workers expect and what they experience? *ILR Review, 72*(1), 3–38.

Lafer, G., & Loustaunau, L. (2020). *Fear at work: An inside account of how employers threaten, intimidate, and harass workers to stop them from exercising their right to collective bargaining*. Economic Policy Institute. https://www.epi.org/publication/fear-at-work-how-employers-scare-workers-out-of-unionizing/

Laschinger, H. K. S., Finegan, J. E., Shamian, J., & Wilk, P. (2004). A longitudinal analysis of the impact of workplace empowerment on work satisfaction. *Journal of Organisational Behaviour, 25*(4), 527–545.

LePine, J. A., & Van Dyne, L. (1998). Predicting voice behavior in work groups. *Journal of Applied Psychology, 83*(6), 853.

Lewin, D. (2001). IR and HR perspectives on workplace conflict: What can each learn from the other? *Human Resource Management Review, 11*(4), 453–485.

Marchington, M., & Kynighou, A. (2012). The dynamics of employee involvement and participation during turbulent times. *The International Journal of Human Resource Management, 23*(16), 3336–3354.

McCarthy, J. (2022). *U.S. approval of labor unions at highest point since 1965*. Gallup. https://news.gallup.com/poll/398303/approval-labor-unions-highest-point-1965.aspx

McClean, E. J., Martin, S. R., Emich, K. J., & Woodruff, C. T. (2018). The social consequences of voice: An examination of voice type and gender on status and subsequent leader emergence. *Academy of Management Journal, 61*(5), 1869–1891.

McKenna, M. (2015). *Tomato pickers expand case for workers' rights*. National Geographic. https://www.nationalgeographic.com/culture/article/tomato-pickers-expand-case-for-workers-rights

Morrison, E. W. (2011). Employee voice behaviour: Integration and directions for future research. *Academy of Management Annals, 5*(1), 373–412.

Morrison, E. W. (2014). Employee voice and silence. *Annual Review of Organizational Psychology & Organisational Behaviour, 1*(1), 173–197.

Morrison, E. W. (2023). Employee voice and silence: Taking stock a decade later. *Annual Review of Organisational Psychology and Organisational Behaviour, 10*, 79–107.

Mowbray, P. K., Wilkinson, A., & Tse, H. H. (2015). An integrative review of employee voice: Identifying a common conceptualization and research agenda. *International Journal of Management Reviews, 17*(3), 382–400.

Nelson, M. W., & Proell, C. A. (2018). Is silence golden? Audit team leader reactions to subordinates who speak up "in the moment" and at performance appraisal. *The Accounting Review, 93*(6), 281–300.

Park, J. Y., & Nawakitphaitoon, K. (2018). The cross-cultural study of LMX and individual employee voice: The moderating role of conflict avoidance. *Human Resource Management Journal, 28*(1), 14–30.

Peterson, C., Maier, S. F., & Seligman, M. E. (1993). *Learned helplessness: A theory for the age of personal control.* Oxford University Press.

Rothenberg, S. (2003). Knowledge content and worker participation in environmental management at NUMMI. *Journal of Management Studies, 40*(7), 1783–1802.

Schneider, B., Yost, A. B., Kropp, A., Kind, C., & Lam, H. (2018). Workforce engagement: What it is, what drives it, and why it matters for organisational performance. *Journal of Organisational Behaviour, 39*(4), 462–480.

Sojourner, A., & Yang, J. (2015). *Effects of unionization on workplace-safety enforcement: Regression-discontinuity evidence.* IZA Discussion Papers 9610, Institute of Labor Economics (IZA).

Taiyi Yan, T., Tangirala, S., Vadera, A. K., & Ekkirala, S. (2022). How employees learn to speak up from their leaders: Gender congruity effects in the development of voice self-efficacy. *Journal of Applied Psychology, 107*(4), 650.

Tangirala, S., & Ramanujam, R. (2012). Ask and you shall hear (but not always): Examining the relationship between manager consultation and employee voice. *Personnel Psychology, 65*(2), 251–282.

U.S. Department of Labor. The Union Advantage. https://www.dol.gov/general/workcenter/union-advantage#:~:text=Workers%20with%20union%20representation%20enjoy,%241%2C169%2Fweek).&text=When%20more%20workers%20have%20unions,union%20and%20non%2Dunion%20workers

Ulrich, D., & Brockbank, W. (2005). *The HR value proposition.* Harvard Business Press.

Van Dyne, L., & LePine, J. A. (1998). Helping and voice extra-role behaviours: Evidence of construct and predictive validity. *Academy of Management Journal, 41*(1), 108–119.

Walsh, D. (2018). Alt-labor, explained. https://mitsloan.mit.edu/ideas-made-to-matter/alt-labor-explained

Walumbwa, F. O., & Schaubroeck, J. (2009). Leader personality traits and employee voice behaviour: Mediating roles of ethical leadership and work group psychological safety. *Journal of Applied Psychology, 94*(5), 1275.

Weil, D. (1991). Enforcing OSHA: The role of labour unions. *Industrial Relations: A Journal of Economy and Society, 30*(1), 20–36.

Weiss, M., & Morrison, E. W. (2019). Speaking up and moving up: How voice can enhance employees' social status. *Journal of Organisational Behaviour, 40*(1), 5–19.

4

Employee Voice and Engagement: An Assessment of Greek Organisations

Nadia K. Kougiannou

Introduction

There is extensive literature on employee voice and engagement in the Anglo-American world, but we know much less about how employee voice operates in less advanced economies (Pyman et al., 2016). This chapter explores the evolving concepts of employee voice and engagement, which have emerged as important areas of research and management in the last three decades. This growth in interest can be linked to increasing globalisation, deregulation, and a search for competitive advantage in the current environment (Holland & Kougiannou, 2021). The chapter looks to define and explain the role of employee voice and engagement and their crucial role in establishing an effective workplace underpinned by efficient communications within the context of Greek organisations. This chapter looks to assess the state of employee voice and engagement within Greek organisations by exploring recent publications

N. K. Kougiannou (✉)
Nottingham Trent University, Nottingham, UK
e-mail: nadia.kougiannou@ntu.ac.uk

T. Ajibade Adisa et al. (eds.), *Employee Voice in the Global North*,
https://doi.org/10.1007/978-3-031-31123-9_4

that focused on these concepts within the Greek context. There is little doubt that communication in the workplace has been fundamentally reshaped in recent years (Holland & Kougiannou, 2021), especially so in Greece, where employment relations have been impacted not only by the recent crises (e.g. COVID-19 pandemic, cost-of-living crisis, etc.) but also by one of the worst economic crisis of its recent history (Prouska et al., 2022). These changes have had a significant effect on the structure of the employment relationship, not least on the nature of employee voice and employee engagement in the workplace. The move from a collective to an individual approach to managing the workplace has seen an increasing focus on direct communications between employers and employees at all levels, but more so in less unionised workplace areas (Holland & Kougiannou, 2021). This change has seen the emergence of substantial research and interest in establishing how employee voice channels can be adapted and managed effectively in an evolving work environment.

Although research has emphasised the organisational and individual factors that influence employee voice and engagement at work, it is less known how these concepts are affected by the economic context, particularly when this context is one of intensive and long-term economic crisis, followed by consecutive crises (e.g. COVID-19 pandemic, cost-of-living crisis, etc.). It seems that employee voice and, more so, employee engagement have not been greatly investigated within a financial crisis context. Given the particular gaps in research on employee voice and engagement in a context of almost constant crises, it is crucial to explore the state of employee voice and engagement within the Greek context, a context characterised by prolonged and consecutive crises (e.g. ten-year-long economic crisis, followed by COVID-19 pandemic and cost-of-living crises). Such macro-turbulence influences employees' experience with work, given the higher job insecurity and stress that prevail, as well as decreased pay, benefits, training and development opportunities (Prouska et al., 2022). This conceptual chapter contributes to employee voice and engagement knowledge by assessing the state of these two concepts within Greek organisations and proposes future research directions. This chapter is organised into four main sections. The first part provides an introduction and recent debates on the conceptualisation of employee voice and engagement. The second part discusses the Greek context, including the economic crisis, working conditions, and the nature of the employment relationship in Greek organisations. The third part offers an assessment of the state of employee voice and engagement in Greece based on recent empirical publications that tackle these issues. A summary and future research directions are presented in the final part.

What Is Employee Voice

For more than a century, research on the broad fields of industrial relations (IRs) and human resource management (HRM) has attempted to understand the role of unions in providing a representative voice to promote workplace inclusion for employees (Townsend et al., 2022). However, the topic of employee voice and associated streams of research has broadened in recent decades to include multiple forms, such as grievance procedures (Kirk, 2018) alongside union and non-union employee channels for representative participation (Cullinane et al., 2017; Lewin, 2014). Attention has also concerned informal voice and the extent to which internal mechanisms may compete against or complement one another, for example individual speak-up arrangements alongside collective consultation (Townsend et al., 2022).

The voice literature suggests that employees will have multiple motivations for voice across diverse workplace settings. Some streams of literature focus on particular contexts or specific voice arrangements: 'voice processes' (Dundon et al., 2005); specific 'channels of voice' (Pyman et al., 2006); 'voice systems' (Marchington, 2007); or 'voice episodes' (Wilkinson et al., 2018). Other research streams typically look at different voice behaviours at an individual level: motivational traits, prosocial intentions, individual differences, or employee commitment and satisfaction with voice (Morrison, 2011, 2014). In its simplest form, employee voice arrangements are associated with formal and informal systems or networks for employees and management to communicate about workplace issues. It is how workers raise concerns with management and how management raises issues with workers and gains insight into the workers' reactions (Kougiannou & Holland, 2022). Voice is a broad term, often used interchangeably with concepts such as participation, engagement, involvement, and empowerment and has been mostly examined through two paradigms, namely the industrial relations (IRs) and organisational behaviour (OB) paradigms (Prouska & Psychogios, 2018). Within the IR paradigm, employee voice is broadly defined as the ways and means through which employees attempt to have a say and potentially influence organisational affairs about issues that affect their work and the interests of owners and managers (Wilkinson et al., 2014). On the other hand, the OB paradigm views voice as 'prosocial', assuming employees communicate ideas, suggestions, or opinions about work issues to benefit the organisation (Barry & Wilkinson, 2016). For the assessment of voice in Greek organisations, this chapter adopts an integrative approach (Mowbray et al., 2015), allowing the examination of the context of voice with a consideration of the role of power at work.

By taking an integrative approach to voice, the chapter focuses on how these voice mechanisms develop and what their major challenges are within the Greek context. As noted, the main changes made in the organisation of work and employment have fundamentally impacted employee voice. As a result, what has emerged in the last three decades has been the development of multiple channels of voice, best described as direct, indirect, and hybrid voices (Holland & Kougiannou, 2021):

- Direct voice refers to direct communication between individual employees and their immediate manager(s), emphasises the enhancement of productivity and employee commitment, and is characterised as 'prosocial'.
- Indirect voice is often seen through the prism of the employee representative, such as trade unions, with an emphasis on negotiating workplace terms and conditions, and is mainly associated with the IR paradigm.
- A hybrid voice system involves both direct and indirect mechanisms.

Prior research has emphasised the significance of employee voice for work groups, units, organisations, and individuals in private and public organisations (Bennett, 2010; Benson & Brown, 2010; Gambarotto & Cammozzo, 2010; Liang & Tang, 2010; Morrison, 2011, 2014). For example, it has been shown that employee voice enhances the effectiveness of team and organisational operation and performance through the sharing of employees' ideas and opinions (Detert et al., 2013; MacKenzie et al., 2011), it brings about advantageous effects on the quality and productivity of the organisation (Wilkinson & Fay, 2011), it facilitates organisational learning through the successful implementation of new practices and methods within a team (Edmondson, 2003), and it can be the source of novel ideas (Liang & Tang, 2010). Furthermore, at an individual level, employee voice is likely to increase work engagement (Rees et al., 2013), reduce turnover intentions, and improve involvement in higher-level decision-making (McClean et al., 2013). As one can deduce from the above, voice is a broad term that often is used interchangeably with concepts such as involvement and participation, empowerment, and engagement (Prouska & Psychogios, 2018; Wilkinson & Fay, 2011). Additionally, employee voice has been identified as one of the pillars of employee engagement (MacLeod & Clarke, 2009). As such, it is prudent to discuss employee engagement before exploring its state within Greek organisations.

What Is Employee Engagement

The MacLeod Review (MacLeod & Clarke, 2009) propelled the concept of employee engagement into the consciousness of organisations, practitioners, and academics (Yalabik et al., 2013). Findings from the review highlighted the positive links between employee engagement and organisational outcomes (e.g. May et al., 2004; Yalabik et al., 2013; Soane et al., 2013). Consequently, organisations, policymakers, and academics began to pay greater attention to employee engagement (Bailey et al., 2017). However, although there is an increased awareness and interest in employee engagement, there is an apparent 'knowing-doing' gap attributed to a lack of rigorous research and a gap between practitioner and academic focus (Jenkins & Delbridge, 2013; Shuck, 2011).

Four major approaches are widely used to define the concept of employee engagement (Fragouli & Louka, 2021): (a) the need-satisfying approach (Kahn, 1990), (b) the burnout-antithesis approach (Maslach et al., 2001), (c) the satisfaction-engagement approach (Harter et al., 2002), and (d) the multidimensional approach (Saks, 2006). Kahn (1990) conceptualised employee engagement as the concurrent expression of one's preferred self and the promotion of connection to others. He suggested that meaningfulness, safety, and availability were very important in understanding why a person would become engaged in their work. According to Kahn (1990), meaningfulness is the positive 'sense of return on investments of self in role performance' (Kahn, 1990, p. 705), while safety is the ability to show one's self 'without fear or negative consequences to self-image, status, or career' (Kahn, 1990, p. 705) and availability was the 'sense of possessing the physical, emotional, and psychological resources necessary' (Kahn, 1990, p. 705) to complete one's work.

In contrast, Maslach et al. (2001) posited that employee engagement is the positive antithesis to burnout, defining burnout as the erosion of engagement. The authors defined engagement as 'a persistent, positive affective-motivational state of fulfilment in employees characterised by high levels of activation and pleasure' (p. 417). At the same time, burnout is work that becomes unpleasant, unfulfilling, and meaningless (Maslach et al., 2001, p. 416). Maslach and Leiter (2008) essentially rephrased burnout as an erosion of engagement with the job. Accordingly, engagement is characterised by energy, involvement, and efficacy—the direct opposites of the three burnout dimensions (Xanthopoulou, Bakker, Arnold, Kantas, & Demerouti, 2012). According to this approach, anyone not experiencing burnout should be engaged. Schaufeli et al. (2002, p. 74) define engagement as a 'positive, fulfilling, work-related state of mind that is characterised by vigour, dedication, and absorption'. However, the authors use the term 'work engagement' for this definition. Harter et al.'s (2002, p. 417) approach encompasses Kahn's (1990) and Maslach et al.'s (2001) engagement frameworks and defines employee engagement as an 'individual's involvement and satisfaction with as well as enthusiasm for work'. The fourth and final approach to employee engagement is based on a multidimensional perspective (Fragouli & Louka, 2021). According to Saks (2006), employee engagement was developed from cognitive (Kahn, 1990; Maslach et al., 2001), emotional (Harter et al., 2002; Kahn, 1990), and behavioural elements (Harter et al., 2002; Maslach et al., 2001) separating job engagement and organisational engagement. Extending Schaufeli et al.'s (2002) model, this research suggested that engagement could be experienced emotionally and cognitively and manifested behaviourally. Saks (2006) paralleled Schaufeli et al.'s (2002), Kahn's (1990), and Harter et al.'s (2002) models by viewing the development of engagement as the absorption of a person's resources into their work. All frameworks suggest that employees should readily have the physical, emotional, and psychological resources to complete their work for absorption to occur (Fragouli & Louka, 2021). Without them, burnout develops (Maslach et al., 2001; Schaufeli et al., 2002), and employees eventually disengage. Furthermore, Macey and Schneider (2008), extending Saks's (2006) model, suggested that each state of engagement (cognitive-emotional-behavioural) builds on the next, eventually leading to absolute employee engagement.

Organisations need engaged employees and are looking for ways to develop this workforce (Bakker & Schaufeli, 2008). Research has shown that organisations with high levels of employee engagement report positive organisational outcomes (Kular et al., 2008). Moreover, Welch (2011) suggests that employee engagement is the most crucial factor that can drive an organisation's success and effectiveness. However, employee engagement is not only needed in balanced situations. Research evidence draws attention to employee engagement as a tool that can lead to organisation success, productivity, and effectiveness during times of crisis (Welch, 2011; Saji, 2014; Kelleher, 2009). Arguably, this is more salient within contexts of deep and long crises and weak institutional bases (Prouska et al., 2022), such as Greece. Next, the Greek context is discussed, with a particular focus on the economic crisis and consequent working conditions in Greek organisations.

The Greek Context

Greece is a country-member of the European Union, with a central role in the financial and business development in the Balkans and South-Eastern Europe (Nikolaou et al., 2008). Greece is a peripheral country in the European Union that influences and is influenced by the Balkan and the Black Sea countries, whose cultural and economic context is somewhat different from the West-European countries (Katou & Budhwar, 2012). Greece might be primarily considered a West-European country as a member of the EU, but it is also extensively influenced by the Middle East and Mediterranean national culture. Greece has weak institutional bases and is characterised by unique labour relations and institutional conditions (Mihail & Kloutsiniotis, 2016; Prouska & Psychogios, 2018).

A striking dualism characterises the Greek economy in terms of the private sector (Mihail & Kloutsiniotis, 2016). On the one hand, there is a class of professionally managed firms, including the subsidiaries of multinationals. On the other hand, there are numerous small and medium enterprises (SMEs), mostly family owned and traditionally managed by their founders or small proprietors (Mihail & Kloutsiniotis, 2016). SMEs perform 99% of industrial business activities, and although they demonstrate low productivity, they tend to maintain an increased employment rate (Psychogios & Wood, 2010). It can be argued that the practice of HRM in Greece is also dualistic. Indeed, larger employers are more inclined to follow the law and be unionised, which makes the practice of HRM more consistent and regulated. In contrast, the HRM policies in SMEs are likely to be unprocedural, flexible, highly personal, but also arbitrary (Mihail & Kloutsiniotis, 2016), and with little in the way of formalised mechanisms for involvement and participation, which is often matched by poor terms of employment and working conditions (Psychogios & Wood, 2010). Specifically, SMEs are characterised by relatively weak job security, while the lack of resources forces them to rely mainly on on-the-job training rather than on external courses (Psychogios & Wood, 2010).

The Greek Economic Crisis and Its Effect on the Employment Relationship

The Greek economic crisis was triggered by the global economic recession in 2008. As a result, since 2010, the Greek government has adopted several austerity programmes to reduce public debt (Fragouli & Louka, 2021). The main elements of the fiscal consolidation programmes for the public sector focused on: the reduction of employees' salaries, increase in several types of indirect taxes, and recruitment freeze (Kouretas & Vlamis, 2010; Markovits et al., 2014). Moreover, the Greek government focused on competitiveness measures targeting the private sector, such as a reduction in the minimum wage, abolition of collective wage agreements, and the liberalisation of several professions (Christopoulou & Monastiriotis, 2014). However, these measures caused a vicious cycle of depression and a worsening crisis (Fragouli & Louka, 2021). Greek organisations struggled to survive in this climate, with the most affected sectors being construction, trade, tourism, services, and banking (Epitropaki, 2011). In response to the challenges faced, many Greek organisations dismissed employees and reduced salaries and other benefits. The effects were severe for many work-related attitudes, such as employee voice and engagement, psychological climate, job fit, affective commitment, and ethical leadership (Fragouli & Louka, 2021).

The Greek crisis also led to endogenous and exogenous institutional change (Williams & Vorley, 2015). Greek institutions are traditionally weak (Prouska & Kapsali, 2011) and have become even more dysfunctional since the crisis in regulating labour markets and securing viable and sustainable growth (Kornelakis & Voskeritsian, 2014). Greek financial institutions have been deteriorating since the beginning of the crisis when the country entered a strict austerity regime with extensive market reforms (Samitas & Polyzos, 2016). Since 2009 Greece has been experiencing a decline in wages and an increase in part-time and fixed-term employment, resulting in increased job insecurity (Leschke et al., 2012). Greece suffered significantly from the crisis, with a near collapse of its economy and austerity measures having a critical impact on the labour force, particularly among younger workers (Psychogios et al., 2016). Greece experienced a 22% increase in job insecurity during the crisis (2008–2012) compared to an EU-27 average of 4% and a 0.7% increase in temporary employment compared to an EU-27 average of −0.6% in the same period (Eurofound, 2016). Among EU member states, the highest unemployment rates were observed in Greece (24.6%) (Eurostat, 2016a). In addition, Greece reduced its minimum wage by 22% since 2010, the highest cut in the EU (Eurofound, 2016). The national minimum wage in 2016 stood at €683 per month, compared to the UK

(€1529) (Eurostat, 2016b). The minimum wage was cut to €586 in 2012 and, since 2016, it has been raised three times, to €713, with a further rise in 2023 to €751 per month.

This long-term crisis's effects have negatively impacted many Greek companies (Arghyrou & Tsoukalas, 2010), especially SMEs (Prouska & Psychogios, 2018). The Greek business system is dominated by SMEs, primarily small (counting less than 50 employees) family businesses with concentrated ownership structures within a few large holders (Prouska & Kapsali, 2011). These firms have been negatively impacted since 2009; not only did they have to counter and overcome increased taxation, but they also had to cope with the inability of the country's banks to support them financially. Also, many small and micro companies had liquidity problems, being unable to pay their suppliers and employees (Kouretas & Vlamis, 2010). This problem intensified in June 2015 when capital controls were implemented to stop a likely bank run due to the political instability in the country (Samitas & Polyzos, 2016). Moreover, increased layoffs and decreased salaries have led to high uncertainty and employee dissatisfaction (Arghyrou & Tsoukalas, 2010). The European Job Quality Index (Leschke et al., 2012) ranked Greece as the worst performer, highlighting a decline in full-time employment and wages and increased job insecurity. With companies employing fewer people, workloads increased significantly for those remaining, with a rise in bullying behaviour (Giorgi et al., 2015).

In sum, the economic crisis led to changes in management style and cost-cutting strategies, worsening the working conditions. As a result, employees experienced redundancies, increased working hours, and reductions in pay and development opportunities, all of which led to job insecurity, work overload, demotivation, and well-being issues.

Working Conditions in Greek Organisations

The Greek industrial relations system is bifurcated: the state sector and large firms are strongly unionised and regulated, but there are many SMEs and a significant underground economy. Smaller enterprises make up the bulk of the Greek economy, lack trade union representation, and have a culture of non-compliance with labour law (Mihail, 2004). This leads to non-procedural and informal practices within an environment of poor employment and working conditions (Wood et al., 2015).

The comparative capitalisms literature categorises Greece in the 'Mediterranean' model of South European countries, with limited state intervention in the regulation of working conditions, a restricted influence of organised labour on working conditions in the private sector and low job tenure, making it unattractive for employers and uninteresting for employees to invest in training (Amable, 2003; Psychogios et al., 2020). This leads to lower employee skill levels, low-quality work organisation, and low wage rates (Holman, 2013).

Among the Mediterranean countries, Greece has some of the 'cheapest' labour, the lowest levels of productivity, and the lowest minimum wage (Prouska & Kapsali, 2011). This can be explained through the country's socioeconomic, political, and historical context (Psychogios et al., 2020). In the late twentieth century, Greece attempted to imitate the industrialisation process of northern Europe and North America but never overcame the underdevelopment of domestic institutions and infrastructures caused by its turbulent political and economic history (Psychogios et al., 2020). Moreover, since the last century, Greece has been affected by numerous political and military events, including, most recently, monetary integration with the EU and the latest global 'crunch' (Kapsali & Butler, 2011). As a result, Greece was financially 'exhausted', needing economic aid with the resulting foreign interference in internal affairs.

Apart from this reduction of sovereignty, geopolitical factors affected the economy and made it difficult to attract foreign direct investment. Frequent changes in political regimes and economic policies led to a lack of a consistent national strategy and an underdeveloped institutional base that could provide 'guarantees' for investors (Psychogios et al., 2020). Businesses needed to be small (low-cost, low-investment, and short-term oriented) and agile; this made for a volatile landscape with a high rate of self-employment and micro-family owned enterprises (Prouska & Kapsali, 2011). This system could not sustain large manufacturing, and the economy focused on services and small-scale agriculture. Overall, the institutional basis is weak and fragile (Psychogios et al., 2020).

Entry into the Eurozone in 2001 was the first step towards the current systemic crisis. Greek organisations were impacted negatively because the economy was not ready for the constraints imposed (Gibson et al., 2012), and successive governments failed to recognise the consequences. The issue of Greek debt resurfaced after the 2008 global financial crisis. The effects were catastrophic for many companies that faced significant financial difficulties with a spillover effect on their suppliers and employees (Kouretas & Vlamis, 2010).

The severity of the impact of the 2007 global financial crisis varied considerably between economies worldwide (Johnstone et al., 2019), with some countries experiencing significant austerity cuts while others resisted such measures (Eurofound, 2013). Although research talks about a 'post-crisis' period (Kornelakis et al., 2017), recovery has not yet been achieved by all affected economies. Institutionally weaker economies have struggled to bounce back to pre-crisis levels, with knock-on effects on working conditions (Prouska et al., 2022). In Greece, for example, worsening working conditions have become the norm for many workers as the crisis led to regressive institutional employment changes (Psychogios et al., 2020).

The most recent European survey on working conditions shows that the work environment of Greek employees is significantly more demanding and less resourceful (Eurofound, 2019). More specifically, Greek employees work longer hours, are at a higher risk exposure level, perceive lower levels of autonomy and voice at work, have lower task rotation, and receive significantly less training (Eurofound, 2019). Also, Greek employees are among the first in Europe to report that their work negatively affects their health (Xanthopoulou et al., 2012). These differences are significant because theoretical models explaining burnout and engagement suggest that demanding work environments (i.e. characterised by a high workload, high risks, and cognitive demands) are responsible for employee burnout. In contrast, resourceful work environments (i.e. characterised by high levels of autonomy, support, and employee-friendly practices) relate to employee engagement (Demerouti et al., 2001). Furthermore, the level of unemployment has been historically significantly higher in Greece (Eurofound, 2007, 2012, 2019). These results suggest that Greek employees are more likely to be burned out and less likely to be engaged.

Employee Voice and Engagement in Greece

Research has studied firms' responses to the crisis through restructuring and downsizing, changing working time arrangements, implementing pay freezes, or reducing pay and rewards (Teague & Roche, 2014; Wood et al., 2015). Such strategies have implications for employee motivation, productivity, loyalty, well-being (Ogbonnaya et al., 2019), and, arguably, employee voice and engagement. At the national policy level, the ILO (2015) has recorded a general decline in collective bargaining due to the termination of national general agreements and the abolishment of policy support for multi-employer bargaining—particularly in countries hardest hit by the crisis, such as Greece. Since the global financial crisis (2008) and the Eurozone crisis (2010), research has focused on the consequences of these crises on institutional arrangements across different models of capitalism (e.g. Hassel, 2014; Heyes et al., 2012; Lallement, 2011). There has been a particular interest in how European peripheral economies responded to the crisis, considering the impact on their debt and banking systems (Tsolacos, 2014). In addition, research has been conducted on the impact of the crisis on HRM (Psychogios & Wood, 2010), working conditions (Psychogios et al., 2016), and employee health and well-being (Kondilis et al., 2013). But there is a lack of research, particularly on how countries with weak institutional bases, such as Greece, operating in long-term economic turbulence and almost constant crisis (economic, COVID-19, cost-of-living, etc.), have responded to these labour issues, particularly on how the crisis has affected voice at work in these contexts. Although in most of these economies, the crisis seems to have brought new balances into the financial operation of their systems, in Greece, the situation remained critical and turbulent (Prouska & Psychogios, 2018). The Greek crisis passed through various phases, and although stabilisation was observed in aspects of the system, turbulence dominated the system at the end (Wood et al., 2015). This indicates that the crisis in Greece, in contrast to other economies, particularly those in western and northern Europe, has been institutionalised and has taken a long-term form (O'Reilly et al., 2011).

The economic crisis brought more labour market deregulation, with a higher effect on employee voice, limiting the extent to which employees can 'be heard', especially on issues related to organisational decision-making (Wood et al., 2015). In SMEs, employee voice has been traditionally marginalised (Featherstone, 2008). Before the crisis, employee representation was highly fragmented, with high levels of centralisation of collective bargaining, especially in the public sector, leaving many small enterprises uncovered by collective bargaining agreements (Featherstone, 2008). In addition, a significant percentage of employees do not have the opportunity to join a trade union since 96% of firms in the country employ less than the minimum number of 21 employees required for a union to be established (Kouzis, 2000). This means that official employee voice is limited in the Greek private sector, especially in smaller firms.

Eurofound (2019) data shows that an official structure for employee representation is present in 29% of EU27 establishments, with Greece having the lowest proportion in all categories. Larger establishments are much more likely to have an employee representation structure (76%) than medium-sized (51%) or small (23%) establishments. However, structures for employee representation are least common in Greece (2%), with barely any presence. The proportion of small establishments with an employee representation structure is also lowest in Greece (1%), with a similar picture for medium-sized establishments with an employee representation, where Greece has the lowest proportion (7%) again. Finally, the proportion of large establishments with employee representation is lowest in Malta (24%) and Greece (25%). In the majority, if not all, of establishments in Greece that reported the presence of a body for employee representation, this is a trade union delegation.

In the broader IR context, Greece's entrance into the Eurozone (Makridimitris, 2001; Michalopoulos & Psychogios, 2003) and the increased competition for products and services in the single European market (Mandaraka & Kormentza, 2000) could lead to enhanced forms of voice through new patterns of employee representation (Psychogios & Szamosi, 2007). However, the crisis created a rapid decentralisation of collective bargaining to the enterprise level (since 2011) and a decrease in the number of labour market regulations deriving from sector-level and occupational collective employment agreements (Ioannou & Papadimitriou, 2013). Greek trade unions are considered a politicised form of employee representation with strong confrontational and militant strategies, making IR highly conflictual in collective negotiations (Mihail, 2004). However, since 2009, there has been a decline in trade unionism with an evident relaxation in the strictness of employment protection for regular contracts, temporary contracts, and dismissals (Prouska & Psychogios, 2018). Although unions are the most important form of employee representation, the law also provides for work council structures.

These are only found in a few companies, and where they exist, they work closely with the local union, while where there is no union in place, there will not be a works council (ETUI, 2022). The crisis also resulted in the emergence of 'associations of persons' (Prouska & Psychogios, 2018)—a 2011 law enables these associations to operate without a time limitation and with authority to sign collective agreements for companies of any size, provided there is no union in place, and 60% of the workforce is a member of the association (ETUI, 2022). But representatives of these associations have no permanent mandate and no protection against mistreatment by the employer (Prouska & Psychogios, 2018). In terms of the incidence of collective action in Greece, it is moderately high (Wallace & O'Sullivan, 2006). However, although general strikes have been organised throughout Greece since 2010 to protest against the Memorandum, pay, and working conditions, particularly from workers in large organisations (Lampousaki, 2014), employees from smaller enterprises do not often have this collective avenue for expressing voice (Kouzis, 2000).

Employee voice in Greek SMEs is practised differently than in large organisations due to a lack of formalisation (Psychogios et al., 2016). Most businesses are non-unionised, and only a few have some formal representation at work (Prouska & Psychogios, 2018). There is an apparent absence of work councils in the workplace (Lampousaki, 2011) and a weakening of the role and power of trade unions (Ioannou & Papadimitriou, 2013). The literature on Greece has explored how larger employers are inclined to promote unionisation, with some large companies having very active unions in the private sector (Ioannou &

Papadimitriou, 2013). In SMEs, the situation is different; employee voice is mainly driven by management-employee relationships, making smaller employers less keen to engage in creating and developing unions (Prouska & Kapsali, 2011).

Many economists consider the economic crisis of 2008 the worst since the Great Depression of the 1930s (Fragouli & Louka, 2021). Bell and Blanchflower (2011), who studied the effects of the economic crisis on world labour markets, highlight that it influenced employment, personal approaches in life, and attitudes to employment and work situations. Employee engagement is one of the most affected by the crisis work-related attitudes (Fragouli & Louka, 2021). A survey conducted by the global consulting firm Watson Wyatt in 2009 highlighted that levels of employee engagement dropped 9% over 2008. The study also revealed that the levels of engagement of the companies' top performers dropped 25% over 2008 (Fragouli & Louka, 2021).

Furthermore, evidence shows that during an economic crisis, employees are forced to produce more for less (Covey, 2004) with fewer resources (Buckingham & Coffman, 1999) while having unclear job demands in a climate of low managerial support (Covey, 2004). As a result, employees get more disengaged in the workplace (Cartwright & Holmes, 2006; Harter et al., 2002). In addition, employee engagement practices are often among the first programmes companies postpone or remove during a crisis as they try to reduce costs (Van Rooy et al., 2011). However, highly engaged employees are essential during a crisis as they are the force that helps the company get through it (Van Rooy et al., 2011). Welch (2011) argues that organisations should improve employee engagement to deal with crises. He highlights that employee engagement can drive organisation success and effectiveness and is more needed in crises. According to Saji (2014), attention should be drawn to understanding the value of employee engagement in a crisis. The article argues that during a crisis, a company needs engaged employees to be saved and to keep its customers happy. Research has shown (Welch, 2011; Kelleher, 2009) that the full power of employee engagement can drive organisational success and effectiveness while saving a company from the threat of a severe economic downturn.

Conclusion

The focus of this chapter has been to evaluate concepts of employee voice and employee engagement in Greek organisations. The chapter aimed to define and explain the role of employee voice and engagement, the key part they play, and how they are impacted by the context of Greek organisations. The Greek context was chosen to examine the subtleties of employee voice and engagement because weak institutional foundations characterise it in terms of employment policies, employment protection, industrial relations, and social protection (Prouska & Psychogios, 2018). There is little doubt that employee voice and engagement in the workplace have been fundamentally reshaped in recent years (Holland & Kougiannou, 2021), especially so in Greece, where employment relations have been impacted not only by the recent crises (e.g. COVID-19 pandemic, cost-of-living crisis, etc.) but also by one of the worst economic crisis of its recent history (Prouska et al., 2022). As noted in this chapter, these changes have had a significant effect on the structure of the employment relationship, not least on the nature of employee voice and employee engagement in the workplace.

There are substantial practical implications as the practices that were adopted to deal with the economic crisis, such as restructuring and downsizing, abolition of collective wage agreements, labour deregulation, and reducing pay and rewards, had a direct negative impact on employee voice, limiting the extent employees can 'be heard', especially on issues related to organisational decision-making. The crisis created a rapid decentralisation of collective bargaining to the enterprise level (since 2011) and a decrease in labour market regulations. Additionally, there has been a decline in trade unionism. In Greek SMEs, the situation is different and arguably more challenging; employee voice, when present, is mainly driven by management-employee relationships and takes mostly direct forms making smaller employers less keen to engage in the creation and development of unions. Most businesses are non-unionised, and only a few have some type of formal representation at work. The institutionalisation of adverse working conditions raises significant issues with employee voice and representation in the workplace. Adverse and worsening working conditions also mean managing implications for employee engagement.

There are also theoretical implications as currently there is limited literature on countries where long-term institutional weaknesses combine with turbulent economic conditions and long-term crises (Prouska & Psychogios, 2018). Additionally, there is limited literature comparing different crises and their effects on labour, employment, and employee relations (Psychogios et al., 2020). Future research can bring to the forefront how employees operate during periods of crisis and change, with a specific focus on the effects of crises on employee voice and engagement. Lastly, future research should focus on issues emerging from periods of ongoing crises, the strain that might impose, and their impact on working conditions. Studies specific to measuring working conditions in climates of almost constant crisis, such as the Greek context, could shed additional light on employee voice and engagement issues.

References

Amable, B. (2003). *The diversity of modern capitalism*. Oxford University Press.

Arghyrou, M., & Tsoukalas, J. (2010). The Greek debt crisis: Likely causes, mechanics and outcomes. *The World Economy, 34*, 173–191.

Bailey, C., Madden, A., Alfes, K., & Fletcher, L. (2017). The meaning, antecedents and outcomes of employee engagement: A narrative synthesis. *International Journal of Management Reviews, 19*(1), 31–53.

Bakker, A. B., & Schaufeli, W. B. (2008). Positive organisational behavior: Engaged employees in flourishing organisations. *Journal of Organizational Behavior: The International Journal of Industrial, Occupational and Organizational Psychology and Behavior, 29*(2), 147–154.

Barry, M., & Wilkinson, A. (2016). Prosocial or pro-management? A critique of the conception of employee voice as a prosocial behaviour within organisational behaviour. *British Journal of Industrial Relations, 54*(2), 261–284.

Bell, D. N., & Blanchflower, D. G. (2011). Young people and the Great Recession. *Oxford Review of Economic Policy, 27*(2), 241–267.

Bennett, T. (2010). Employee voice initiatives in the public sector: Views from the workplace. *International Journal of Public Sector Management, 23*(5), 444–455.

Benson, J., & Brown, M. (2010). Employee voice: Does union membership matter? *Human Resource Management Journal, 20*(1), 80–99.
Buckingham, M., & Coffman, C. (1999). *First, break all the rules; What the world's greatest managers do differently*. Simon and Schuster.
Cartwright, S., & Holmes, N. (2006). The meaning of work: The challenge of regaining employee engagement and reducing cynicism. *Human Resource Management Review, 16*, 199–208.
Christopoulou, R., & Monastiriotis, V. (2014). The public-private duality in wage reforms & adjustments during the Greek crisis. EIAMEP Crisis Observatory, Research Paper No. 9.
Covey, S. R. (2004). *The 8th habit: From effectiveness to greatness*. Simon and Schuster.
Cullinane, N., Hickland, E., Dundon, T., Dobbins, T., & Donaghey, J. (2017). Triggering employee voice under the European Information and Consultation Directive: A non-union case study. *Economic and Industrial Democracy, 38*(4), 629–655.
Demerouti, E., Bakker, A. B., Nachreiner, F., & Schaufeli, W. B. (2001). The job demands-resources model of burnout. *Journal of Applied Psychology, 86*(3), 499.
Detert, J. R., Burris, E. R., Harrison, D. A., & Martin, S. (2013). Voice flows to and around leaders: Understanding when units are helped or hurt by employee voice. *Administrative Science Quarterly, 58*(4), 624–668.
Dundon, T., Wilkinson, A., Marchington, M., & Ackers, P. (2005). The management of voice in nonunion organisations: managers' perspectives. *Employee Relations 27*(3), 307–320.
Edmondson, A. C. (2003). Speaking up in the operating room: How team leaders promote learning in interdisciplinary action teams. *Journal of Management Studies, 40*(6), 1419–1452.
Epitropaki, O. (2011). Human resource management strategies during the economic crisis. Retrieved from ALBA Graduate Business School website. http://www.alba.edu.gr/RCI/Documents/rci_2011%20olga%20final.pdf
ETUI. (2022). Greece—Workplace representation. https://worker-participation.eu/national-industrial-relations/countries/greece
Eurofound. (2007). Fourth European working conditions survey. Publications Office of the European Union, Luxembourg.
Eurofound. (2012). Fifth European working conditions survey. Publications Office of the European Union, Luxembourg.

Eurofound. (2013). Impact of the crisis on working conditions in Europe. http://www.eurofound.europa.eu/sites/default/files/ef_files/docs/ewco/tn1212025s/tn1212025s.pdf

Eurofound. (2016). Impact of the crisis on working conditions in Europe—Impact on employment conditions. http://www.eurofound.europa.eu/observatories/eurwork/comparative-information/impact-of-the-crisis-on-working-conditions-in-europe

Eurofound. (2019). European Company Survey 2019: Workplace practices unlocking employee potential. https://www.eurofound.europa.eu/publications/flagship-report/2020/european-company-survey-2019-workplace-practices-unlocking-employee-potential

Eurostat. (2016a). Unemployment statistics. http://ec.europa.eu/eurostat/statistics-explained/index.php/Unemployment_statistics

Eurostat. (2016b). Monthly minimum wages. http://appsso.eurostat.ec.europa.eu/nui/show.do

Featherstone, K. (2008). *Varieties of capitalism and the Greek case: Explaining the constraints on domestic reform*. GreeSE Paper No. 11, Hellenic Observatory, Papers on Greece and Southeast Europe. London: London School of Economics.

Fragouli, E., & Louka, X. (2021). Employee engagement in a crisis situation: the case of Greece. In *British Academy of Management (BAM) Conference 2021 on Recovering from Covid: Responsible Management and Reshaping the Economy*; 31 Aug–03 Sep 2021, Manchester, U.K.

Gambarotto, F., & Cammozzo, A. (2010). Dreams of silence: Employee voice and innovation in a public sector community of practice. *Innovation: Organization & Management, 12*(2), 166–179.

Gibson, H., Hall, S., & Tavlas, G. (2012). The Greek financial crisis: Growing imbalances and sovereign spreads. *Journal of International Money and Finance, 31*(3), 498–516.

Giorgi, G., Shoss, M. K., & Leon-Perez, J. M. (2015). Going beyond workplace stressors: Economic crisis and perceived employability in relation to psychological distress and job satisfaction. *International Journal of Stress Management, 22*(2), 137–158.

Harter, J. K., Schmidt, F. L., & Hayes, T. L. (2002). Business-unit-level relationship between employee satisfaction, employee engagement, and business outcomes: A meta-analysis. *Journal of Applied Psychology, 87*(2), 268.

Hassel, A. (2014). The paradox of liberalisation—Understanding dualism and the recovery of the German political economy. *British Journal of Industrial Relations, 52*, 57–81.

Heyes, J., Lewis, P., & Clark, I. (2012). Varieties of capitalism, neoliberalism and the economic crisis of 2008. *Industrial Relations Journal, 43*, 222–241.

Holland, P., & Kougiannou, N. (2021). Employee voice. In N. Dodd, C. Brewster, & P. Holland (Eds.), *Contemporary issues in human resources management* (5th ed., pp. 295–314). Oxford University Press.

Holman, D. (2013). Job types and job quality in Europe. *Human Relations, 66*(4), 475–502.

ILO. (2015). Collective bargaining coverage down as a result of the global financial crisis. http://www.ilo.org/global/about-the-ilo/newsroom/news/WCMS_415612/lang–en/index.htm

Ioannou, C., & Papadimitriou, K. (2013). *Collective bargaining in Greece in 2011 and 2012: Trends, breakthroughs and prospects (in Greek).* Athens: OMED (Organisation for Mediation and Arbitration).

Jenkins, S., & Delbridge, R. (2013). Context matters: Examining 'soft' and 'hard' approaches to employee engagement in two workplaces. *The International Journal of Human Resource Management, 24*(14), 2670–2691.

Johnstone, S., Saridakis, G., & Wilkinson, A. (2019). The global financial crisis, work and employment: Ten years on. *Economic and Industrial Democracy, 40*, 455–468.

Kahn, W. (1990). Psychological conditions of personal engagement and disengagement at work. *Academy of Management Journal, 33*, 692–724.

Kapsali, M., & Butler, J. (2011). Politics. In R. Prouska & M. Kapsali (Eds.), *Business and management practices in Greece: A comparative context* (pp. 3–25). Palgrave Macmillan.

Katou, A., & Budhwar, P. (2012). The link between HR practices, psychological contract fulfillment, and organisational performance: The case of the Greek service sector. *Thunderbird International Business Review, 54*, 793–809.

Kelleher, T. (2009). Conversational voice, communicated commitment, and public relations outcomes in interactive online communication. *Journal of Communication, 59*(1), 172–188.

Kirk, E. (2018). The (re)organisation of conflict at work: Mobilisation, countermobilisation and the displacement of grievance expressions. *Economic and Industrial Democracy, 39*(4), 639–660.

Kondilis, E., Giannakopoulos, S., Gavana, M., Ierodiakonou, I., Waitzkin, H., & Benos, A. (2013). Economic crisis, restrictive policies, and the population's health and health care: The Greek case. *American Journal of Public Health, 103*, 973–979.

Kornelakis, A., Veliziotis, M., & Voskeritsian, H. (2017). How can competitiveness be achieved in post-crisis Europe? Deregulating employment relations or enhancing high performance work practices? *The International Journal of Human Resource Management, 28*, 2957–2976.

Kornelakis, A., & Voskeritsian, H. (2014). The transformation of employment regulation in Greece: Towards a dysfunctional liberal market economy? *Relations Industrielles, 69*, 344–365.

Kougiannou, N., & Holland, P. (2022). Employee voice and silence in the digital era. In *The Emerald handbook of work, workplaces and disruptive issues in HRM* (pp. 513–531). Emerald Publishing Limited.

Kouretas, P. G., & Vlamis, P. (2010). The Greek crisis: Causes and implications. *Panoeconomicus, 57*(4), 391–404.

Kouzis, Y. (2000). The impact of EMU on labor relations. *Επιθεώρηση Εργασιακών Σχέσεων (in Greek), 18*, 57–66.

Kular, S., Gatenby, M., Rees, C., Soane, E., & Truss, K. (2008). Employee engagement: A literature review. Kingston University, Kingston Business School. http://eprints.kingston.ac.uk/4192/1/19wempen.pdf

Lallement, M. (2011). Europe and the economic crisis: Forms of labour market adjustment and varieties of capitalism. *Work, Employment and Society, 25*, 627–641.

Lampousaki, S. (2011). Greece: EIRO CAR on SMEs in the crisis: Employment, industrial relations and local partnership. http://www.eurofound.europa.eu/observatories/eurwork/comparative-information/national-contributions/greece/greeceeiro-car-on-smes-in-the-crisis-employment-industrial-relations-and-local-partnership

Lampousaki, S. (2014). Greece: Industrial relations profile. EurWORK, European Observatory of Working Life. http://www.eurofound.europa.eu/observatories/eurwork/comparative-information/national-contributions/greece/greeceindustrial-relations-profile

Leschke, J., Watt, A., & Finn, M. (2012). *Job quality in the crisis—An update of the Job Quality Index (JQI)*. Working Paper 2012.07. Brussels: European Trade Institute.

Lewin, D. (2014). Individual voice: Grievance and other procedures. In A. Wilkinson, J. Donaghey, T. Dundon, & R. Freeman (Eds.), *The handbook of research on employee voice* (pp. 281–297). Edward Elgar Press.

Liang, J., & Tang, J. (2010). A multi-level study on employee voice: Evidence from a chain of retail stores. *Frontiers of Business Research in China, 4*(4), 542–561.

Macey, W. H., & Schneider, B. (2008). The meaning of employee engagement. *Industrial and Organizational Psychology, 1*, 3–30.

MacKenzie, S. B., Podsakoff, P. M., & Podsakoff, N. P. (2011). Challenging-oriented organisational citizenship behaviors and organisational effectiveness: Do challenge-oriented behaviors really have an impact on the organisation's bottom line? *Personnel Psychology, 64*(3), 559–592.

MacLeod, D., & Clarke, N. (2009). *Engaging for success: Enhancing performance through employee engagement*. London: Department for Business, Innovation and Skills.

Makridimitris, A. (2001). Public administration in the political system: The Government, the Prime Minister, the Ministers. In P. E. Spiliotopoulos & A. Makridimitris (Eds.), *Public administration in Greece* (pp. 19–44). Sakkoulas.

Mandaraka, M., & Kormentza, I. (2000). Greece faces up to the EU packaging regulation: Businesses reveal their plans to meet the new legislative environment. *Environmental Management and Health, 11*, 7–19.

Marchington, M. (2007). Employee voice systems. In P. Boxall, J. Purcell, & P. Wright (Eds.), *The Oxford handbook of human resource management* (pp. 231–250). Oxford University Press.

Markovits, Y., Boer, D., & Dick, R. (2014). Economic crisis and the employee: The effects of economic crisis on employee job satisfaction, commitment and self-regulation. *European Management Journal, 32*(3), 413–422.

Maslach, C., & Leiter, M. P. (2008). Early predictors of job burnout and engagement. *Journal of Applied Psychology, 93*, 498–512.

Maslach, C., Schaufeli, W. B., & Leiter, M. P. (2001). Job burnout. *Annual Review of Psychology, 52*, 397–422.

May, D. R., Gilson, R. L., & Harter, L. M. (2004). The psychological conditions of meaningfulness, safety and availability and the engagement of the human spirit at work. *Journal of Occupational and Organizational Psychology, 77*(1), 11–37.

McClean, E. J., Burris, E. R., & Detert, J. R. (2013). When does voice lead to exit? It depends on leadership. *The Academy of Management Journal, 56*(2), 525–548.

Michalopoulos, N., & Psychogios, A. (2003). Knowledge management and public organisations: How well does the model apply to Greece? *Chinese Public Administration Review, 2*, 64–80.

Mihail, D. M. (2004). Labour flexibility in Greek SMEs. *Personnel Review, 33*, 549–560.

Mihail, D. M., & Kloutsiniotis, P. V. (2016). The effects of high-performance work systems on hospital employees' work-related well-being: Evidence from Greece. *European Management Journal, 34*(4), 424–438.

Morrison, E. W. (2011). Employee voice behavior: Integration and directions for future research. *The Academy of Management Annals, 5*(1), 373–412.

Morrison, E. W. (2014). Employee voice and silence. *The Annual Review of Organizational Psychology and Organizational Behavior, 1*(1), 173–197.

Mowbray, P. K., Wilkinson, A., & Tse, H. H. (2015). An integrative review of employee voice: Identifying a common conceptualisation and research agenda. *International Journal of Management Reviews, 17*(3), 382–400.

Nikolaou, I., Vakola, M., & Bourantas, D. (2008). Who speaks up at work? Dispositional influences on employees' voice behavior. *Personnel Review, 37*(6), 666–679.

O'Reilly, J., Lain, D., Sheehan, M., Smale, B., & Stuart, M. (2011). Managing uncertainty: The crisis, its consequences and the global workforce. *Work, Employment and Society, 25*, 581–595.

Ogbonnaya, C., Gahan, P., & Eib, C. (2019). Recessionary changes at work and employee well-being: The protective roles of national and workplace institutions. *European Journal of Industrial Relations, 25*, 377–393.

Prouska, R., & Kapsali, M. (Eds.). (2011). *Business and management practices in Greece: A comparative context*. Palgrave Macmillan.

Prouska, R., Nyfoudi, M., Psychogios, A., Szamosi, L. T., & Wilkinson, A. (2022). Solidarity in action at a time of crisis: The role of employee voice in relation to communication and horizontal solidarity behaviour. *British Journal of Management*. Online Early View, 1–20.

Prouska, R., & Psychogios, A. (2018). Do not say a word! Conceptualising employee silence in a long-term crisis context. *The International Journal of Human Resource Management, 29*(5), 885–914.

Psychogios, A., Brewster, C., & Parry, E. (2016). Western European HRM: Reactions and adjustment to crises. Chap. 7 in M. Dickmann, C. Brewster, & P. Sparrow (Eds.), *International human resource management: Contemporary issues in Europe* (3rd ed., pp. 115–134). Routledge.

Psychogios, A., & Szamosi, L. T. (2007). Exploring the Greek national business system: Towards a modernisation agenda. *EuroMed Journal of Business, 2*, 7–22.

Psychogios, A., Szamosi, L. T., Prouska, R., & Brewster, C. (2020). Varieties of crisis and working conditions: A comparative study of Greece and Serbia. *European Journal of Industrial Relations, 26*(1), 91–106.

Psychogios, A. G., & Wood, G. (2010). Human resource management in Greece in comparative perspective: Alternative institutionalist perspectives and empirical realities. *The International Journal of Human Resource Management, 21*(14), 2614–2630.

Pyman, A., Cooper, B., Teicher, J., & Holland, P. (2006). A comparison of the effectiveness of employee voice arrangements in Australia. *Industrial Relations Journal, 37*(5), 543–559.

Pyman, A., Gollan, P. J., Wilkinson, A., Xu, C., & Kalfa, S. (Eds.). (2016). *Employee voice in emerging economies*. Emerald Group Publishing.

Rees, C., Alfes, K., & Gatenby, M. (2013). Employee voice and engagement: Connections and consequences. *The International Journal of Human Resource Management, 24*(14), 2780–2798.

Saji, B. (2014). Employee engagement and its role during crisis management: A conceptual model. *European Journal of Business and Management, 6*(19), 110–117.

Saks, A. M. (2006). Antecedents and consequences of employee engagement. *Journal of Managerial Psychology, 21*, 600–619.

Samitas, A., & Polyzos, S. (2016). Freeing Greece from capital controls: Were the restrictions enforced in time? *Research in International Business and Finance, 37*, 196–213.

Schaufeli, W. B., Salanova, M., Gonzalez-Roma, V., & Bakker, A. B. (2002). The measurement of engagement and burnout: A two sample confirmatory factor analytic approach. *Journal of Happiness Studies, 3*, 71–92.

Shuck, B. (2011). *Four emerging perspectives of employee engagement: An integrative literature review*. SAGE Publications.

Soane, E., Shantz, A., Alfes, K., Truss, C., Rees, C., & Gatenby, M. (2013). The association of meaningfulness, well-being, and engagement with absenteeism: A moderated mediation model. *Human Resource Management, 52*(3), 441–456.

Teague, P., & Roche, W. K. (2014). Recessionary bundles: HR practices in the Irish economic crisis. *Human Resource Management Journal, 24*, 176–192.

Townsend, K., Wilkinson, A., Dundon, T., & Mowbray, P. K. (2022). Tracking employee voice: Developing the concept of voice pathways. *Asia Pacific Journal of Human Resources, 60*(2), 283–304.

Tsolacos, S. (2014). A prolonged financial crisis: Adjustments and prospects in Eurozone's southern markets. *Journal of Property Investment & Finance, 32*, 94–102.

Van Rooy, D. L., Whitman, D. S., Hart, D., & Caleo, S. (2011). Measuring employee engagement during a financial downturn: Business imperative or nuisance? *Journal of Business and Psychology, 26*(2), 147–152.

Wallace, J., & O'Sullivan, M. (2006). Contemporary strike trends since 1980: Peering through the wrong end of a telescope. In M. J. Morley, P. Gunnigle, & D. G. Collings (Eds.), *Global industrial relations* (pp. 273–291). Routledge.

Welch, M. (2011). The evolution of the employee engagement concept: Communication implications. *Corporate Communications: An International Journal, 16*, 328–346.

Wilkinson, A., Donaghey, J., Dundon, T., & Freeman, R. (2014). Employee voice: Charting new terrain. In A. Wilkinson, J. Donaghey, T. Dundon, & R. Freeman (Eds.), *The handbook of research on employee voice* (pp. 3–16). Edward Elgar Press.

Wilkinson, A., & Fay, C. H. (2011). Guest editors' note: New times for employee voice? *Human Resource Management, 50*(1), 65–74.

Wilkinson, A., Gollan, P., Kalfa, S., & Xu, C. (2018). Voices unheard: Employee voice in the new century. *International Journal of Human Resource Management, 29*(5), 711–724.

Williams, N., & Vorley, T. (2015). The impact of institutional change on entrepreneurship in a crisis-hit economy: The case of Greece. *Entrepreneurship & Regional Development, 27*, 28–49.

Wood, G., Szamosi, L. T., Psychogios, A., Sarvanidis, S., & Fotopoulou, D. (2015). Rethinking Greek capitalism through the lens of industrial relations reform: A view until the 2015 referendum. *Relations Industrielles, 70*, 698–717.

Xanthopoulou, D., Bakker, A. B., Kantas, A., & Demerouti, E. (2012). Measuring burnout and work engagement: Factor structure, invariance, and latent mean differences across Greece and the Netherlands. *International Journal of Business Science & Applied Management, 7*(2), 40–52.

Yalabik, Z. Y., Popaitoon, P., Chowne, J. A., & Rayton, B. A. (2013). Work engagement as a mediator between employee attitudes and outcomes. *The International Journal of Human Resource Management, 24*(14), 2799–2823.

5

Employee Voice in Portugal: Exploring Alternative Trajectories and Channels of Voice

Pedro Mendonça

Introduction to the Conceptualisation of Employee Voice Trajectories

The academic concept of 'voice' was popularised by Freeman and Medoff (1984) who argued that promoting voice amongst employees could, on the one hand, lead to employees' participation in the production process and as result impact positively on quality and productivity; and on the other hand, it could help mitigate 'bubbling' problems which left unaddressed could result in even bigger issues. A framework for voice proposed by Wilkinson et al. (2004) differentiated along two-by-two dimensions. These were argued to be (i) direct (based on employees themselves) and indirect (based on a union or collective grouping), and (ii) shared and contested agendas. A later study elaborated the conceptualisation of voice to argue that it could be petitioned individually or collectively and channelled formally and informally (Mowbray et al., 2015).

P. Mendonça (✉)
Heriot-Watt University, Edinburgh, UK
e-mail: p.mendonca@hw.ac.uk

T. Ajibade Adisa et al. (eds.), *Employee Voice in the Global North*,
https://doi.org/10.1007/978-3-031-31123-9_5

Therefore, voice can be expressed via representation, recognition and union membership, and via company-sponsored participation mechanisms, such as joint consultative committees and direct employee involvement (Millward et al., 2000).

This chapter contends that the absence or constrain of a type of worker voice, such as collective and formal, does not necessarily result in absence of voice (or as it is commonly conceptualised, silencing [Kougiannou & Mendonça, 2021]); rather, this chapter suggests a shift in or re-direction of the trajectories of voice that enhance the role of some actors and reduce that of others. Voice therefore is not a static and zero-sum concept, but rather a changing construct, that is a result of a contested process undertaken at various levels (macro, meso and micro), and enacted at local level by employers and employees. Therein the theoretical thrust in this chapter is that actors, be they employers, employees or state action, can shape and reshape institutional structures that create and realign trajectories of employee voice that are more collective or individual, and more formal or informal (Mowbray et al., 2015). In this chapter, employee voice centres on how state intervention has reshaped employment relationship structures in Portugal with the aim to constrain and marginalise collective voice (such as trade unions and collective bargaining structures). Therefore, this chapter contends that alternative trajectories of voice emerge from constrains enacted by the employer or state as resistance to immediate manifestations of exploitation. In doing so, it engages empirically with the case study of gig economy activity in Portugal, with particular focus on food delivery couriers in Porto and Lisbon. The case study shows how food delivery couriers realign their voice in the absence of formalised collective employee voice in the form of union representation due to workers' peripheral position in the labour market and their limited rights to collective representation.

This chapter will firstly discuss the complex developments of employment relations in Portugal. In doing so, it shows how the Portuguese employment context has shifted towards more decentralised employment relations with heightened focus on labour flexibilisation resulting in labour market segmentation and fragmentation. Secondly, the chapter will discuss what impacts these developments have for worker representation and voice, and later contextualise the context and dynamics of gig work in general. Empirically, this chapter will show how gig workers attempt to find new trajectories of voice and representation to make amends to the lack of inherent formal and collective representation. The chapter will finish by discussing theoretically the implication of constrains to worker voice in Portugal and its impacts on a peripheral workforce such as those operating in the gig economy.

Employment Relations in Portugal

The understanding of worker voice requires framing at national and macro levels, involving the Portuguese employment regulatory framework and the industrial relations context. In Portugal, the form workers voice their interests and demands is typically institutionalised largely pluralist in manner where tripartite agreements and law-making processes are the result of negotiations between social partners and the government (Eurofound, 2016). However, the 2008 economic crisis and the subsequent debt bailout led the Portuguese government to agree a memorandum of understanding (MoU) with so-called Troika institutions: the European Commission, European Central Bank and International Monetary Fund. The negotiation of the MoU integrated many of the previously agreed proposals in a tripartite agreement (Campos Lima, 2016). However, there was an acceleration of decentralisation of employment relations and a focus on labour flexibilisation resulting in increasing labour market segmentation and fragmentation. These factors are seen as constraining drivers of worker voice. The following discussion centres on the elaboration of these factors and how they potentially constrain employee voice at macro and local levels. The last decade has been a defining moment for worker voice in Portugal, stemming from both key regulatory changes that have reconfigured the employment relationship context and increasing pressures to set up new systems of individualised employee representation at workplace level. The European Directive on Employee Information and Consultation provides the supra-national context to strengthen the notion of worker voice in European member states. In Portugal worker voice macro structures have increasingly become more decentralised due to various amendments in the legislation covering the employment relationship, the 2009 Labour Code (Código de Trabalho), which regulates private and public sectors. As a response to a concertation agreement led by the Troika, the 2009 Labour Code was subject to various amendments between 2011 and 2014, aimed at increasing labour market flexibility and decentralising collective bargaining (Law 23/2012). Primarily, the amendments enabled the postponement of collective agreements in companies, as well as shortened the validity periods of the same collective agreements (Law 55/2014). In essence, since the 2012 economic crisis and subsequent social concertation agreement signed with the Troika, Portugal labour context experienced various regulatory changes, which accentuate ongoing processes of decentralisation of employment relations (Koukiadaki et al., 2016). There is a degree of uncertainty in the literature regarding the loss of coverage and union density in Portugal (Addison et al., 2015). For instance, focusing on new collective agreements, Schulten and Müller (2014, p. 102) and Rigby and García Calavia (2018) report sharp declines in bargaining coverage and sectoral multi-employer agreements. Távora and González (2016) argue that although the number of new collective agreements have indeed declined, the number of workers covered by valid agreements have remained relatively stable over the 2012 crisis. However, it has been documented in the past decade the erosion of collective bargaining structures and trade union influence in Portuguese workplaces. As Table 5.1 shows, the percentage of employees covered in collective bargaining agreements have been steadily decreasing, suggesting that decentralisation results in an erosion of effective collective structures that represent employees and voice their concerns.

Table 5.1 Collective wage bargaining coverage of employees

Year	Percentage of employees covered (%)
2011	91.4
2013	89.1
2016	87.5
2017	86.5
2018	86.2

Source: Eurofound (2022)

According to Costa (2012), these include reducing trade union autonomy, as new agreements undermine multi-employer collective agreements in favour of company-level agreements. In particular, the concertation agreement establishes new clauses enabling companies to diverge from sectoral and industry agreements (Rigby & García Calavia, 2018). Employers are thereafter able to suspend collective agreements on the grounds of economic reason. Lastly, the agreement has also resulted in a lesser level of supervision from the national regulatory body (Autoridade para as Condições de Trabalho) as firms are no longer required to submit their working time schedule or agreement on working time exemptions (Costa, 2012). An increasingly decentralised corporatist model of participation and partnership among the social partners (government, unions and employers) set the basis for more individualised worker voice mechanisms.

In a new political cycle (2015–2019), the government of the Socialist Party took the initiative of a wide range of legislative changes, partly with the aim to reverse regulatory changes enacted by the Troika and the right-wing coalitional government at the time. For instance, several newly produced laws were introduced to combat modern forms of forced labour, considering not only the criminal responsibility of subcontractors and temporary staffing agencies but also the responsibility of company users. In the public sector, the most important changes were the reversal of nominal wages cuts that had been in place since 2011 and the re-establishment of the 35-hour week in the public sector, through the second amendment to the General Labour Law in Public Functions (Eurofound, 2022). But most importantly to this chapter is that in 2017 the Resolution 82/2017 (in Eurofound, 2022) established new directives on the extension of collective agreements. Although the new directives included new criteria with focus on inclusiveness and reduction of inequality (introducing transparency rules to prevent wage discrimination), these did not establish new terms for the collective bargaining agreements and therefore workers continue to be at the will of employers' discretion in terms of working conditions (such as wages and changes in working time) (Eurofound, 2022).

In 2019, the Law 93/2019 that came into force on 1 October 2019, introduced significant changes to the Labour Code (in Campos Lima & Perísta, 2020; Campos Lima, 2020). The newly introduced legal framework aimed at preventing the alarming growth in labour market segmentation by reducing the duration of fixed-term contracts to a maximum of two years and of three renewals. It also restricted the use of fixed-term contracts only to temporary needs and created an 'additional contribution for excessive turnover' to be applied to companies with an annual share of fixed-term contracts higher than the sector average turnover (a measure planned to take effect in practice in 2021). In addition, two measures introduced by this law created heightened risks of precariousness which furthered labour market segmentation and fragmentation in the Portuguese context. As Dias et al. (2020) show the segmentation of the labour market in Portugal has been growing and cuts across most of the country's economic activities. One of the key issues in segmentation in Portugal relates to the distinction between the insiders and outsiders of the labour market. In other words, the core workers (who have full time with permanent contracts) and the peripheral workers (who have temporary or fixed-term contracts). These distinct groups of workers have access to different social security rights and job security regimes. Moreover, peripheral workers face risks in job mobility as they are more prone to remain in peripheral labour market employment with poorer working conditions. It is then only natural that this labour market segmentation and fragmentation produces diverging interests for the workers.

Therefore, a problematic issue identified by Távora and González (2016) is that the decline of new sectoral- and industry-level agreements may result in greater employee vulnerability to unilateral demands made by employers at workplace-level. Moreover, Campos Lima (2016) contends that the social concertation agreement coupled with the policies implemented throughout the years when Troika institutions were active in Portugal exacerbates an already ongoing process labour market segmentation and of decentralisation of employment relations, constraining even further collective employee representation and voice at a national and workplace levels. This clear path towards increasing labour market segmentation and workforce fragmentation is critical for declining effectiveness of collective structures of employee representation and employee voice. This impact will be elaborated in the following section, which will help us understand the emergence of new channels and trajectories of worker voice.

The Impact of Employment Relations Segmentation/Fragmentation on Worker Representation and Voice

Labour market fragmentation deeply affects collective worker voice of both the core and peripheral workforces (Adăscăliței et al., 2022). Institutions of workers' representation, such as trade unions, are usually formed along organisational and industrial demarcations that are broken by pressures created by employee fragmentation and division between the core workers and the peripheral workers (Mendonça, 2020). Such divisions are aggravated and further deepened by a competition between different groups of workers (Mendonça & Kougiannou, 2022). Studies conducted by Hammer and Riisgaard (2015) and Mendonça and Adăscăliței (2020) show how the interdependencies between the employer-employee relationship and the market pressures produce changing contours of the workforce and, consequently, of workers capacity to effectively exert voice. The two studies focus on how market pressures demand companies to hire and employ workers on different contractual statuses, resulting in fragmented workforces. For Hammer and Riisgaard (2015), fragmentation of the workforce is an effective divide-and-rule strategy as it weakens labour by inhibiting solidarity and employee collective voice. It inhibits it because, as Doellgast and Greer (2007) argue, this fragmentation process ends up rendering obsolete some parts of the institutional arrangements of industrial relations (as shown in the previous section). Moreover, fragmentation produces increasing divisions amongst workers. Firstly, because fragmentation rearranges the foundation in which different workplaces or departments within the same company (e.g. shop floor workers and office workers in a manufacturing context) are interlinked amongst each other. Secondly, this rearrangement often entails the restructuring and re-organisation of the workplace, producing a multi-tiered workforce, where workers undertake the same job but are separated by their contractual status (Barrientos, 2013). As Hyman (1997, p. 521) argues, such differentiation ends up eroding "egalitarian commitments" as it generates the dispersion of workers' interests.

At the same time, the dispersion of workers' interests creates difficult conditions for trade unions to coordinate and organise in workplaces. Trade unions are made to make concessions with the employer, which usually results in further fragmentation of workforces (through temporary work agencies) or employing a bigger percentage of temporary workers in order to keep costs low, and comply with cost requirements (Kalleberg, 2011). Consequently, trade unions may find themselves having to deal with a fluctuating, fragmented and vulnerable—in terms of employment—workforce. This vagary of the market generates a segmented and fragmented workforce within the company, which is naturally challenging for trade unions and the formation of an effective collective voice (Mendonça, 2020). The literature suggests that workforce segmentation and fragmentation lead to rivalry among workers, making solidarity and mobilisation of collective interests and voice difficult (Mendonça & Kougiannou, 2022; Hyman, 2001).

Worker Voice in Platform-Based Delivery Work

Since 2017, the delivery of food and goods intermediated by digital platforms such as Uber Eats, Glovo and Bolt has grown significantly in Portugal, particularly in Lisbon and Porto (Boavida et al., 2021). Platform-based delivery companies have been characterised as lean platforms (Srnicek, 2017) that use self-learning algorithms to automatically and autonomously govern the rules to control and intermediate the supply/demand between producers, couriers and consumers (Duggan et al., 2020). They are characterised as lean because the use of algorithmic management and artificial intelligence enables platform companies to strip back any human management interaction (Mendonça & Kougiannou, 2022). Platforms and algorithms can then set the work conditions, identify the task, allocate it to individuals and manage their performance with minimum human intervention (Rosenblat, 2018). In this sense, algorithmic management is a controlling system responsible for making and executing decisions affecting labour and workers' working lives, where there is limited human involvement and oversight over the labour process (Duggan et al., 2020).

Delivery couriers in Portugal are categorised within the employment relationship with platform companies as independent contractors or self-employed (Boavida et al., 2021). This categorisation and consequent employment and working conditions place delivery workers as a peripheral workforce within the labour market. The use of self-employment status enables platform companies to attract and engage workers with a no-frills process and reduce costs by eliminating many of the labour and time costs involved (Srnicek, 2017). This is crucial to enable companies in efficiently coordinating labour supply-demand that is necessary to fulfil the orders made by customers to producers (such as restaurants). Although self-employment implies individuals having the autonomy to control when to work and how much money they want to make, researchers have emphasised that this relationship enables gig economy platform companies to save on direct and indirect overhead costs (Ivanova et al., 2018), access a wider pool of potential recruits (Campbell, 2018; Meijerink & Keegan, 2019) and gain prerogative over when and why an individual can be fired (van Doorn, 2017). Therefore, this employment status has been widely discussed as being more conducive to companies' particular business needs (De Stefano, 2016; Huws & Joyce, 2016). At the same time, delivery workers are subject to insecure and unstable piece rate pay and they are also stripped from most basic employment and social rights, such as sick or holiday pay and an hourly minimum wage (Mendonça et al., 2023). What is more, responsibilities and costs are further externalised to the independent contractors who are required to possess specific work requirements such as health insurance, working gear and a mode of transport (bike, moped, car) to participate in the labour process (Goods et al., 2019). Often, these services are offered by the platform companies themselves who are paid a monthly fee so that platform workers can access (through rent) the much-needed 'tools' necessary to undertake the work (Mendonça et al., 2023). In Portugal, this peripheral position is emphasised by the lack of access to collective bargaining structures and formal collective representation that voices the delivery workers' concerns and interests (Boavida et al., 2021).

The compounding effect of algorithmic management coupled to the self-employed status imposed on delivery workers operates as an efficient mechanism that drives workers to silence, that is the lack of having access to effective voice mechanisms. The removal of human interaction enables platform companies to more efficiently manage labour process and workers' performance (Cant, 2019), but can in the same way act as a barrier for voice (Kougiannou & Mendonça, 2021). The use of algorithmic management and lack of human interaction centralises communication channels in the platform company. Workers are then forced to contact the platform company via email or complete a form through the app. The responses are often automated and mediated by a 'bot' that assesses the message through key words in the text (Rosenblat, 2018).

Another barrier relates to the employment relationship based on insecure and precarious conditions further constrains workers to speak up due to fear of having their account terminated or being target with less orders. Delivery workers' status in delivery platform work as self-employed means they are not covered by collective bargaining (Mendonça & Kougiannou, 2022) and are less protected in terms of employment and health and safety (Cant, 2019), which can also create an imbalanced bargaining relationship and accentuate divisions. Therefore, workers find themselves less powerful and increasingly pressured to manage the risks inherent to the job on their own. Such constraints barriers to worker organising can be mitigated when a 'reserve army of labour' is small, and companies cannot easily cover their labour needs through external recruitment (Flecker et al., 2013).

In delivery platform work, the employment relationship is coupled with workers typically experiencing disperse work settings due to the lack of a physical workplace as well as high levels of colleagues' turnover (Rosenblat, 2018). The issue of dispersed workplace setting becomes crucial for the definition of common voice and interests, which can become hampered by a fragmented and dispersed workforce (Wood et al., 2018). Recent research in food delivery gig work suggests that gig workers may be segmented in terms of dependence and attachment to the job (Joyce et al., 2019; Veen et al., 2020). As discussed previously, fragmented and dispersed workforces have been identified as a major obstacle to collective voice, as workers often see themselves as separated from other workers in the workplace and ultimately engage in individual competition with one another (Gumbrell-McCormick & Hyman, 2013). This fragmentation of the workforce is particularly relevant in the context of platform-enabled delivery work. For instance, Mendonça and Kougiannou (2022) show that platform companies can make last-minute changes in the algorithmic to produce changes in the labour process and workforce configurations. This in turn produces fragmentation in the workforce and makes different groups of platform workers being concern with different issues. As a result, different workers bargain for specific conditions (such as pay) while others voice concerns over having less orders being allocated to them, making this an effective divide-and-rule strategy promoted by the platform company.

Therefore, removing the capacity for workers to have a say within these processes can result in a less representative working relationship. However, when trying to voice and resolve issues of concern, workers, by using technology, consider varying factors to determine which mechanism to use (Kougiannou & Mendonça, 2021) to react to these restrictions and barriers. In specific types of app-work, such as the transport of goods and people, workers are necessarily embedded in particular places, such as cities (Wood et al., 2018). These conditions may offer potential sites in which communities of workers are able to coalesce with the aim of making their voice heard and influence platforms and clients (Cant, 2019). Therefore, workers' propensity for self-organisation and willingness to voice their concerns is prone to happen despite the adversarial conditions created by platform capitalism and algorithmic management. Similarly, technology can be used by food delivery couriers to boost worker solidarity and counterbalance power disparities that are reproduced by algorithmic management (Mendonça & Kougiannou, 2022). This context, where the 'workplace' conditions are not only influenced by the organisation but also by the local economy and city environment, offers an opportunity to examine a range of voice mechanisms that workers utilise to achieve change in the workplace, aimed at different stakeholders.

Methods

This chapter focuses on delivery platform work in Portugal as an extended sectoral case study (Burawoy, 2009). Delivery platform work in Portugal started to be established around 2016 with companies such as Glovo and Uber Eats. There are no definite and accurate numbers of how many workers are engaged in delivery platform work in Portugal due to the high rate of turnover (Boavida et al., 2021). Qualitative research was conducted between November 2021 and September 2022 in the cities of Lisbon and Porto. Data is drawn from a total of five face-to-face and online semi-structured interviews with three trade union officers and two delivery platform workers. Purposive sampling was used to select information-rich participants to accommodate an in-depth study (Patton, 2014). In the first stage, one semi-structured interview was conducted with one trade unionist in Lisbon, in which themes such as the labour process and issues related to collective bargaining and representation and difference voice trajectories were explored. The trade unionist acted as gatekeeper and provided access to other informants participating in this study. In the second stage, an additional four semi-structured interviews were conducted with four informants (two trade unionists and two delivery platform workers). The interviews with the two trade union officers were conducted online since they were located in Porto, where the same themes as the first interview were explored. The interviews with the two delivery platform workers were conducted face-to-face in Lisbon. The interviews with delivery platform workers were structured around themes such as worker voice in delivery platform work (with focus on informal and formal approaches to voice), the labour process, employment conditions, contractual terms and trade union action.

The delivery platform workers were engaged with different delivery platform companies at the time of data collection. Due to increasing tensions between management and the participants (workers and trade union officers), informants' identity was anonymised. To overcome the limited number of interviews and due to the lack of management response to requests to participate in the study, data were also collected from desk research: companies and trade unions' official documents and media items, public statements from key stakeholders such as policymakers and company representatives. Desk research was in understanding the institutional development of voice trajectories in platform work in Portugal. Data were thematically analysed in Nvivo using parental nodes and child nodes, which were linked to particular topics of interest, such as the company's low-cost business model, precarious work and trade union activity (Yin, 2003). Data triangulation procedures were followed (Creswell & Miller, 2000) using three data sources: (i) semi-structured interviews with trade unionists and delivery platform workers; (ii) the companies' and trade unions' official documents; (iii) media items.

Findings

Dynamics of Voice in Platform-Based Delivery in Portugal

Legal Framework for Collective Voice and Representation for Delivery Platform Workers in Portugal

In Portugal, delivery platform workers are categorised as self-employed independent contractors. This categorisation of delivery platform workers results in constraining access to formal voice representation (through a trade union). Data drawing from desk research show that there is labour law framework regulating specific platform workers (named as TVDE Law, which covers workers engaged with ride-hailing services), but this excludes coverage of workers who are self-employed and provide services of food and parcel delivery mediated by digital platforms (such as Uber Eats, Glovo and Bold). Given that TVDE Law only covers platform workers engaged with ride-hailing services, there is a regulatory void that is promoted by state, which results in lack of coverage of a large share platform workers engaged with food delivery services. The TVDE Law in Portugal therefore does not consider the reality experienced by platform workers as whole. As a result, in terms of collective bargaining for platform workers, the Portuguese regulatory framework does not provide the possibility of independent contractors to have access to collective bargaining, which is similar to other European legal frameworks such as the UK or Italy (De Stefano, 2016). Similar situation relates to collective representation where delivery platform workers are not formally seen as being represented by trade unions. Nonetheless, the data collected in this study from interviews with trade union officers show that delivery platform workers are indeed represented by a branch of the Portuguese trade union confederation (CGTP), who promotes collective actions and represents workers' collective interests (this is further elaborated below).

The absence of state intervention at national level is seen in this study not as a withdrawal by the state from the regulatory space; rather, it is a re-configuration of the same space. This re-configuration enhances and constrains the role of different social actors. Although Portugal typically holds a pluralist approach to employment relations, the active absence of state intervention in regulating delivery platform workers' employment relationship with their counterpart platform companies gives space for the latter to potentially capture the regulatory space and shape working conditions such as pay and working time schedules in a way that is conducive of their business strategy and goals. Moreover, it is noteworthy that the current regulatory framework, the TVDE Law, that covers some platform workers by excluding delivery platform workers, results in the striking fragmentation of the platform gig workforce in Portugal. This creates fissures in the platform gig workforce, who naturally experience differences in working and employment conditions and as a consequence in their specific interests as workers. It is then expected increasing difficulties and constrains for formal collective institutions such as trade unions to effectively represent platform workers as whole.

Informal Voice: Using Different Voice Trajectories to Build Up Formal Voice and Institutional Representation

Given the lack of institutional support, delivery platform workers explored the opportunity to create new trajectories and modes of voice. Exercising voice was not only made by engaging with platform companies through the formal company channels (such as the company's chatbot or filling in forms) but also by engaging with the wider public, political actors (such as the Bloco de Esquerda and the Portuguese Communist Party, PCP), the local restaurants and, in later stages, the formal trade union confederation of Portugal—CGTP.

In the early stages of setting up informal voice mechanisms, delivery platform workers reported to engage with different modes of voice. Which type of voice mechanism they used depended on the issue or topic of concern. For example, data from interviews with delivery platform workers show that Facebook group discussion was used to post multiple messages with the aim to notify workers about roadworks, road closures and road accidents in the city so that couriers can modify their delivery routes accordingly. The Facebook Messenger and WhatsApp application were also being used by workers to provide support for more immediate issues on the job and for providing advice for the newer members of the group. These topics were usually connected with flat tyres, advice about deliveries and online polls about key issues of the job such as pay and working time schedules.

As noted above, there is a tendency for delivery platform workers to get in touch with each other and form supporting networks by using social media platforms. These were the basis to develop further trajectories of voice. One of which related to the engagement with the wider public in order to raise awareness of the issues that affected this employment activity. Data from desk research show that this was done informally through multiple newspaper articles and interviews in local radios with some platform workers. With the same objective of raising their voice profile and impact, delivery platform workers asked local restaurants to improve working conditions for them such as being able to shelter from weather conditions inside the restaurant or use the toilet facilities. This activity was crucial to make platform workers' poor employment conditions more visible not only for the public but also to the political parties sitting in parliament. Political parties such as Bloco de Esquerda and the Portuguese Communist Party (PCP) started to engage with the workers' demands for fairer pay and more employment security, which resulted in several debates in parliament and activities promoted by both parties to raise the voice profile of these gig workers. For instance, a mini documentary was produced by the Bloco de Esquerda regarding the precarious conditions that delivery platform workers were subject to (Esquerda, 30 de Abril 2021). Moreover, delivery platform workers have also experienced enhanced voice as a result of associations that attempt to make workers' struggles heard in the mainstream media. For instance, the *Precários Inflexíveis* (an association of precarious workers that gives voice to workers who lie at the margins of the society and do not have access to effective voice mechanisms) often formulates demands for the delivery platform workers and they have mentioned workers challenges in various media outlets. The outcome has resulted in more visibility for platform workers not only in parliamentary debates but also for society as a whole.

Formal Collective Voice: Union Representation and Strikes

Trade union renewal of membership support relies on aiming at economic sectors where conditions are favourable to accrue a stable and loyal base of membership. This is typical from traditional manufacturing or larger service workplaces, where workers are employed through traditional contractual arrangement, that is permanent full-time contracts. In a sector such as platform delivery, trade unions may face various challenges to represent, organise and mobilise workers. One trade union officer reported that in April 2022, delivery platform workers in Porto went on strike with the full support of CGTP hospitality northern branch. Already in the past, delivery platform workers had engaged in collective action to bring their demands and collective voice forward. Interviewees mentioned that the initial contact between delivery platform workers and the union representatives was made in 2016 after an accident involving a delivery platform worker. This first contact was made through social media outlets, which indicates how important the previous informal networking and organising dynamics were. However, one interviewed union officer refers that the first attempts to make contact were unsuccessful due to the vulnerable positions of many migrant workers who constitute the bulk of the workforce in the platform delivery in Portugal. This challenge is seen in other national contexts such as the UK (Mendonça et al., 2023). Trade union officers also highlighted the self-employment status as another barrier for collective organising and voice. According to the interviewees, trade unions find difficult to organise and mobilise workers that have unstable employment relationships. This becomes one of the major constrains for union representation and collective bargaining because it translates into the high level of turnover amongst delivery platform workers. The data collected during desk research and in interviews suggest that the average length of time working within the delivery activity is of ten months. Delivery platform workers reported that after they have started working in delivery platform sector, they were already looking to take other opportunities in other sectors of the economy. The reality of this dynamic can make building formal collective representation throughout trade union a constant challenge. This is because trade unions struggle to maintain a significantly relevant membership density that gives weight to workers' voice and demands. Yet, another struggle mentioned by trade unionists relates to the mobile nature work of delivery platform work, which means that workers do not have a fixed workplace or site where they assemble or undertake the labour process. This becomes challenging for trade unions who need to spend significant resources to contact delivery platform workers with high risk of failure.

Despite these struggles the union branch was able to organise a strike action in April 2022, and although the action was consigned to the city of Porto, there were some previous actions in the city of Lisbon as well. According to the interviewed trade union officers, in the strike action in Porto, delivery platform workers demanded better working conditions and fairer pay. One union officer reported that "workers are demanding for a pay increase for each kilometre of €0,80 and a piece rate pay for each delivery, which has to be a minimum of €2,50, which is accrued €1 if there is a waiting time of over 10 minutes, as well as a daily €1 bonus for each hour of work". In addition to this, workers were also demanding a pay surge of €10 for extreme weather conditions, a health care insurance to compensate for the high health and safety risks incurred by delivery platform workers, and that the company complied with the national monthly minimum wage. Lastly, the demands included the recognition of employment rights such as sick and holiday pay as well as start of negotiations for structured and systematic collective bargaining.

However, as it stands, the interviewed union officers reported that platform companies have refused to meet all the workers' demands for better working and employment conditions. What is more, platform companies did not propose any counteroffer, which implies that companies are not willing to negotiate. The trade union officers reported that platform companies justify their decisions of not negotiation by arguing that there is a new supra-national legal framework being drafted at European level. The trade union has been attempting to represent the delivery platform workers since 2017—when platform companies initiated activity in Portugal—and arguing that delivery platform workers fulfil all the preconditions to the categorised as employees. However, the Portuguese regulatory and inspecting body (Autoridade para as Condições de Trabalho) has not yet coerced platform companies to fulfil their duty of recognising delivery platform workers as employees. Given how particularly strike-prone delivery platform workers are, it is interesting to note that in the data collected for this study strike was seen as one form of voice out of the several the workers could choose to use in their efforts to make their voice heard. The formal union representation of workers' voice was the basis to sought after formal recognition of employment rights and collective bargaining.

Discussion and Conclusion

This chapter aimed at developing a conceptual understanding of new trajectories of voice in platform work, with a particular focus on (i) workers' motivations in building new and developing existing voice channels; (ii) the content and purpose of these different voice channels; (iii) the outcomes in terms of voice effectiveness and employment conditions and working lives. Across the different institutional and employment dynamics described above, delivery platform workers were able to develop different trajectories of worker voice. These include informal collective voice that has built up to more formalised forms of representation and voice. As it stands, delivery platform workers together with trade unions are attempting to build up institutional recognition as employees to get access to the much-needed full employment rights.

One of the key contributions of this chapter is that although workers are not given a formal voice representation, this does not translate into absence of voice. It rather shows that a tension between company and worker prevails, which then results in workers pursuing other trajectories to voice their concerns. Importantly, these trajectories of voice are typically starting as informal forms of voice, which are away from managerial monitoring mechanisms, that then build up to more formal collective forms of representation and voice. This voice-building strategy enables workers to coordinate between them and draw collaborations with other actors more effectively. The informal forms of voice heavily relied on technology and social media as a more direct channel of voice, to promote workers' common interests and demands, as well as to provide immediate support and advice to newly entry delivery workers.

The formal collective voice, through the action of trade union representation and strike, is seen as necessary to strengthen collective bargaining and to attempt to shape institutional legal frameworks. The collective actions in the form of strikes continue today connected to the CGTP branch that represents workers from the hospitality sector. However, it is clear that strike action is not enough to get effective concessions from platform companies or to get state recognition and bring the regulatory framework forward. The development of networks between delivery platform workers, unions and political parties holds the potential for more sustainable development of effective worker voice and its formal representation. What emerges from the informal networks (informal collective voice), the attempts of union organising (formal collective voice) and its legal campaigns, is that there is a rationale of influence and of representation that is specific to delivery platform work. That is, self-organising informal voice mechanisms that then produce attempts to formalise voice representation by trade unions emerge from this specific digital platform labour process.

These novel and not-so-novel voice mechanisms represent different trajectories of voice that are shaped and reshaped as some forms (such as the formal collective voice) are constrained. In Portugal, at macro level, there is a focus on the pluralist approach to regulating employment relations, but the recent economic crisis and subsequent intervention enacted by the government and Troika resulted in an environment more conducive of management's unilateral decision-making in setting up business models that are in contraction with the regulatory framework of Portugal. This was the case with Uber entering the market of ride-hailing and the government at the time setting up a specific law that fit Uber's business and employment model needs. This new tailor-made regulatory setting enhanced capacity to capture the regulatory space and alter working and employment conditions, which became a key strategy in coping with cost-driven market demands and intense competition. This was the case for delivery platform workers who had to accept changes in pay structures and working time schedules. The changes entailed a move from a pluralist context to a more liberal economy, where many important aspects of employment conditions are negotiated at workplace level by employer and employee. Beyond extending research fieldwork with more interviewees, future studies should aim to comparatively evaluate the different voice mechanisms that platform workers develop considering different platforms they work for and sectoral activity (such as food and parcel delivery, ride-hailing, warehouse work); national regulatory framework and demographics (such as gender and ethnicity).

References

Adăscăliței, D., Heyes, J., & Mendonça, P. (2022). The intensification of work in Europe: A multilevel analysis. *British Journal of Industrial Relations, 60*(2), 324–347.

Addison, J., Portugal, P., & Vilares, H. (2015). Unions and collective bargaining in the wake of the great recession. IZA Discussion Paper No. 8943.

Barrientos, S. (2013). 'Labour chains': Analysing the role of labour contractors in global production networks. *The Journal of Development Studies, 49*(8), 1058–1071.

Boavida, N., Moniz, A., Naumann, R., Roque, I., & Azevedo, R. (2021). Case studies on digital labour platforms in Portugal: 2nd National Report of Project Crowdwork.

Burawoy, M. (2009). *The extended case method: Four countries, four decades, four great transformations, and one theoretical tradition*. University of California Press.

Campbell, H. (2018). *The rideshare guide*. Simon & Schuster.

Campos Lima, M. (2016). O desmantelamento do regime de negociação coletiva em Portugal, os desafios e as alternativas. *Cadernos do Observatório sobre Crises e Alternativas, 8*, 1–54.
Campos Lima, M. P. (2020). Reconfiguring labour market and CB institutions in Portugal: Turning the page on internal devaluation mechanisms? In A. C. Santos & N. Teles (Eds.), *Financialisation in the European periphery: Work and social reproduction in Portugal* (pp. 103–126). Routledge.
Campos Lima, M. P., & Perísta, H. (2020). Country Report: Portugal, NEWEFIN: New Employment Forms and Challenges to Industrial Relations.
Cant, C. (2019). *Riding for deliveroo: Resistance in the new economy*. Polity.
Costa, H. (2012). From Europe as a model to Europe as austerity: The impact of the crisis on Portuguese trade unions. *Transfer: European Review of Labour and Research, 18*(4), 397–410.
Creswell, J. W., & Miller, D. L. (2000). Determining validity in qualitative inquiry. *Theory into Practice, 39*, 124–130.
De Stefano, V. (2016). The rise of the 'just-in-time workforce': On-demand work, crowdwork, and labour protection in the 'gig-economy'. *Comparative Labour Law & Policy Journal, 37*(2), 471–504.
Dias, J., Kovács, I., & da Conceição Cerdeira, M. (2020). Mudanças recentes na estrutura de emprego em Portugal segmentação e polarização. *Sociologia On Line. Revista da Associação Portuguesa de Sociologia (APS), 22*, 112–137.
Doellgast, V., & Greer, I. (2007). Vertical disintegration and the disorganization of German industrial relations. *British Journal of Industrial Relations, 45*(1), 55–76.
Duggan, J., Sherman, U., Carbery, R., & McDonnell, A. (2020). Algorithmic management and app-work in the gig economy: A research agenda for employment relations and HRM. *Human Resource Management Journal, 30*, 114–132.
Esquerda. (2021). "ESTAFADOS", um mini-documentário sobre a precariedade laboral dos trabalhadores estafetas. Estreia no Primeiro de Maio, Dia do Trabalhador, nas redes sociais do Bloco de Esquerda, 31 April 2021. Retrieved October 22, 2022, from https://www.esquerda.net/videos/estafados-teaser/74133
Eurofound. (2016). *Working time developments in the 21st century: Work duration and its regulation in the EU*. Publications Office of the European Union, Luxemburg.

Eurofound. (2022). *Living and working in Portugal.* Publications Office of the European Union, Luxemburg. https://www.eurofound.europa.eu/country/portugal#

Flecker, J., Haidinger, B., & Schönauer, A. (2013). Divide and serve: The labour process in service value chains and networks. *Competition & Change, 17*(1), 6–23.

Freeman, R., & Medoff, J. (1984). *What do unions do?* Basic Books.

Goods, C., Veen, A., & Barratt, T. (2019). "Is your gig any good?" Analysing job quality in the Australian platform-based food-delivery sector. *Journal of Industrial Relations, 61*(4), 502–527.

Gumbrell-McCormick, R., & Hyman, R. (2013). *Trade unions in Western Europe: Hard times, hard choices.* Oxford University Press.

Hammer, N., & Riisgaard, L. (2015). Labour and segmentation in value chains. In K. Newsome, P. Taylor, A. Rainnie, & J. Bair (Eds.), *Putting labour in its place: Labour process analysis and global value chains* (pp. 83–99). Palgrave Macmillan.

Huws, U., & Joyce, S. (2016). Crowd working survey: Size of UK's 'Gig Economy' revealed for the first time University of Hertfordshire. Retrieved March 7, 2021, from http://englishbulletin.adapt.it/wp-content/uploads/2016/02/crowd-working-surveypdf1.pdf

Hyman, R. (1997). Trade unions and interest representation in the context of globalisation. *Transfer: European Review of Labour and Research, 3*(3), 515–533.

Hyman, R. (2001). *Understanding European trade unionism: Between market, class and society.* Sage.

Ivanova, M., Bronowicka, J., Kocher, E., & Degner, A. (2018). The app as a boss? Control and autonomy in application-based management. Retrieved April 14, 2021, from https://opus4.kobv.de/opus4-euv/frontdoor/deliver/index/docId/388/file/ArbeitGrenzeFlussVol02.pdf

Joyce, S., Stuart, M., Forde, C., & Valizade, D. (2019). Work and social protection in the platform economy in Europe. *Advances in Industrial and Labour Relations, 25*, 153–184.

Kalleberg, A. (2011). *Good jobs, bad jobs.* New York.

Kougiannou, N. K., & Mendonça, P. (2021). Breaking the managerial silencing of worker voice in platform capitalism: The rise of a food courier network. *British Journal of Management, 32*(3), 744–759.

Koukiadaki, A., Távora, I., & Martínez, L. M. (2016). Continuity and change in joint regulation in Europe: Structural reforms and collective bargaining in manufacturing. *European Journal of Industrial Relations, 22*(3), 189–203.

Meijerink, J., & Keegan, A. (2019). Conceptualising human resource management in the gig economy: Toward a platform ecosystem perspective. *Journal of Managerial Psychology, 34*(4), 214–232.

Mendonça, P. (2020). Trade union responses to precarious employment: The role of power resources in defending precarious flight attendants at Ryanair. *Transfer: European Review of Labour and Research, 26*(4), 431–445.

Mendonça, P., & Adăscăliței, D. (2020). Trade union power resources within the supply chain: Marketisation, marginalisation, mobilisation. *Work, Employment and Society, 34*(6), 1062–1078.

Mendonça, P., & Kougiannou, N. K. (2022). Disconnecting labour: The impact of intraplatform algorithmic changes on the labour process and workers' capacity to organise collectively. *New Technology, Work and Employment.*

Mendonça, P., Kougiannou, N. K., & Clark, I. (2023). Informalization in gig food delivery in the UK: The case of hyper-flexible and precarious work. *Industrial Relations: A Journal of Economy and Society, 62*(1), 60–77

Millward, N., Bryson, A., & Forth, J. (2000). *All change at work: British employment relations 1980–1998 as portrayed by the Workplace Industrial Relations Survey Series.* Routledge.

Mowbray, P. K., Wilkinson, A., & Tse, H. H. (2015). An integrative review of employee voice: Identifying a common conceptualization and research agenda. *International Journal of Management Reviews, 17*(3), 382–400.

Patton, M. (2014). *Qualitative research & evaluation methods: Integrating theory and practice.* Sage.

Rigby, M., & García Calavia, M. A. (2018). Institutional resources as a source of trade union power in Southern Europe. *European Journal of Industrial Relations, 24*(2), 129–143.

Rosenblat, A. (2018). *Uberland: How algorithms are rewriting the rules of work.* University of California Press.

Schulten, T., & Müller, T. (2014). *Wages and collective bargaining during the European economic crisis: Developments in European manufacturing industry.* IndustriALL.

Srnicek, N. (2017). The challenges of platform capitalism: Understanding the logic of a new business model. *Juncture, 23*, 254–257.

Távora, I., & González, P. (2016). Labour market regulation and collective bargaining in Portugal during the crisis: Continuity and change. *European Journal of Industrial Relations, 22*(3), 251–265.

van Doorn, N. (2017). Platform labour: On the gendered and racialised exploitation of low-income service work in the "on-demand" economy. *Information, Communication and Society, 20*(6), 898–914.

Veen, A., Barratt, T., & Goods, C. (2020). Platform-capital's 'app-etite' for control: A labour process analysis of food-delivery work in Australia. *Work, Employment and Society, 34*(3), 388–406.

Wilkinson, A., Dundon, T., Marchington, M., & Ackers, P. (2004). Changing patterns of employee voice: Case studies from the UK and Republic of Ireland. *Journal of Industrial Relations, 46*(3), 298–322.

Wood, A. J., Lehdonvirta, V., & Graham, M. (2018). Workers of the Internet unite? Online freelancer organisation among remote gig economy workers in six Asian and African countries. *New Technology, Work and Employment, 33*, 95–112.

Yin, R. (2003). *Case study research: Design and methods* (3rd ed.). Sage.

6

The Perspectives of Legal Regulations and Employee Voice: Insights from Sweden

Laura Carlson

Introduction

Sweden has a single-channel collective employee voice model with the trade unions solely negotiating the majority of employment issues, both collective and individual, with the employers and employer organizations. This bipartite corporatism involving the social partners, trade unions, and employer organizations is characteristic of the Nordic labour law models that have been in place since the turn of the twentieth century. Corporatist and corporatism as used in this chapter are defined as the "concertation of economic and social policies amongst interest associations and state actors" (Jochem, 2003, p. 114). The Nordic systems reflect Kahn-Freund's collective laissez-faire, "What the State has not given, the State cannot take away" (1959, p. 244). The Nordic governments legislate restrictively "in fields where self-regulation of corporate actors seems possible, particularly with structures that allow for

L. Carlson (✉)
Stockholm University, Stockholm, Sweden
e-mail: laura.carlson@juridicum.su.se

T. Ajibade Adisa et al. (eds.), *Employee Voice in the Global North*,
https://doi.org/10.1007/978-3-031-31123-9_6

centralised decision-making that reflect the general interest" (Götz, 2022). Collective agreements are "regarded as a higher, more desirable form of regulation than the direct state intervention through legislation" (Kettunen, 1997, p. 166). Collective agreements between the central labour and employer organizations creating this model were entered into already by 1899 (Denmark), 1902 (Norway), and 1906 (Sweden).

Employee voice as stated above is exercised almost exclusively through the labour unions in Sweden. Employees receive information, are consulted, and are part of codetermination/joint decision-making only through the unions and employee participation in unions, defined by Kwon et al. (2016) as indirect employee voice mechanisms. The Swedish labour unions are tenacious in retaining this power and privilege, as seen below with respect to the feedback concerning the EU minimum wage and pay transparency directives. This chapter first presents the development of the Swedish (and Nordic) labour law model based on single-channel employee voice. Collective bargaining, industrial action, and codetermination as between employers and labour unions are next addressed. The structure of labour unions as well as the relationship to the members are then set out. Employee grievances are taken up as an example of individual employee voice in action, demonstrating the monopoly on power the unions have with respect to individual employee grievances. The lack of access to justice mechanisms that could enable individual employee voice, particularly with respect to issues of grievances, including questions such as discrimination, underscores the privilege that the labour law model in Sweden has created between the social partners.

By way of background, Sweden is a civil law country that belongs to the Nordic law family, comprising Denmark, Finland, Iceland, Norway, and Sweden. One of the singular characteristics in the Nordic legal family is the preference for self-autonomy by large central organizations, which can be seen in the legal fields of labour law, landlord-tenant law, and arbitration. An example here is that neither Denmark, Finland, Norway, nor Sweden has any minimum wage legislation, leaving it to the social partners, the employers, employer organizations, and labour unions, to regulate. Sweden's population today is 10.2 million with an active workforce of almost 5 million. Almost 20% of the population was born outside of Sweden (Kjellberg, 2022). Unemployment in Sweden in 2021 is 8.8% (SCB, 2022). Both the employer and employee sides were significantly organized already by the turn of the twentieth century, and both sides were in general, and to a very significant extent still are, sceptical of legislative solutions. Today both the employer and employee sides are still highly organized, with Swedish employers currently having an organizational density of almost 90% and Swedish employees one of approximately 70% (Kjellberg, 2022). Union membership exists even at professional levels, such as for professors, judges, and physicians.

The Development of the Swedish Labour Law Model

The modern Swedish labour movement, in many ways the successor of the guild corporatist system, began in earnest already in the 1880s (Carlson, 2018). The December Compromise of 1906, still in place, is the Swedish central private sector collective agreement reached between the private employer umbrella organization, *Svenska Arbetsgivareföreningen* (SAF), and the primary blue-collar private employee umbrella organization, *Landsorganisation i Sverige* (LO). Both are still in place today. The agreement still sets out the mainframe for the present-day Swedish labour law model in which the social partners, and not the state, resolve labour market issues. The degree of aversion to legislation by the labour market parties can already be seen with the passage of the first collective agreements act (*Lag* 1928:253 *om kollektivavtal*) and the creation of a Labour Court in 1928 (*Lag* 1928:254 *om arbetsdomstol*). These employee-friendly developments faced protests by over a quarter of a million workers. The 1920s and 1930s marked the birth of the Swedish welfare state, the folk home (*folkhemmet*), which coincided with the finalization of the Swedish labour law model. The welfare state, comprising public services such as insurance, education, and medical care, emerged in parallel to the completion of the labour law model, in many instances with the individual trade unions providing, authorizing, and administering social benefits, such as unemployment and sickness insurances. The central labour market organizations, SAF and LO, entered into the 1938 Basic Agreement, reinforcing the Swedish model of self-regulations by the social partners and the state's expressed policy of neutrality as to labour issues by refraining from legislation. Its rules concerning industrial action and that the social partners should resolve disputes through negotiations are still in place.

The following period up to the 1970s is often characterized as one of harmony in the labour market, achieved under this system of self-regulation and political cooperation. The folk home and the labour law model resulted in a pattern of civil society, courts, and lawmakers much different compared to more pluralistic systems such as the Anglo-American legal systems. Swedish civil society, in the form of the social partners, worked in conjunction with lawmakers with respect to labour market issues, creating rather than challenging existing structures, such as structural gender discrimination (Lijphart, 2012). The Labour Court, comprising members appointed by the social partners, is still the sole interpreter of labour legislation, with its decisions often being the first and last instance for the parties, given that its judgements cannot be appealed. Until 1990, LO members were automatically enrolled as members of the Social Democrats political party, founded by the LO in 1889. This process of collective affiliation, after decades of criticism, was finally removed by the 1987 Congress of Social Democrats, effective 1990 (Santesson, 2010). The Social Democrats remained in power uninterrupted from 1932 to 1976. Currently there are four collective agreements that are key as to the regulation of social partners: the 1938 Basic Agreement (*Saltsjöbadsavtalet*), basically defining the Swedish model; the 1982 Agreement on Efficiency and Participation (*Utvecklingsavtalet*) between SAF, LO, and PTK (*Privattjänstemannakartellen*, the Council for Negotiation and Co-operation), setting out how the codetermination act is to be applied by the social partners; the 2016 Agreement on Industrial Development and Wage Formation (*Industriavtalet*), addressing the procedures concerning wage negotiations; and the most recent 2022 LO, PTK, and the Confederation of Swedish Enterprise Basic agreement on security, transition, and employment protection (*Omställningsavtal*). The aversion to legislative solutions is also reflected in the fact that in private law generally, the majority of Swedish legislation is gap-filling (*dispositive*), meaning the parties to a transaction have the right to contract out of the law. With respect to labour legislation, on the national levels the social partners have historically had the opportunity to contract out of labour law through central agreements, sometimes with the requirement of a higher level of protection, but not always. One example of this gap-filling function can be seen with the 1979 and 1991 acts concerning equal treatment between men and women, *lag* (SFS 1979:1118) *om jämställdhet mellan kvinnor och män i arbetslivet* and *Jämställdhetslag* (SFS 1991:433). Equality Agreements were entered into by the majority of social partners in the private sector to opt out of these acts and out of the Equality Ombudsman's jurisdiction. These Equality Agreements in essence provided no protections against sex discrimination, but simply opted out of the acts and the jurisdiction of the Ombudsman, gutting the possibility of any effective enforcement of the legislation. The 1991 Equal Treatment Act was finally amended in 1994 to be mandatory and no longer gap-filling. A greater number of statutory provisions are now mandatory, particularly those enacted for Sweden to be in compliance with EU law requirements. In such cases, collective agreements can have higher degrees of protection, but still must provide at least the statutory floor of such protections.

The primary statutes in labour law are the 1976 Employment (Co-Determination in the Workplace) Act (*lag* 1976:580 *om medbestämmande i arbetslivet*) and the 1982 Employment Protection Act (*lag* 1982:80 *om anställningsskydd*). There are no explicit statutory definitions of employee, employer, or employee or employer organization (SOU, 1975, p. 1; Adlercreutz, 1964). This lacuna is deliberate in that the legislator reasoned that such definitions would facilitate circumvention and that the courts could most suitably define the parties in the case at hand. Trade unions are legal persons within the category of non-profit voluntary unincorporated associations (*ideella föreningar*) for which there is no explicit legislation (aside from certain tax provisions) nor any legal definition. The Act governing for-profit unincorporated associations (*lag* 1987:667 *om ekonomiska föreningar*), a form of commercial cooperative, is to some extent applied by analogy. Consequently, trade unions have no statutory requirements as to gaining legal personhood. There is no procedure in the Swedish labour law system for trade union recognition by employers. Trade unions that have first entered into a collective agreement with an employer have certain priority rights as "established" or "signatory" unions (*kollektivavtalsbärande fackföreningar*) under the Employment (Co-Determination in the Workplace) Act, a system that is argued to encourage employers to enter into collective agreements with only the historically larger, central trade unions (Flodgren, 1978). An example of this system of self-regulation at work is the absence of minimum wage legislation in Sweden. Wages are set in collective agreements that do not have *ergo omnes* effect; in other words, they are not made generally applicable by statute to parties other than those to the agreement. There is certain room for individual negotiations for wages, but these are usually with wage scales as still set by the social partners.

Collective Bargaining

The Employment (Co-Determination in the Workplace) Act sets out categories of negotiation between the social partners: a general right in §10 which can be invoked by any trade union regardless of whether there is a collective agreement; a primary right under §11 which must be invoked by the employer; and rights under §12 and §13 which can be invoked by the established and other trade unions, respectively. Collective bargaining occurs at the national, sector, and local levels. There has been a movement from the national centralization of agreements that dominated most of the twentieth century to terms of employment, particularly wages, being negotiated more at the local level. Central agreements now typically concern either procedural agreements (such as the 1938 Basic Agreement), agreements on the conditions of employment, or, to a degree, framework wage regulation agreements. Central collective agreements, often referred to as recommended agreements, can be entered into between the umbrella organizations, but such agreements must be adopted at the member level within these organizations to have effect at that level. Such agreements can also be binding on all member organizations if a certain threshold number of organizations ratifies the agreement.

The general right to negotiate (*allmän förhandlingsrätt*) in section 10 of the Employment (Co-Determination in the Workplace) Act defines this right as belonging to an employee organization "to negotiate with an employer on any matter relating to the relationship between the employer and any member of the organisation who is, or has been, employed by that employer." This right is regardless of whether the union is the established one. If an employee organization approaches an employer with the objective of reaching a collective agreement, the employer must attend the negotiations and discuss the demands presented, a duty sanctioned under the act by damages. Such an obligation to negotiate exists even if the union only has one member at the workplace. This general right to negotiate does not create any obligation on either party to reach an agreement.

The primary right to negotiate (*primär förhandlingsrätt*) is set out under §11 of the Act. It entails that an employer, before deciding on any important alterations to its activities, must initiate negotiations with the established trade union to which it is bound by collective agreement. The objective of this right is to compel employers to receive input from the employees before taking certain decisions. The rule is also applicable where an employer wishes to make major alterations to the terms of employment or conditions of work in relation to an employee. In certain cases, an employer may make and effect a decision prior to fulfilling its duty to negotiate. However, the Labour Court has interpreted "important alterations" fairly broadly, requiring not only formal but also substantive compliance. The Court has found in several cases that the employer acted too late, as the decision had already been made informally prior to consultation with the trade union. This right to negotiate, however, is limited simply to the fact that once the negotiations are concluded, the employer is free to make any decision it considers best for the company.

An employer is obliged to negotiate even in matters not involving major alterations, if a trade union party to a collective agreement with the employer, but not the established union, so requests under §12. In certain cases, a trade union not bound by a collective agreement has a right to negotiate under §13, namely where a matter specifically concerns the work or employment conditions of an employee belonging to that union. Under §14 the employer may also be requested to negotiate in these types of matters by a central organization of employees. An employer not bound by any collective agreement must negotiate with all the trade unions involved, that is all unions having at least one member employee affected by the measure under consideration, before a decision on collective dismissals or transfer of an undertaking can be made. Upon the request of an employee party under §32 of the act, the parties are to negotiate as to a collective agreement concerning the employees' right to codetermination. This section encourages the parties to a collective agreement regulating wages and similar matters to enter into agreements about entering into codetermination agreements concerning the conclusion and termination of contracts of employment, the management and distribution of work, and conducting of operations in general.

The Legal Status of Collective Agreements

There is no statutory requirement that an employer has to have a collective agreement. However, the threat of industrial action, particularly secondary action, acts as a very strong incentive. An employer can be bound by several collective agreements regarding its workforce. Employers not members of an employer organization can sign a simplified form of an already existing collective agreement, a tie-in agreement (*hängavtal*), usually containing a minimal number of terms and conditions mirroring those found in the sector collective agreement. Collective agreements are legally binding both for the parties to the agreement and for their members (Schmidt, 1997, p. 78). The legislation does not explicitly regulate the legal effects of collective agreements with regard to employees who are members of different unions or not members of unions at all. A collective agreement can be applied in practice (but is not required by statute) to employees of other unions not having an applicable collective agreement at that workplace. This can follow explicitly from the collective agreement or implicitly under the case law of the Labour Court, which often finds that collective agreements contain implied (in the absence of explicit) commitments by employers to not apply other terms of employment to those employees outside the collective agreement (AD 1990 no. 33). This broader application ensures that the terms of the collective agreement are not circumvented, for example, by employers hiring employees not covered by the agreement at lower costs.

The social partners have fairly extensive freedom regarding the content of collective agreements. According to the Employment (Co-Determination in the Workplace) Act, collective agreements are to be in writing and concern employment terms and conditions or the general relationship between employees and employers. This is the extent of the statutory regulation. The primary issues addressed in collective agreements tend to be wages and employment terms and conditions. This lack of regulation as to the content of collective agreements is seen as a strength. Collective agreements allow the social partners to adapt the terms and conditions of employment to each trade/sector. The parties to the agreement are free to negotiate the terms affecting employees and employers within the specific sector and at a specific workplace. In addition to collective agreements, individual terms in the employment contracts can be entered into between employers and individual employees that may not be in conflict with the applicable collective agreement. Because of the duty to keep the industrial peace while a collective agreement is in place, collective agreements are typically renegotiated prior to their expiration. There are about 650 collective agreements, covering approximately 90% of the Swedish workforce. Those employees not directly covered by a collective agreement, nor those employees who indirectly are covered by a collective agreement through the agreement of the social partners, have no protections other than the minimal ones in the legislation. More than 450 collective agreements are scheduled for renegotiation in 2023, covering approximately 2.2 million employees (Medlingsinstitut, 2022). Renegotiation procedures are addressed by collective agreement; for example, the 2016 Agreement on Industrial Development and Wage Formation (*industriavtal*) contains timetables for bargaining to ensure that bargaining commences in enough time that a new collective agreement can be successfully negotiated before the existing one expires to allow the duty to keep the industrial peace to remain intact.

Industrial Action and the Peace Obligation

Only the social partners can take lawful industrial action; individual employees acting on their own are seen as taking unlawful action. Two main categories of industrial conflict are set out: rights and interest disputes. Rights disputes concern issues covered by collective agreements and ultimately must be taken by one of the social partners to the Labour Court for resolution. Where there is a collective agreement at a workplace, the parties bound to the collective agreement are deemed to have waived their right to take industrial action and are under a duty of peace (*fredsplikt*). As soon as a collective agreement is reached, the right of the parties to take industrial action in principle ceases according to Sections 41–42 of the Employment (Co-Determination in the Workplace) Act. Neither may industrial action be taken in order to amend a collective agreement. This is also seen as a rights dispute and must be first negotiated and then, failing a resolution by the parties, ultimately taken to the Labour Court. The collective agreements function as industrial peace instruments act as an incentive for employers to sign collective agreements. A party to a collective agreement, however, is generally entitled to take secondary action (*sympatiåtgärder*) without restriction in order to assist another party in an ongoing lawful labour conflict.

If no collective agreement is in place between the social partners, and they cannot come to an agreement, the social partners are normally free to take industrial action (*stridsåtgärder*), a right constitutionally protected by Article 14 of the Second Chapter of the Instrument of Government. Such conflicts are deemed interest disputes for which industrial action is an appropriate resolution mechanism. Industrial action is not defined by statute, but rather purposely not defined to allow for greater flexibility and protection of rights. Industrial action can take the form of a strike, lockout, or boycott, or any similar measure against the other party, failing any provision to the contrary by law or agreement. The 1938 Basic Agreement sets out self-regulation procedures concerning blue-collar industrial actions, with respect to negotiations as well as to handling conflicts threatening essential public services.

The National Mediation Office (*Medlingsinstitut*) is currently authorized to provide assistance in resolving industrial disputes through mediation. In the event a strike is seen as potential concerning a vital societal operation, the social partners are to first attempt to settle the dispute before industrial action is taken. If they are unable to do so, the proposed industrial action is to be taken up to a council comprised members from the social partners to determine if it concerns an essential public service. Such conflicts seldom reach the Council. If still unresolved, the Parliament is empowered under the Instrument of Government to intervene only in certain, very limited cases of industrial action. One of the most recent examples is the 1971 nurses strike that affected 44,500 works and the State intervened in after 30 days. A temporary law (1971:50) was passed that gave the State the right to prolong the collective agreements, thus extinguishing the conflict. An indication of the efficacy of the Swedish model is provided in the statistics concerning industrial action. In 2021 11 working days were lost in Sweden due to conflicts; in 2020 zero days were lost (Medlingsinstitut, 2022).

Collective Employee Consultation: Codetermination

As the Swedish labour law model is single-channel, there are no Works Councils other than as required by EU law (Medlingsinstitut, 2022). The social partners have been given the power to self-police the enforcement of the collective agreements and legislation, and they have the right generally to institute proceedings on behalf of their members. The employers' prerogative, historically basically unlimited as set out in the 1906 December Compromise, has been successively circumscribed in the intervening decades, arguably beginning with the Basic Agreement in 1938 limiting the right of employers to freely terminate employment. This erosion of the employers' prerogative can be seen as making way for a parallel expansion of the rights of employees through trade unions to influence the employer's decision-making processes through codetermination. The term "codetermination" has a contextual meaning. For example, the components comprising codetermination in the German system differ from those in the Swedish system. Some Swedish scholars prefer the English term "joint regulation" (Eklund et al., 2008).

The structure of codetermination and trade union influence comprises the following:

- the primary right to negotiate and the employer's duty to consult with the trade unions;
- the right of interpretation by the union as to certain issues under the collective agreements such as the employee's duty to perform work;
- the trade union's right to information;
- the trade union's right to veto certain employer decisions as to the use of temporary agency labour;
- statutory rights for trade union representatives, including paid time off to conduct union activities;
- the establishment and rights of employee safety delegates at the workplace; and
- mandatory representation of employees on the board of directors for private corporations and public entities.

The primary right to negotiate can be seen as the central component in employee consultation, as the employer has to initiate negotiations with the union before taking decisions that can be viewed as significant in the workplace. Several of the collective agreements set up procedures for the provision of information to employees through trade unions, such as the 2016 Agreement and the 1982 Agreement on Efficiency and Participation between SAF, LO, and PTK, which contain information procedures during paid working time, including hiring experts to interpret the information so that employees can be fully informed.

The Act on Board Representation (Private Sector Employees) (*lag 1987:1245 om styrelserepresentation för de privatanställda*) mandates employee representation within boards of directors for corporations, commercial cooperatives, and other types of organizations such as banks and insurance companies. Under this act, two members of the board of directors in such an organization are to act as representatives of the employees if the organization has at least 25 employees, while 3 members may be appointed in certain organizations having at least 1000 employees. However, the number of employee members is never to exceed the number of other board members so that employee members are always to be at most one half, and more likely in the minority. The local trade unions bound by the applicable collective agreement are to appoint the employee directors. The employee directors are to have the same rights and obligations, including a duty of confidentiality in certain areas, as regular board members. A similar right to representation on boards of directors of public entities in the public sector is set out in the Personnel Representation Regulation (*personalföreträdarförordning 1987:1101*).

Trade Union Structure and Membership

The social partners are represented by strong centralized organizations, each having a hierarchy comprising umbrella organizations, national sector organizations belonging to the umbrella organizations, then local/regional and club organizations belonging to the national sector organizations. There are only a few radical trade unions, such as the Syndicalists, with the vast majority being reform trade unions. Under the umbrella organizations, the national organizations are organized mostly by industry or employer, with only a few still organized by craft or trade. Under the national organizations, there may also be local clubs for particular workplaces. As there are no direct statutory regulations governing the formation or operations of any of these organizations, the bylaws (*stadgar*) as adopted by their members alone govern the organizations, elections, recognition, governance, and the taking of decisions concerning industrial action.

On the national umbrella level, as well as the national sector levels, the organizations' governance structures are similar. Congresses (*kongresser*) are to be held at regular intervals; in the majority of cases, these intervals are longer than one year, sometimes up to every fourth year. For example, the bylaws of Industrifacket Metall 2017 state in §14(1) that the ordinary congress is to be held every third year. Byggnads holds its congresses at least every four years: councils (*representantskap/förbundfullmäktige*) and boards (*förbundstyrelse*) make decisions in the periods between congresses if authorized to do so in the bylaws. The national sector unions are members of the umbrella organizations, sending representatives to these, and the local unions are members of the national sector organizations, sending representatives to these. Individuals are members of the local unions. The LO bylaws require member unions to enact certain provisions, for example that the national sector's board is to make any decisions as to accepting, rejecting, or terminating a collective agreement, as well as concerning taking industrial action. In general, LO members are to obtain opinions from the LO Board before taking any significant decision. Members of LO must allow all workers in their area of operation to be members. This clause in the LO bylaws allows the rejected individual union members to appeal to the LO regarding a local union's decision against allowing membership (Schmidt, 1962). The national unions are not to strike (primary or secondary) without the consent of the LO Board where the strike or potential employee action concerns more than 3% of the national union's members. Where the national union has followed LO's procedures and been granted permission to take industrial action, the national union has the right to strike compensation from LO. In the same vein, every national union member has the duty to contribute to LO's strike fund. LO and several of its union members have significant assets. From the most recent publicly available annual accounts 2021, for example, it can be seen that the LO group had stated assets in 2021 of £470 million. That same year a national union, Industrifacket Metall, had £872 million in assets.

Trade Union Duties to Members

The bylaws of the labour market organizations also define the mutual rights and duties between the members and the organizations. There is no Swedish legislation explicitly regulating the internal affairs of labour market organizations. However, the 2008 Discrimination Act (*diskrimineringslag* 2008:567) expressly prohibits unlawful discrimination by employee and employer organizations on the basis of sex, transgender identity or expression, ethnicity, religion or other belief, disability, sexual orientation, or age with respect to employment, labour market policy, professional recognition, and membership in organizations. There are no specific statutory duties that trade unions must fulfil as regards their members that can give rise to a member claim. The most common remedy for a union member is to leave the union. Under the statutory framework of the labour law model, trade unions represent member employees on both the collective and the individual levels. Unions can conclude collective agreements that bind their members. Unions are also to negotiate with an employer on behalf of employee members. Local signatory unions have the right to nominate a safety delegate at a workplace as well as employee representatives on the company's board of directors (Källström, 1979, p. 104). The union can also decide to pursue an employee member grievance, first through negotiations with the employer and then, if unsuccessful, by bringing a case to the Labour Court. The decision to pursue a case is at the sole discretion of the trade union as there is no general duty of fair representation by trade unions as to their members. LO and *Tjänstemannens central organisation* (TCO), the Swedish Confederation of Professional Employees, have a joint law firm, LO-TCO rättsskydd AB, that provides help to union members in the areas of occupational injuries and employment disputes. A member of an LO or TCO union first needs to apply to the union for legal aid, after which the union assesses the merits of the case with regard to whether there is a reasonable chance of success. If approved by the union, the member then can use the services of the law firm.

By way of example, the bylaws of the Swedish Association of Health Professionals (*Vårdförbundet*) state that members have the right to free assistance in matters concerning employment, but decisions as to litigation assistance that can be seen as costly are to be taken by the Board of the Union under Section 3.3 of the Union's bylaws, with no appeal procedure in place. The bylaws of the finance sector union provide a similar benefit, in that members have the right, after three months' membership, to apply for assistance with advice, negotiations, or legal aid with respect to an employment issue. The union council decides the form and extent of the assistance to be provided. Members have the right to request that the council hears a matter in which the member feels a decision has been wrongly taken by the union. A member can appeal a decision of the board in writing within 30 days after notice of the decision has been given, and the appeal is then heard by the ordinary congress, which is held every third year. The statute of limitations in employment issues is generally very short, measured in terms of weeks and months. The requirement that the member wait until the ordinary annual congress for a decision concerning support in litigation—which could take as much as three years—means the claim would long have been barred by the time the congress addressed the decision.

General legal principles as found in the areas of contracts or agency can also regulate the relationship between the union and its members. Those legal areas not covered by collective agreements or labour law are to be regulated by general private law. An example can be seen in a case brought by an employee against a trade union that had negotiated away certain vested rights of the employee in relation to the employer. The Labour Court found that the trade union had not explicitly been given authority by the employee to negotiate issues concerning vested rights and that trade unions generally only had the mandate to negotiate as to future employment issues. Thus, the union had acted outside the scope of its authority under general rules of agency. It can also be mentioned here that there is no overriding principle of fiduciary duties in Swedish law generally; any such duty must be based on explicit agreement or law. Trade unions are to follow general principles of procedural fairness, for example with decisions as to expelling members or concerning member benefits. A general principle of equal treatment of members is argued in the legal scholarship (Hemström & Giertz, 2014).

Pursuing Employee Grievances

With respect to employee grievances generally, unions represent their members in any negotiations regarding the grievance to the extent the union deems sufficient, and have the possibility (but not duty) of representing members in litigation. There, however, is no duty whatsoever to represent non-member employees. It is estimated in that well over 90% of employment termination disputes in Sweden are settled out of court, but there are no official statistics on this number or how they are settled, particularly with respect to discrimination claims (Votinius, 2016, p. 239). This system is very much based on a collective and not individual approach.

Cases involving the social partners, including where a union represents an employee, are to be brought directly to the Labour Court as it has exclusive jurisdiction in such issues. The Labour Court's primary task historically was to resolve labour law issues, disputes regarding the interpretation and application of collective agreements, and the non-strike regulations of the Collective Agreements Act. The present expanded jurisdiction of the Labour Court over most issues of labour and employment law has several causes: collective agreements now exist in most of the labour market, having been extended in the 1970s to include salaried private employees and the public sector; much labour law was codified in the 1970s package; and there was an expansion in certain areas due to EU membership so that the Labour Court's jurisdiction was broadened to include even employment law issues brought by unions on behalf of members, such as discrimination claims. The composition of the Labour Court, as well as the relevant procedure, is regulated in the Labour Disputes (Judicial Procedure) Act (*lag* 1974:371 *om rättegången i arbetstvister*) and to the extent a specific issue is not regulated there, the procedural rules as found in the Code of Judicial Procedure are applicable. A judging panel for the Labour Court consists of at most seven members in total. Typically, three are nonpartisan members: a chair and a vice-chair trained in law, and an expert in the labour market. Another four members are partisan, with two appointed by the employer organizations and two by the employee organizations. This is not so different, for example, to composition of the employment tribunals in the UK, however, with the caveat that the judgements of the Labour Court cannot be appealed.

The Labour Court is limited in the relief it can grant. It can grant a motion for a declaratory judgement (*fastställesletalan*), such as whether an employment relationship exists; order performance based on a legal obligation (*fullgörelsetalan*); or declare invalid certain acts by the social partners, as well as collective agreements or clauses therein contained (*ogiltigförklaring*). The other primary remedy that the Labour Court can award is damages to either the individual employer or employee, the organization, or both. The damages are modest on a comparative scale. For example, in discrimination cases, the average of damages for the 2010s has been £5000 (as against the average trial costs and fees per party of £15,000) (Carlson, 2017, p. 129). The Labour Court has no equitable remedies, such as the authority to order an employer to hire an individual, nor can punitive damages be awarded. There is no modern case law relying on principles such as, for example, natural justice. As stated above, the Labour Court is the final instance, and its judgments cannot be appealed to any higher Swedish court.

With respect to the costs of pursuing an employee grievance after unsuccessful negotiations, if the union chooses to litigate the case, it bears all the costs and fees, and the case is brought directly to the Labour Court. If the individual employee brings the employment grievance, it must be to the general courts, which judgement can be then appealed to the Labour Court. Sweden generally follows the English rule with respect to trial costs and fees, which means that the non-prevailing party pays the trial costs and fees for both parties. According to §5(2) of the 1974 Labour Disputes (Judicial Procedure) Act, the Labour Court may also order that each party bear its own costs if the losing party had reasonable cause to have the dispute tried, but this reallocation is seldom invoked by the Court, and then the Court is even-handed between losing employers and losing employees. In the majority of employee grievances, the individual employee member has no mechanism to force a union to litigate a claim, and the unions have no duty to provide legal assistance; in other words, there is no duty of representation. The employee's only redress as against the union is to withdraw membership. Trade unions have the right of first refusal with respect to bringing certain claims on behalf of an employee. By way of example, the union can decide (and often does) to not litigate a discrimination claim on behalf of a member. The number of discrimination cases taken by the unions to the Labour Court is historically very low, one case in 2021, four cases in 2020 with a nadir reached in 2019 of no discrimination cases heard by the Labour Court. Added to this is the complication of the very short statute of limitations in employment claims. For example, if the claim concerns unlawful dismissal, notice has to be given to the employer of the alleged unlawfulness within two weeks of the notice of dismissal, and if negotiations are not held, the case has to be filed within a second period of two weeks, or, where negotiations are held, two weeks after the end of negotiations. An individual with an unlawful dismissal claim consequently must receive a response from the union within two weeks or be barred from bringing the claim. Employers terminating employment during holidays exacerbate these procedural difficulties as the prescription times have few exceptions.

If the individual employee pursues litigation of the grievance, they risk liability for the trial costs and fees of both parties and two instances, both before the general court and before the Labour Court. For example, in the case AD 2006 no. 54, a former employee argued that his employment termination was unlawful as it was based on sexual harassment of another employee as well as due notice of termination was not given. The employee prevailed in the trial court (applying the case law of the Labour Court) and was awarded £6700 in damages for the unlawful termination and £1230 for the employer's failure to give notice. On appeal by the employer, the Labour Court departed from its earlier case law and found that the termination based on sexual harassment was lawful but that the former employee was correct in that he did not receive proper notice, for which the Labour Court awarded him £400 in damages. Determining that the former employee had not prevailed as to the majority of the issues in the case, the Labour Court ordered him to pay the employer's trial costs and fees before the Labour Court of £ 4000, as well as for the trial proceedings in the amount of £14,750—a total of £19,000.

There is a limited right to receive legal aid (e.g. an individual cannot have assets and yearly income of more than £206,000), with a ceiling of one hundred hours of legal advice. If the individual is a member of a trade union, the trade union is to be contacted before legal aid can be provided. If an individual has legal assistance coverage as part of their home insurance, the insurance coverage is to be used instead. With respect to home insurance covering legal assistance, the range of coverage varies per policy, often from £6000 to £16,000, regularly with a deductible of 20%. Some policies also cover liability for the other party's fees up to 80%. A caveat here, though, is that most, if not all, insurance policies exempt employee employment disputes, referring instead to the trade unions as the avenue for pursuing such claims (regardless of whether the insured is a union member). Given the financial risks for plaintiffs, many claimants have opted to take employment claims to the small claims court, which has a ceiling of approximately £17,000 in damages (with a filing fee of £72) but a limited risk of being found liable to pay the other party's trial costs and fees. Given this limit in damages, it is questionable whether this can be seen as a suitable or deterrent alternative from an access to justice perspective.

The Swedish labour law model is unabashedly concerned with the social partners and collective solutions to labour market issues. Union members have no statutory rights with respect to the unions, and no voice with regard to employers except through the unions or through pursuing litigation themselves. Elaborate procedures have been put in place concerning the negotiations between the social partners, with extensive rights as to industrial action and secondary or sympathetic actions lawful. The claim could be made that the Swedish trade unions are some of the strongest in the world, with little or no legal accountability. The low damages awarded and the relatively higher attorneys' costs and fees create a significant deterrent for individuals considering the pursuit of employment grievances. Litigation is arguably not an affordable option for most individual plaintiffs. This is particularly true in light of the fact that such cases often involve employment grievances in terms of hiring or firing, and consequently individuals who are unemployed.

Individual Employee Voice: Access to Justice

The unions in Sweden are the central means for their members as to negotiations with employers. With respect to individual employees exerting voice outside the collective, and several challenges can be identified. In the case of employee grievances, the collective continues to be integral, with grievances to be raised by members through the union. In the event the union decides to not further pursue a grievance, which it can do so fairly freely after the first negotiations with the employer, the employee must litigate the issue in the general courts. If it is a question of discrimination, the employee can turn to the Discrimination Ombudsman (*Diskrimineringsombudsmannen* DO), but as a rule they have not litigated individual cases.

As to the individual, when reviewing different procedural mechanisms that can be seen as facilitating access to justice, most of these are not taken up in the Swedish legal system. Sweden generally is a defendant-friendly judicial forum with few concessions to access to justice issues. To begin with, an employee with the claim to invalidate a wrongful termination has very short limitations periods in which to file. With respect to a wrongful termination claim, the employee has to notify the employer within two weeks, other employment claims four months under section 40 of the Employment Protection Act. Amendments to pleadings are limited, with complaints to be filed based on facts and to include already at the time of filing a list of the evidence. There are limited discovery mechanisms with weak sanctions for failures to produce discovery, mostly in the form of insignificant fines. Recordkeeping requirements as to employers were added in 2018, mostly however more systematically in relation to equal pay and gender, and no other variables, and not as systematically with respect to employment hires or terminations on any grounds. Statistical evidence as a rule is not used. The shifted burden of proof in discrimination cases is applied more often as a shared burden of proof. Equity is not an institution in Swedish law, so equitable remedies are not available, such as ordering employers to hire discriminated applicants. Damages can be reduced to zero if this is deemed fair by the court. Punitive damages are not available generally in Swedish law. Economic damages are only awarded where the plaintiff is already an employee. Nominal damages are awarded by the Labour Court in modest amounts, typically somewhere between £2000 and £5000. A third category of damages, discrimination damages, was introduced by the 2008 Discrimination Act comprising "enhanced" damages so that employers would be deterred from discriminating. The Labour Court has at the time of this writing awarded discrimination damages in 16 cases, with an average award of £5000 per plaintiff. Sweden arguably can be seen as the Nordic country that has stayed truest to the dominance of labour law corporatism in the human rights area of discrimination law (Bauge & Løvdal, 2022).

In essence, there is at best limited legal aid and no contingent fees or pro bono systems. There is no reallocation of costs and fees as to employee claims in an effort to make litigation generally more affordable and consequently accessible. Any awarded amounts of damages are not high and greatly outpaced by the trial costs and fees. The loser pays rule is applied, and where the unions take up the claims, they then pay the costs and fees. Certain employees have opted to take claims against employers to small claims courts to avoid the economic risks of costs and fees, but then the damages are set at a ceiling of £1700, a negligible sum for most employers. This lack of development with respect to damages must also be assessed against the trial costs and fees as awarded by the Labour Court. The Labour Court can order that each party bear its own costs if the losing party had reasonable cause to have the dispute tried under Section 5(2) of the 1974 Labour Disputes (Judicial Procedure) Act (1974:3711). The Court has seldom done so and then almost evenly in favour of employers and employees. Losing is also not defined as losing the case, but losing the issues pled. For example, in AD 2020 nr. 13, the discrimination award of £6000 was offset by the fact that the Labour Court ordered the union to pay 4/5's of the employer's trial costs and fees, £11,000. The plaintiff had not been successful on the claim of indirect discrimination, nor did the plaintiff receive the full amount of damages initially pleaded of £14,000, but only £6000. The plaintiff, losing on these two issues that did not in any way entail more evidence or legal work, resulted in the employer recovering 4/5 of its trial costs and fees.

The Court can be seen as assuming an equality of arms that outside the relationship between the social partners does not exist. By way of example, the amount of trial costs and fees as awarded by the Labour Court in employment discrimination cases demonstrates a trend that deviates radically from the static amounts of damages, with trial costs and fees increasing, taking into account inflation, by approximately 153% since the 1980s. The average trial costs and fees in the 1980s was almost in parity with the damages awarded, £1500 in damages and £1700 in trial costs and fees awarded, £5000 and £6000 respectively after inflation (Carlson, 2016). Consequently, during the 45-year time span in which the discrimination laws have been in place, the amounts of damages per plaintiff have remained basically unchanged even after the implementation of enhanced discrimination damages, while the trial costs and fees have risen 153%. To this risk calculation can be added the success rates of the different claims, with the lowest success rate for claims of ethnic discrimination; only 2 of over 30 such cases have been brought successfully by plaintiffs, a less than 6% chance of prevailing.

The case law of the Labour Court also demonstrates a consistency of result and approach as to claims of employment discrimination. The significance of precedent is not recognized by the Labour Court, as seen from a 2017 case brought by a deaf university lecturer concerning the decision not to hire, AD 2017 no. 51. The Labour Court found no discrimination as the costs of interpreters was a continual cost that other employees with disabilities could not benefit from. The Labour Court's assessment was solely a financial one, that the costs for interpreters was not proportional, without taking into consideration any broader societal aspects of integration. This lack of a broader discussion was brought up by The Committee on the Rights of Persons with Disabilities in its decision (CRPD, 2018) concerning this case at §8:10:

> However, [the Committee] also notes the Court's conclusion that the sign language interpretation provided to the author would not have benefited other potential employees with hearing impairment. The Committee considers that this reasoning focussed on the specific measure taken for the author, but failed to take into account the negative impact of the Court's assessment in more general terms, by discouraging potential employers from considering the possibility to employ individuals with hearing impairment for positions similar to the one the author applied to.

This can be contrasted with the UK Supreme Court's holding in R (UNISON) v Lord Chancellor [2017] UKSC 51, that access to justice is a constitutional principle under both UK and European law, with the Court underscoring the need for litigation not just for the individual but also to effect change in society. The EU Commission's Proposal for a Directive of the European Parliament and of the Council to strengthen the application of the principle of equal pay for equal work or work of equal value between men and women through pay transparency and enforcement mechanisms for a directive on pay transparency also has a focus on access to justice as necessary to enforce rights.

That the non-recognition of individual access to justice mechanisms, and the sole focus on collective voice and rights, is a conscious policy by the social partners can be seen with the Swedish feedback to several recent EU directive proposals. EU discrimination law has been placing an ever-greater emphasis on empowering individual employee voice and bringing discrimination claims successfully, focusing on access to justice mechanisms as well as deterring and effective damages. However, the individual human right not to suffer unlawful discrimination in employment has been placed within the Swedish corporatist labour law system, giving rise to a dissonance between the exercise of collective rights and individual rights. Recent examples of this can be seen with the feedback given by several Swedish social partners concerning the EU Commission's proposal (2021) for a directive concerning pay transparency and enforcement mechanisms in March 2021. Both approaches in the proposed directive, creating pay transparency and increasing access to justice mechanisms, challenge the corporativism of the Swedish labour law model.

Three Swedish social partners responded in the first round of the Commission feedback open 6 January–3 February 2020, TCO (Feedback F504753, 2020), the Swedish Association of Local Authorities and Regions (Feedback F504693, 2020), and the Confederation of Swedish Enterprise (Feedback F503430, 2020). Four of the nineteen responses received to date in the second feedback round (15 April 2021–6 October 2021) by the Commission were from Swedish social partners, the Swedish Trade Union Confederation—*Landsorganisationen i Sverige* (LO) (Feedback F2256513, 2021), the Swedish Confederation of Transport Enterprises (*Biltrafikens arbetsgivareförbund*) (Feedback F2353025, 2021), TCO (Feedback F256513, 2021), and *Unionen* (Feedback F2660595, 2021). All these feedback statements emphasize the importance of the Swedish collective model not only in setting wages but also in the collective model with respect to resolving conflicts. LO makes the argument specifically that a reallocation of costs and fees is not necessary as it is almost exclusively the Equality Ombudsman or the unions that litigate equal pay claims, and that such a reallocation would result in an increase in claims. As seen from these statements by the social partners, the lack of access to justice mechanisms is a conscious choice, as equality of arms needs only be between the social partners, and not between employers and workers, in basically any question concerning employment, but here, specifically with respect to discrimination claims. Similar arguments as to the primacy of the labour law model are made in feedback by the Swedish social partners with respect to the Commission proposal for a directive on adequate minimum wages in the European Union.

The trends with respect to damages and trial costs and fees, combined with the low success rates, create a significant deterrent for plaintiffs to bring employment claims, in essence blocking access to justice. Litigation is arguably not an affordable option for most plaintiffs. Though the Swedish Discrimination Ombudsman (DO) and the trade unions can litigate certain claims, they most often choose not to do so. The trade unions have no duty of fair representation, meaning that with respect to their members, after the first set of negotiations with the employer, they can decline defending a member on a claim of discrimination, and with respect to non-member they have no obligations. There are also no procedural due process protections with respect to the decisions by unions as to representation as can be found, for example in the UK Ministry of Justice, Claims Management Relation-Code of Practice for the provision of Regulated Claims Management Services by Trade Unions (2006). Neither does DO have any explicit obligation to investigate discrimination employment complaints as lodged with the DO nor to act upon them.

The Swedish labour law system can be seen as one of the purest single-channel collective employee voice systems, focusing on the collective of employees as represented solely by the labour unions. The Swedish labour law model is about the social partners and collective solutions to labour market issues. In other words, the individual employee, as seen from the feedback by the social partners above to the proposed EU directives on pay transparency and minimum wages, is not to exercise voice except through the unions or litigation. Union members have no statutory rights regarding their unions. Elaborate procedures have been put in place concerning the negotiations between the social partners, with extensive rights as to industrial action. The Swedish system is one of the few globally where secondary industrial actions are lawful as long as the primary action is lawful. This extensive right of the unions can be contrasted with the rights of employees under Swedish law. There are no internal individual employee grievance procedures under law for employers to follow.

This can be seen in contrast, for example, with the German right for the individual employee to raise a grievance based on an implied term in the employment agreement, derived by the courts from the employer's duty of care (Waas, 2016, p. 148). This duty requires the employer to consider the employee's moral rights and wellbeing, thus to hear the employee when grievances are raised as to unfair or disadvantaged treatment. German employees also have the right, as set out in the German Works Constitution Act, to raise a grievance through the works council or individually bring a grievance in the absence of a works council. There are no mediation/agency procedures in Sweden outside of the unions for individual employee complaints, such as with Acas and the Certification Officer in the UK, and the National Labor Relations Board, Department of Labor, Wage and Hour Division, or Equal Employment Opportunity Commission in the United States. The Swedish Discrimination Ombudsman has the mandate to take up employment discrimination cases, but does so rarely. In essence, employees have little recourse outside their unions with respect to negotiations with employers.

Insights from Sweden

Given the predominant role of the social partners in the Swedish labour law model, and the monopoly of the Labour Court with respect to employment issues, the corporatist interests are set squarely in contrast with the individual interests. In some ways, in Sweden human rights, such as protection from unlawful employment discrimination, hinge upon union membership for assertion, as individuals raising such claims on their own are faced with too great of an economic risk with respect to trial costs and fees. The judgements of the Labour Court clearly show an assumption of equality of arms regardless of whether it is an individual or union bringing the case. Where an individual brings the case, the economic risks are even greater as there are two, not one, judicial instances for which the trial costs and fees can be ordered.

The Swedish system most closely mirrors Kahn-Freund's collective laissez-faire. The trade unions are the gatekeepers as to employee voice, and the employer and employee organizations are treated as equally strong—a presumption in the law that mirrors a reality in existence since the 1930s. The focus on the social partners and self-regulation has entailed that individual members are not empowered. It is an accepted proposition that the Swedish system is built on a system of collective justice—a communitarian approach to the law and its role in society. This has also meant that procedural guarantees for individuals are not in place to any extent and that there is no natural justice reasoning by the courts, no duty of fair representation by which to hold unions accountable, no overriding duty of care. This is not to say that the Swedish legal system is necessarily fundamentally unfair, but simply that individual employee voice has not been a focus in this very communitarian system that works for the collective rather than the individual.

References

Adlercreutz, A. (1964) *Arbetstagarbegreppet*. Gleerup.

Bauge, M., & Løvdal, L. (2022). Access to justice in discrimination cases in Norway. In L. Carlson (Ed.), *Scandinavian studies in law* (Vol. 68, pp. 373–402). Equality Law.

Carlson, L. (2016). Addressing unlawful discrimination: The Swedish journey. In L. Carlson, Ö. Edström, & B. Nyström (Eds.), *Globalization, fragmentation, labour and employment law: A Swedish perspective* (pp. 139–160). Lustus.

Carlson, L. (2017). Discrimination damages—Promoting or preventing access to justice? In M. Rönnmar & J. Votinius (Eds.), *Festskrift till Ann Numhauser-Henning* (p. 129). Juristförlaget i Lund.

Carlson, L. (2018). *Workers, collectivism, and the law—Grappling with democracy*. Elgar.

CRPD. (2018). CRPD/C/23/D/45/2018, Communication no 45/2018.

Eklund, R., Sigeman, T., & Carlson, L. (2008). *Swedish labour and employment law: Cases and materials* (pp. 426–434). Iustus förlag.

EU Commission's proposal. (2021) Brussels, 4.3.2021, COM (2021) 93 final, 2021/0050 (COD) Proposal for a Directive of the European Parliament and of the Council to strengthen the application of the principle of equal pay for equal work or work of equal value between men and women through pay transparency and enforcement mechanisms {SEC (2021) 101 final} - {SWD (2021) 41 final} - {SWD (2021).

Feedback F2256513. (2021). Gender pay gap—Transparency on pay for men and women, feedback from: The Swedish Trade Union Confederation-Landsorganisationen i Sverige (LO), LO's yttrande över EU:s förslag till direktiv om åtgärder för transparens vid lönesättning, submitted on 12 April 2021.

Feedback F2353025. (2021). Gender pay gap—Transparency on pay for men and women, feedback from: The Swedish Confederation of Transport Enterprise, submitted on 3 June 2021.
Feedback F256513. (2021). Gender pay gap—Transparency on pay for men and women, feedback from: The Swedish Confederation of Professional Employees (Tjänstemännens Centralorganisation (TCO), The initial position of TCO on the European Commission proposal for a pay transparency directive, submitted on 2 July 2021.
Feedback F2660595. (2021). Gender pay gap—Transparency on pay for men and women, feedback from: Unionen, submitted on 2 July 2021.
Feedback F503430. (2020). Gender pay gap—Transparency on pay for men and women, feedback from: Confederation of Swedish Enterprise, submitted on 31 January 2020.
Feedback F504693. (2020). Gender pay gap—Transparency on pay for men and women, feedback from: Swedish Association of Local Authorities and Regions, submitted on 03 February 2020.
Feedback F504753. (2020). Gender pay gap—transparency on pay for men and women, feedback from: Tjänstemännens Centralorganisation (TCO), submitted on 03 February 2020.
Flodgren, B. (1978). *Fackföreningen och rätten* (p. 126). Norstedts.
Götz, N. (2022). *Corporatism and the Nordic countries*. Nordics.info. Aarhus University. Retrieved January 5, 2023, from https://nordics.info/show/artikel/corporatism-the-influence-of-trade-unions-and-interest-groups/
Hemström, C., & Giertz, M. (2014). *Bolag, föreningar, stiftelser: en introduction* (8th ed.). Norstedts Juridik AB.
Jochem, S. (2003). Nordic corporatism and welfare state reforms, Denmark and Sweden compared. In G. Lehmbruch & F. van Waarden (Eds.), *Renegotiating the welfare state* (p. 114). Routledge.
Kahn-Freund, O. (1959). Labour law. In M. Ginsberg (Ed.), *Law and public opinion in Britain in the twentieth century* (p. 244). London.
Källström, K. (1979). *Lokala kollektivavtal—Om lokal parters rättsliga ställning inom fackliga organisationer* (p. 104). Liber.
Kettunen, P. (1997). The society of virtuous circles. In P. Kettunen & H. Eskola (Eds.), *Models, modernity and the myrdals* (pp. 153–177, 166). University of Helsinki Press.
Kjellberg, A. (2022). *Facklig organisationsgrad ur ett nordiskt perspektiv*. Lund.

Kwon, B., Farndale, E., & Park, J. G. (2016). Employee voice and work engagement: Macro, meso and micro-level drivers of convergence? *Human Resource Management Review, 26*, 327–337.

Legislative Bill (1971:50). Kungl. Maj:ts proposition till riksdagen med förslag till lag om förnyad giltighet av vissa kollektivavtal.

Lijphart, J. (2012). *Patterns of democracy—Government forms and performances in thirty-six countries* (2nd ed., pp. 158–173). Yale.

Medlingsinstitut. (2022). *Gällande avtal*. Retrieved January 5, 2023, from https://www.mi.se/forhandling-avtal/gallande-avtal/

Santesson, P. (2010) *När Socialdemokraterna skulle avskaffa kollektivanslutningen*. Retrieved January 5, 2023, from https://inslag.se/journal/2010/3/10/nar-socialdemokraterna-skulle-avskaffa-kollektivanslutningen.html

SCB. (2022). *Arbetslöshet i Sverige*. Retrieved January 5, 2023, from https://www.scb.se/hitta-statistik/sverige-i-siffror/samhallets-ekonomi/arbetsloshet-i-sverige/

Schmidt, F. (1962). *Kollektiv arbetsrätt* (4th ed., p. 106). Stockholm.

Schmidt, F. (1997). *Facklig arbetsrätt*, revised by R. Eklund, H. Göransson, K. Källström, & T. Sigeman. Stockholm, p. 98.

SOU. (1975). Legislative Inquiry SOU 1975:1, Demokrati på arbetsplatsen förslag till ny lagstiftning om förhandlingsrätt och kollektivavtal. Stockholm, pp. 722–28.

UK Ministry of Justice (2006). Claims Management Relation-Code of Practice for the provision of Regulated Claims Management Services by Trade Unions.

Votinius, J. (2016). Sweden in resolving individual labour disputes. In M. Ebisui, S. Cooney, & C. Fenwick (Eds.), *Resolving individual labour disputes: A comparative overview* (p. 239). ILO Geneva.

Waas, B. (2016). Germany. In M. Ebisui, S. Cooney, & C. Fenwick (Eds.), *Resolving individual labour disputes: A comparative overview* (p. 148). ILO Geneva.

7

The Role of Employee Voice on Mental Health and Wellbeing: The Case of Poland

Magdalena Gilek

Introduction

Mental health has been an important public health challenge in European countries, even before the Covid-19 pandemic. Based on the European health statistics, in 2019, 13% of the European population reported mental health conditions (such as depression, anxiety or psychosis) (WHO, 2022). The latest wave of the European Health Interview Survey (EHIS) conducted in 2019 revealed that chronic depression was one of the most common mental health problems, reported by 7.2% of the EU population aged 15 and over. Similar trends are observed in Poland, where in 2019 around 4% of the population reported chronic depression (Eurostat, 2019). Work is an important domain in an individual's life that is central to mental health and wellbeing (Warr, 2007). In addition to providing financial stability, work also offers a social status, strengthens a sense of identity and provides opportunities for personal development

M. Gilek (✉)
Edinburgh Napier University, Edinburgh, UK
e-mail: m.gilek@napier.ac.uk

T. Ajibade Adisa et al. (eds.), *Employee Voice in the Global North*,
https://doi.org/10.1007/978-3-031-31123-9_7

(Green, 2006). However, work is not always beneficial for people's mental health. Jobs which are of poor quality can be a source of negative experiences at work (e.g. Butterworth et al., 2011; Nieuwenhuijsen et al., 2010) and being in a poor-quality job can be worse for mental health than remaining unemployed (Butterworth et al., 2013). From an organisational perspective, poor mental health is associated with higher levels of absenteeism, greater employee turnover and loss of productivity, to name just a few (Cooper & Dewe, 2008). Workers who report better mental health are more productive and less subjected to sickness leave, when compared to those with lower psychological wellbeing (Cottini & Lucifora, 2013; Wright, 2010).

Health and safety at work, including mental health, is seen as a crucial component of Corporate Social Responsibility (CSR) and organisations are increasingly understanding they cannot be good externally while experiencing poor social performance internally. Firms that are good in promoting social and mental aspects are increasingly viewed as 'employers of choice' (Zwetsloot & Leka, 2010). These findings combined with an increasing organisational awareness and understanding of mental health following the Covid-19 pandemic have led to efforts to explore ways in which organisations can prevent stress and promote mental health and wellbeing in the workplace. Many theories and models in work psychology emphasise the importance of work environments (such as control, job demands or social support at work) in determining employee mental health and wellbeing. These theories recognise that people's mental health status is influenced by work-related factors such as employee control over the work process, the intensity of work, social support from managers or job security. Therefore, many of the issues that impact on mental health at work are beyond the control of individual employees and the health sector (Noblet & Rodwell, 2010). Given that most working-age adults spent on average around two-thirds of their waking hours at work, the significant amount of time spent in this particular environment combined with social and economic importance of work in society, means that working life is going to have a profound effect on people's mental health (Gini, 2000). Several studies have generated comprehensive scientific evidence which shows the detrimental impact of work-related factors (chronic exposure to high workload, intensity or long working hours and lack of control and social support) on employee mental health (e.g. Bonde, 2008; Cottini & Lucifora, 2013; Jain & Leka, 2019; O'Driscoll & Brough, 2010). Nevertheless, the changing nature of work in the past two decades and the increased use of technology in the workplace have contributed to the increasing importance of other areas for wellbeing in the contemporary workplaces such as job insecurity, long working hours, and managerial support (such as effective communication and feedback). While broad links between the above factors and wellbeing have been established in the literature, less is known about the specific mechanisms between different sets of constructs and wellbeing (Arnold et al., 2020).

Despite the important role that work play in shaping employee mental health, the practice of mental health promotion in the workplace has largely disregarded the impact of the work environment. The evidence shows that individually oriented approaches, that focus on enhancing health-related knowledge, attitudes and behaviours of employees, are the most common strategies that employers use to address work-related stress and promote mental health and wellbeing at work (CIPD, 2020). However, these individually oriented approaches have attracted many criticisms, namely the tendency to focus on individual weaknesses (such as the lack of resilience) at the exclusion of the key sources of stress at work and not delivering sustainable outcomes (Noblet & Rodwell, 2010; Richardson, 2017). There is a growing body of research to suggest that approaches aimed at addressing the wide range of factors impacting on the mental health of individuals, rather than focusing predominantly on enhancing individual health behaviours, are much more likely to provide long-term and sustainable benefits for both workers and organisations (Richardson, 2017; Sivris & Leka, 2015).

With an increasing understanding of mental health and wellbeing at work, key factors affecting mental health are increasingly seen as structural and in contemporary workplaces can include an important role for employee voice. Employee voice can be defined as the ability of employees to communicate their views, concerns, worries and suggestions to the employer, and for these to impact decisions in the workplace (Johnstone & Ackers, 2015). This review explores the role of employee voice as an important work-related factor in relation to mental health in contemporary workplaces, as well as a factor to be manipulated for the promotion of employee wellbeing. The case of employee voice in Poland is used in this chapter, which provides some context for the analysis of factors that are likely to affect voice behaviour and mental health.

What Is Mental Health?

Mental health takes many forms and has no single definition, and can refer to the mental, psychological or emotional elements of individuals as indicated by emotional states and rates of mental illnesses and diseases (Danna & Griffin, 1999; Warr, 1990; Warr, 2013). Mental health is considered as one of the core components in the World Health Organisation's (WHO) definition of general health, which is described as 'a state of complete physical, mental and social wellbeing and not merely the absence of disease or infirmity' (WHO, 2006). This definition indicates that there is no health without mental health, and health is not merely the absence of disease (Sivris & Leka, 2015).

Indeed, the last two decades have seen a shift in the academic literature from an emphasis on disease to a focus on wellbeing and positive aspects of mental health. This shift has been particularly visible in psychological research and influenced by the rise of positive psychology in the late 1990s, which highlighted the importance of focusing not only on curing mental illness but also on making lives of individuals more fulfilling and nurturing human talent (e.g. Seligman, 2012; Seligman & Csikszentmihalyi, 2000). In recent decades, positive mental health has also captured the attention of social scientists and policymakers (e.g. Layard, 2006; Marmot et al., 1997). More recently, the WHO has described mental health as 'a state of wellbeing in which the individual realizes his or her own abilities, can cope with the normal stresses of life, can work productively and fruitfully, and is able to make a contribution to his or her community' (WHO, 2014). While research still tends to highlight the negative aspects of mental health (e.g. depression or anxiety), today researchers agree that mental health is also about the presence of positive psychological states and resources (e.g. Huppert, 2009; Seligman, 2012; Warr, 2013). This definition of mental health provides a more comprehensive understanding of this complex phenomenon and points to the importance of multiple life domains (such as work) for promoting positive wellbeing and preventing mental illness.

The Role of Employee Voice

What Is Employee Voice and Why It Matters in the Context of Mental Health?

The concept of employee voice is very imprecise in the academic literature and can be defined differently across different contexts. It can be broadly defined as a two-way communication between employees and employers. Employee voice is the ability of employees to communicate their views, concerns, worries and suggestions to the employer, and for these to impact decisions in the workplace (Johnstone & Ackers, 2015). A recent definition of employee voice refers to 'all of the ways and means through which employees attempt to have a say about, and influence, their work and the functioning of their organisation' (Wilkinson et al., 2020b, p. 22). This definition recognises that voice can involve and be related to a wide variety of different topics such as working conditions, job quality and work organisation. For this chapter, employee voice is defined as any workplace process that enables employees to have some influence over their work and the conditions under which their work is taking place. The evidence suggests that effective employee voice can contribute to positive individual and organisational outcomes. Participating in decision-making is important for motivation and employee wellbeing, as it provides an opportunity to enhance work experience and the overall quality of working life. Organisations benefit from higher productivity and employee commitment, and reduced workplace absenteeism and staff turnover (Cox et al., 2006; CIPD, 2020; Holland et al., 2011).

In the context of mental health and wellbeing, employee voice can provide a stable mechanism which allows for information to flow between the parties, which contributes to increased knowledge and better decision-making (Holland et al., 2011). This decision-making needs to be sensitive to employees' needs and the context in which work takes place, and therefore, voice can be seen as fundamental when promoting mental health at work. For example, voice means providing employees with the opportunity to report work-related issues that influence their wellbeing or express their views and concerns regarding the existing approaches to promoting mental health, which can be a very powerful channel in developing mental health strategies and/or addressing the key sources of work-related stress in the workplace. The identification of factors affecting mental health, that is often referred to as a 'stress audit', underpins successful design of interventions that aim to reduce stress and improve well-being at work. In general, this process has important implications for the mental health at work, in that it can assist employers to obtain valuable information on the potential factors affecting mental health, as well as determining effective initiatives for reducing stress and improving mental health among workers (O'Driscoll & Brough, 2010). Employees' perceptions are also important in the process of evaluating wellbeing initiatives (Randall & Nielsen, 2010). This evidence points to the importance of employee voice in relation to the effective promotion of mental health and well-being in the workplace.

The Forms of Employee Voice in Contemporary Workplaces

Employees can express their views through individual and collective channels. This may involve speaking directly to line managers or indirectly through their employee representatives and/or trade unions. Direct participation can be seen as an important component of employee voice, as it allows employees to impact the decision-making themselves (i.e. not through managers or representatives) (Holland et al., 2011). Traditionally, employee voice has been expressed and communicated through trade unions, but this has never been the sole channel of employee communication and influence in the workplace. The changing nature of work and the wider labour market, and the decline in trade union representation in the past three decades, have significantly changed the forms and structure of employee voice arrangements, which has seen direct voice channels gaining more importance (Holland et al., 2011; Bryson et al., 2007).

This is particularly the case in Poland, as will be discussed in the following section.

In contemporary organisations employee voice is about representation, participation and involvement, and can take many different forms, depending on the context. This chapter considers the role of individual forms of voice at the workplace level, which expresses employees' perspectives, concerns and needs from work, and therefore is important for mental health and wellbeing. Creating opportunities for individuals to have effective voice in the workplace is a key aspect of ensuring high job quality. Job quality refers to job-level characteristics of work (such as autonomy, social support or work intensity) that have an impact on employee wellbeing (De Bustillo et al., 2011). Employee voice can therefore be considered an important part of job quality (CIPD, 2020).

Employee Voice in Poland

In Poland, as in other advanced economies, workplaces are changing. Major changes include increasing uncertainty and insecurity in employment, the intensification of work and more reliance on technologies in the workplace, which changes the way workers interact with employers and other employees. The diffusion of non-standard forms of employment (temporary, casual and part-time work) in the past decade has influenced job security and the overall quality of work. According to some authors, these changes may contribute to the changing nature of employee voice and the emergence of new forms of voice, such as e-voice where employees communicate their views and frustrations via social media (Dean & Greene, 2017). Industrial relations in Poland and the wider Central and Eastern European region have witnessed a sharp decline in trade union membership and collective bargaining, and reduced influence on public policy (Ivlevs & Veliziotis, 2017; Soulsby et al., 2017). In Poland, gone are days when workers on permanent contract working in factories were represented by trade unions. The trade unions in European countries have been declining over the last 30 years, but this decline is particularly steep in Poland. Following a sharp decline of unions in the 1990s, trade union density in Poland stood at 12.9% in

2019 and the union influence on political decisions is very limited (Wenzel, 2009). In addition, legal barriers to union membership are very pronounced in Poland and some groups of workers are excluded from union membership.

Particularly, the Trade Union Act of 1991 gives the right to organise and join union to polish employees, that is individuals who have an employment contract, whereas other categories of workers (such as self-employed or employees in micro firms) are not eligible. Because micro and medium firms prevail in Poland, 40% of all polish employees are not eligible for the union membership (Kohl, 2009). In total, 73% of workers in Poland report that the organisation does not have a 'trade union, works council or a similar committee' representing employees, which is significantly lower than the EU average of 50% (Eurofound, 2015). The trend of declining union membership has been attributed to the transition of Poland to democracy and the subsequent accession to the EU in 2004, which resulted in a change from a compulsory to a voluntary system of union membership, and to the increase of the private sector that is non-unionised (Ivlevs & Veliziotis, 2017). In addition, the post-socialist legacy in Poland means that unions are traditionally associated with anti-communist struggles and seen as 'welfare agencies', rather than representing employees' interests in the capitalist society. Also, the closures of large and unionised public enterprises contributed to the decline of trade union material resources (Ost, 2005). Consequently, skills and knowledge related to union organising are also relatively limited in Poland, when compared to Western countries.

Similarly, collective bargaining in Poland is mostly company-based, and its coverage is low (Bernaciak, 2015; Wenzel, 2009). The evidence shows that sectoral collective bargaining arrangements are not concluded at all. Currently, in the Polish labour market of approximately 17 million employees, only about 15% are covered by collective labour agreements, but their value is debatable. Polish law regulates the collective bargaining in a complex and unclear way, allowing limited room for manoeuvre for social partners and this makes collective labour agreements unattractive for organisations (Pisarczyk, 2019). Unfortunately, little is known about the trend of declining collective bargaining in the post-communist Europe, due to the lack of good quality quantitative data. Another issue is that small and medium enterprises prevail in these countries, which limits the opportunities for studying formal and indirect forms of employee voice in this region (Williams, 2015). With the decline of union representation and collective bargaining coverage, in many polish workplaces (especially small- and medium-sized companies), workers do not have any formal collective voice mechanisms, which would be independent from the organisation. As a result, other more direct forms of voice become prominent, and these forms of voice are often labelled as 'participation' or 'involvement' (Dundon & Gollan, 2007). For example, this may involve individual voice in the workplace where workers express their views to their line managers. The use of individual voice is difficult to examine in the polish context and there does not seem to be any surveys at national level which would estimate its effectiveness.

In general, the evidence shows that while unions in Eastern European countries can exercise some influence, generally employees must rely on alternative forms of voice and remain weaker in their employment relationship, when compared to Western European countries. Research shows that low satisfaction with Polish employers has contributed to exit and migration of Polish workers in the past two decades (Meardi, 2007). Studies reveal that Eastern European workers relocate to Western countries in search of better employment opportunities (Kahanec & Zimmerman, 2009), but apart from income, job quality (such as personal autonomy or the quality of relationships at work) strongly affects migration decisions (Blanchflower & Lawton, 2008). Therefore, given the sharp decline of collective representational forms of voice in Poland and the issues associated with the quality of work, it is particularly interesting to investigate individual forms of voice, especially those forms that occur at the workplace level. These forms of voice are related to the quality of work that workers do, which we will turn to next.

Job Quality in Poland

The case of employee voice in Poland is used to provide some context for the analysis of factors affecting individual forms of voice at the workplace level. The work environment in Poland is increasingly characterised by anxiety, precariousness and insecurity in employment. Job quality is a multidimensional construct and refers to job-level characteristics of work that have an impact on employee wellbeing and includes pay, intrinsic quality of work (such as autonomy or social support), employment quality (such as job security), health and safety (such as work intensity and working hours) and work-life balance (De Bustillo et al., 2011). Job quality varies greatly within Poland due to increasing deregulation of the labour market which contributed to the polarisation of jobs. In general employees in high-skilled and professional jobs tend to be better paid and receive better working conditions than those employed in manual and service jobs (Meardi, 2007). Studies show that workers in Poland have little control over the work process, poor relationships with their managers and less opportunities for career advancement, when compared to Western countries (Giordano & Kostova, 2002; Cieslik, 2011). Job quality is important in the context of employee voice—it is expected to impact on the ability and/or willingness of polish workers to speak up.

The importance of job quality for employee voice has been highlighted in previous research. For example, a study of high-skilled migrant polish workers in the UK found that the model of the authoritarian manager often prevails in polish workplaces, where relationships are very hierarchical and workers do not have much autonomy and independence over the way they do their jobs and, as a result, are not able to contribute to decision-making in their organisation (Cieslik, 2011). In this context, even if workers have voice, managers may wish to have silent workers and are less likely to be interested in listening to employees' comments and acting on their concerns. For some polish workers, lack of control and poor relationships with managers were some of the key reasons they decided to migrate to Western countries, such as the UK (Cieslik, 2011). In addition, studies examining motives of using voice in the workplace showed that managerial support in terms of their interest and willingness to listen to employees' matters substantially affects employee voice behaviour (Detert & Burris, 2007; Franca & Pahor, 2014). These findings suggest low participation and involvement in decision-making which is likely to inhibit any direct and individual forms of voice in polish workplaces.

Indeed, a recent international survey suggests that this seems to be the case in Poland. The European Company Survey (ECS) conducted in 2019 by Eurofound and Cedefop provides a unique quantitative data on employee voice in Europe and examines different mechanisms that organisations use to engage directly with employees. The latest findings of ECS revealed that only around a fifth of companies in Poland (20%) facilitated the regular direct involvement and participation of workers in organisational decision-making and allowed them a high level of influence last year. This is significantly lower than the average for the EU (31%), and much lower than in Nordic countries such as Sweden (56%) and Denmark (55%), where organisations are characterised by high direct engagement with employees on regular basis (Eurofound and Cedefop, 2020).

Other challenges include high job insecurity, with Poland having the highest share of fixed and non-standard contracts in Europe. Based on the European Working Conditions Survey, only 62% of all employees in Poland report holding a permanent contract, which is significantly lower than in Western countries such as Denmark (83%), Germany (85%), France (81%) or the UK (86%) (Eurofound, 2015). Young professionals find it increasingly more difficult to secure permanent employment, and companies tend to be very reluctant to sign a permanent contract (Cieslik, 2011). Research shows that insecurity in employment may be harmful to employee mental health (Virtanen et al., 2005) and may translate into greater reluctance of polish employees to use voice for fear of adverse career outcomes and may contribute to employee silence (Brinsfield, 2013). Employee silence can be defined as the intentional withholding of seemingly important information, including concerns, questions/or suggestions (Tangirala & Ramanujam, 2008). Researchers have identified a wide range of motives for remaining silent, the key reported reason for silence being a tactic to avoid the risks resulting from speaking up (Detert & Edmondson, 2011). Specifically, some commonly reported reasons include the fear of retaliation, being afraid of negative career consequences, believing that speaking up would not do any good or feeling that managers are not interested to hear about these types of issues and therefore will not act on them (Brinsfield, 2013).

The above findings point to a bleak picture of working environment in Poland which is likely to influence the extent to which employees can engage in voice behaviour. Inefficient management and poor workplace relations combined with low levels of control over the work process are some of the key job characteristics that describe job quality work in polish workplaces. Therefore, at the workplace level, job quality which encompasses important work-related characteristics might affect employees' ability and/or willingness to use voice. Overall, these workplace trends may suggest that employers see more costs than benefits when it comes to employee voice, and employees themselves might be less likely to use voice in the context of poor working conditions and high job insecurity. In other words, employees may perceive the risks of using voice as outweighing the benefits. This is expected to have an influence on employee mental health and wellbeing, which will be the focus of the next section.

Employee Voice and Mental Health and Wellbeing

Mental health and wellbeing are important from organisational perspective. As mentioned at the beginning of the chapter, it can contribute to a wide range of organisational outcomes, such as improved organisational performance (Wright, 2010; Wright & Bonett, 2007). Therefore, for companies to perform well, it is essential that employees communicate their views, concerns and suggestions about work-related issues and their wellbeing, so organisations can better understand employee needs in the workplace and the sources of work-related stress. Many of the contemporary health promotion frameworks and guidelines highlight the need to focus on work environments and on empowering individuals to identify and address work-related issues that affect their health, as well as giving employees more control over their work environments (Noblet & Rodwell, 2010; Zwetsloot & Leka, 2010). This highlights the importance of employee voice for mental health in the workplace. There is a growing body of evidence which shows that strategies focused on addressing the work-related determinants influencing on the wellbeing of workers are much more likely to contribute to more sustainable and long-term benefits for both individuals and organisations, when compared to individually oriented initiatives (such as enhancing employee resilience or promoting healthy lifestyles) (Noblet & Rodwell, 2010).

Nevertheless, as we have seen in this chapter, there is no consensus among researchers on how to define employee voice. One of the recent definitions of employee voice refers to different ways through which employees can express their views and influence their work and the wider functioning of the organisation (Wilkinson et al., 2020a). Therefore, it has been concluded that voice can encompass many different topics such as working conditions, employee rewards and work organisation, and voice can occur through a variety of means: collective and individual, direct and indirect, and formal and informal. In relation to mental health and wellbeing, this chapter considers the role of individual forms of voice at the workplace level, which expresses employees' perspectives, concerns and needs from work. Consequently, voice can be seen as an opportunity for workers to have their interests considered in relation to mental health and acted upon during organisational decision-making (Wilkinson et al., 2020b). Based on psychological theories, people's mental health and wellbeing is directly and indirectly affected by a wide range of work-related factors such as low control over the work process, poor social support, or demanding and stressful working conditions (e.g. Bonde, 2008; Cottini & Lucifora, 2013; O'Driscoll & Brough, 2010). However, to date there has been very little research examining the direct link between employee voice and mental health and wellbeing. Therefore, to understand how employee voice can contribute to wellbeing, three theoretical perspectives are proposed in this chapter, which help identify the potential links and provide an opportunity to understand how voice can be used by organisations to enhance wellbeing and reduce work-related stress.

Theoretical Perspectives

According to the most influential job demands-control (JD-C) theory by Karasek (1979), particularly important for employee mental health is the degree of control that people have over the work environment and the demands placed upon them. Control can be applied to almost any work-related aspect (e.g. control over work pace or decision-making, or how much influence the employee has over policies and procedures). Demands can be cognitive, emotional and physical, and if any of these demands are excessive, then there is a strong research evidence that negative outcomes tend to follow for both the employee and the organisation (Arnold et al., 2020). The strain hypothesis suggests that the combination of high job demands with low control is most detrimental to mental health and gives rise to the so-called high strain jobs. In contrast, jobs in which both control and demands are high contribute to wellbeing and personal growth (the so-called active jobs). The importance of control is emphasised in the JD-C theory. In particular, the emphasis in this theory is on role empowerment, which can lead directly to positive outcomes for employee wellbeing, as well as may serve an important moderating function in alleviating the impact of high job demands. Fox et al. (1993) argue that control allows employees to deal better with the demands they are facing but also fulfils a basic psychological need for control.

To date, a considerable number of studies have supported the strain hypothesis, although the relationship between jobs demands and control is inconclusive (De Lange et al., 2003; Meier et al., 2008). Nevertheless, the JD-C theory helps shed some light on the role of employee voice in relation to control and high job demands. As employee voice includes communicating views and concerns in the expectation that management will listen to employees and act on their feedback to alleviate the reported issues (e.g. high job demands), it may contribute to greater control over the work process. Recent evidence showed that voice provides workers with an opportunity to have some control over their work environment which can positively affect wellbeing (Wilkinson & Barry, 2016). While the pathways between voice, control and demands have not been established in the literature, voice may be important in gaining control and when dealing with work-related stressors (e.g. high job demands).

However, as discussed in the previous section, employees do not always voice their views, concerns or needs. Studies suggest the way that individuals use voice is largely determined by opportunities for employee voice, the way that managers support and react to voice, and the attitudes of management to the value that voice can offer to the functioning of the organisation (Brinsfield, 2013; Wilkinson et al., 2020b). Social support can be defined as helpful interactions with supervisors and other workers (Daniels et al., 2009). Poor managerial support such as lack of effective communication and feedback was found to be related to greater stress and symptoms of depression in earlier studies (Sparks et al., 2001), and therefore, social support from managers might be an important factor necessary to facilitate voice in the workplace. Supervisors and managers are common sources of support at work and can provide various sources of support (such as instrumental support, advice and guidance). Although there is a lot of evidence that support has a significant influence on mental health and wellbeing (e.g. Brough et al., 2009), there has been a debate about the nature of this influence. Three alternative pathways have been suggested (Cooper et al., 2001). The first pathway suggests that higher level of support will have a positive influence on wellbeing. The second pathway points to the mediating effect of social support. Finally, the extended version of the job demand-control model (Johnson & Hall, 1988) proposes that, similarly to job control, social support can operate as a buffering (moderating) variable in the association between job demands and wellbeing. This is called the stress-buffering hypothesis. This theory provides another insight on the importance of managerial support in relation to voice. Creating opportunities for employees to have effective voice that is acted upon through managerial support is considered a crucial aspect of ensuring good job quality (CIPD, 2020; Franca & Pahor, 2014), which promotes mental health and wellbeing (Cottini & Lucifora, 2013). In that sense social support could act as a potential mediator between voice and wellbeing.

The role of managers is often viewed in the previous literature as a key work-related factor affecting employees' willingness to speak up (Detert & Burris, 2007; Franca & Pahor, 2014). From theoretical perspective, employees depend on managers in terms of resources, especially in hierarchical settings. Managers have power to devote attention and resources to the concerns raised by employees (Pfeffer & Salancik, 1978). Managers also have the power to provide rewards and punishments, and this influence over employees' pay, working conditions and career outcomes makes managers' behaviours important in the context of employees' willingness to use voice (Depret & Fiske, 1993). When managers are supportive and send signals that they are willing to listen to and act on employee voice, employees perceive fewer costs from speaking up and their motivation to use voice is likely to be higher (Detert & Burris, 2007).

Finally, individuals may also use voice as a means to regulate personal resources and as a response to work-related stress. The Conservation of Resources (COR) theory (Hobfoll, 1989, 2002) helps to explain the relationship between resources, voice and stress. The COR theory states that resources are strongly linked to health and wellbeing. Individuals with many resources are more adaptive, can solve life difficulties better and achieve their goals more successfully than those with fewer resources (Hobfoll, 2002). This leads to lower levels of strain, which in turn enhances wellbeing. Resources are broadly defined as objects, states and conditions, and can include a wide variety of things that individuals value such as material (e.g. shelter or food), social (family), personal (self-esteem) or employment-related (social support) resources (Hobfoll, 2002). The COR theory argues that individuals are motivated to protect their current resources (conservation) and acquire new resources (acquisition). From this basic tenet emerge several principles of the COR theory. The first principle is the 'primacy of resource loss' which is the idea that it is psychologically more damaging for people to lose resources than it is useful for them to gain resources. As a result, it is expected that individuals will engage in behaviours that prevent them from losing resources. The second principle is the 'resource investment' which is the idea that people invest resources in order to protect themselves against resource loss, to recover from losses and also to gain new resources (Hobfoll, 2002).

Stress occurs when resources are threatened with loss, lost or when people fail to acquire resources after substantial resource investments. Because losing resources can cause high psychological distress, individuals work hard to accumulate additional resources to compensate any future losses that might occur (Wright & Hobfoll, 2004). Voice is a behaviour that is not a part of workers' core job responsibilities and therefore requires additional effort and resources. As a result, when individuals engage in voice, they need to devote extra energy and time to that effort (Ng & Feldman, 2012). This resource-depleting nature of voice is more prominent when workers experience high job demands. Some studies suggested that employees who are under stress may reduce their use of voice, because this allows them to conserve the resources (e.g. Bolino & Turnley, 2005; Detert & Burris, 2007). In contrast, other studies found that employees who are under stress may communicate their views and concerns more often, because voice may be key in gaining extra resources to deal with work-related stressors (e.g. Dundon & Gollan, 2007).

The stress–voice relationship has been explored in the study by Ng and Feldman (2012), who conducted a meta-analysis of 55 studies and found that when employees already face job stressors (such as lack of autonomy, poor social relationships with managers or feelings of risk when speaking up about dissatisfaction), they are less likely to communicate their views and concerns, which suggests that using voice under stress may further deplete resources. In other words, individuals who are under stress tend to use less voice as a way of preserving resources. In contrast, employees with lower level of workplace stress are expected to have more resources available to engage in voice, which in turn helps them to accumulate additional resources, that they can use to enhance their wellbeing (Ng & Feldman, 2012).

It is well-known that higher job demands require sustained efforts to cope with work and contribute to psychological and physiological costs (Bakker & Demerouti, 2007). In this case, voice could be seen as an additional demand, rather than a resource (Hirst et al., 2020). Therefore, voice can be perceived by individuals as a demand when employees are in jobs characterised by high job demands or can be viewed as a resource when employees are in jobs with lower level of demands (Ng & Feldman, 2012). In general, the COR theory suggests that job demands might act as a key barrier to employee voice in the workplace. However, it is not clear which demands are the potential barriers to voice, and this area would benefit from more research. Nevertheless, psychological theories of work-related stress help to understand the dynamic relationship between voice and stress, and the psychological motivations for using voice in the workplace. These theories suggests that voice may contribute to more control over the work process and job demands, but at the same time perceived support from managers, job demands and resources in the workplace might be useful in predicting how an employee may use voice in relation to their wellbeing.

Conclusion

Employee voice is crucial to positive organisational outcomes and to implementing a successful wellbeing strategy in the workplace. From employee perspective, individual forms of voice such as expressing themselves and their views, concerns and needs are important in creating good quality work, which is fundamental for mental health and wellbeing at work. From employer perspective, employee voice can assist organisations and managers to obtain valuable information on the potential work-related factors affecting mental health, as well as determining effective initiatives for reducing stress and improving mental health among workers. This is crucial, given that many of the factors that affect mental health in the workplace are structural and beyond the control of individuals themselves.

However, the evidence presented in this chapter shows that little research to date have examined the relationship between employee voice and mental health and wellbeing. Theoretical approaches from work psychology reviewed in this chapter suggest complex associations between voice and stress and help to shed some light on the psychological motivations for using voice in the workplace. While the pathways between voice and mental health are underexplored in the past literature, it seems that stressful work environments (in terms of high job demands and low social support from managers) may inhibit employee voice. Specifically, when faced with high job demands and low managerial support, employees are less likely to use voice. This suggests that employee voice can act as a mechanism through which employees can improve their job quality and wellbeing, but at the same time poor-quality jobs can also act as a barrier to employee voice. This is certainly an underexplored area which would benefit from future research. The case of employee voice in Poland was used in this chapter to provide some context for the analysis of individual forms of voice at the workplace level and helped to shed some light on the factors which may act as barriers to employee voice. Specifically, the evidence presented in this chapter showed that different forms of voice in Poland are under challenge. Based on the European-level data polish workers experience poorer job quality on several dimensions when compared to Western European countries. This can potentially have a negative influence on the ability and willingness of polish workers to use voice, which in turn is expected to have an impact on mental health and wellbeing in the workplace. The case study of Poland highlights the importance of job quality in relation to employee voice.

This chapter has important implications for practice. Employee voice can contribute to many positive organisational outcomes, and it is particularly important when implementing a successful wellbeing strategy. Employees can help in the process of identifying the root causes of work-related stress and poor wellbeing, which is essential in ensuring good mental health among employees. Employee voice can be developed through a wide range of initiatives. This involves enabling individual forms of voice in the workplace and involving employees themselves in the development of the wellbeing policies and practices in an organisation. It also involves providing confidential communication mechanisms through which employees can express their views and concerns on wellbeing issues. Senior leaders and managers all have an important role to play in enabling employees to express themselves and their views in the workplace. It is key that managers demonstrate to employees their interest in and willingness to listen to issues related to job quality and mental health. It is also crucial that managers act on employee voice.

References

Arnold, J., Coyne, I., Randall, R., & Patterson, F. (2020). *Work psychology: Understanding human behaviour in the workplace*. Pearson.

Bakker, A. B., & Demerouti, E. (2007). The job demands-resources model: State of the art. *Journal of Managerial Psychology, 22*(3), 309–328.

Bernaciak, M. (2015). *Beyond the CEE 'black box': Crisis and industrial relations in the new EU member states*. Working Paper 2015.05. Brussels: ETUI.

Blanchflower, D. G., & Lawton, H. (2008). *The impact of the EU on the UK labour market*. IZA, Discussion Paper No. 3696.

Bolino, M. C., & Turnley, W. H. (2005). The personal costs of citizenship behaviour: The relationship between individual initiative and role overload, job stress, and work-family conflict. *The Journal of Applied Psychology, 90*, 740–748.

Bonde, J. P. E. (2008). Psychosocial factors at work and risk of depression: A systematic review of the epidemiological evidence. *Occupational and Environmental Medicine, 65*(7), 438–445.

Brinsfield, C. T. (2013). Employee silence motives. Investigation of dimensionality and development of measures. *Journal of Organizational Behaviour, 34*(5), 671–697.

Brough, P., O'Driscoll, M. P., Kalliath, T. J., Cooper, C. L., & Poelmans, S. A. (2009). *Workplace psychological health: Current research and practice*. Edward Elgar Publishing Limited.

Bryson, A., Gomez, R., Kretschmer, T., & Willman, P. (2007). The diffusion of workplace voice and high-commitment management practices in Britain, 1984–1998. *Industrial and Corporate Change, 16*(3), 395–426.

Butterworth, P., Leach, L. S., Strazdins, L., Olesen, S. C., Rodgers, B., & Broom, D. (2011). The psychosocial quality of work determines whether employment has benefits for mental health: Results from a longitudinal national household panel survey. *Occupational and Environmental Medicine, 68*(11), 806–812.

Butterworth, P., Leach, L. S., McManus, S., & Stansfeld, S. A. (2013). Common mental disorders, unemployment, and psychosocial job quality: Is a poor job better than no job at all? *Psychological Medicine, 43*(8), 1763–1772.

Cieslik, A. (2011). Where do you prefer to work? How the work environment influences return migration decisions from the United Kingdom to Poland. *Journal of Ethnic and Migration Studies, 37*(9), 1367–1383.

CIPD. (2020). Employee voice. *Factsheets*. https://www.cipd.co.uk/knowledge/fundamentals/relations/communication/voice-factsheet.

Cooper, C., & Dewe, P. (2008). Wellbeing—Absenteeism, presenteeism, costs and challenges. *Occupational Medicine, 58*(8), 522–524.

Cooper, C. L., Dewe, P. J., Dewe, P. J., O'Driscoll, M. P., & O'Driscoll, M. P. (2001). *Organisational stress: A review and critique of theory, research, and applications*. SAGE Publications.

Cottini, E., & Lucifora, C. (2013). Mental health and working conditions in Europe. *ILR Review, 66*(4), 958–988.

Cox, A., Zagelmeyer, S., & Marchington, M. (2006). Embedding employee involvement and participation at work. *Human Resource Management Journal, 16*(3), 250–267.

Danna, K., & Griffin, R. W. (1999). Health and wellbeing in the workplace: A review and synthesis of the literature. *Journal of Management, 25*(3), 357–384.

Daniels, K., Boocock, G., Glover, J., Hartley, R., & Holland, J. (2009). An experience sampling study of learning, affect, and the demands control support model. *Journal of Applied Psychology, 94*(4), 1003–1017.

De Bustillo, R. M., Fernández-Macías, E., Antón, J. I., & Esteve, F. (2011). *Measuring more than money: The social economics of job quality.* Edward Elgar Publishing Limited.

De Lange, A. H., Taris, T. W., Kompier, M. A., Houtman, I. L., & Bongers, P. M. (2003). "The very best of the millennium": Longitudinal research and the demand-control-(support) model. *Journal of Occupational Health Psychology, 8*(4), 282–294.

Dean, D., & Greene, A. M. (2017). How do we understand worker silence despite poor conditions–as the actress said to the woman bishop. *Human Relations, 70*(10), 1237–1257.

Depret, E. F., & Fiske, S. T. (1993). Social cognition and power: Some cognitive consequences of social structure as a source of control deprivation. In G. Weary, F. Gleicher, & R. Marsh (Eds.), *Control motivation and social cognition* (pp. 176–202). Springer Verlag.

Detert, J. R., & Burris, E. R. (2007). Leadership behaviour and employee voice: Is the door really open? *Academy of Management Journal, 50*, 869–884.

Detert, J. R., & Edmondson, A. C. (2011). Implicit voice theories: Taken-for-granted rules of self-censorship at work. *Academy of Management Journal, 54*, 461–488.

Dundon, T., & Gollan, P. J. (2007). Re-conceptualizing voice in the non-union workplace. *International Journal of Human Resource Management, 18*, 1182–1198.

Eurofound. (2015). European Working Conditions Survey—Data visualisation. https://www.eurofound.europa.eu/data/european-working-conditions-survey?locale=EN&dataSource=EWCS2017NW&media=png&width=740&question=Q54b&plot=heatMap&countryGroup=linear&subset=agecat_3&subsetValue=All&answer=2%2D%2DYes#

Eurofound and Cedefop. (2020). *European company survey 2019: Workplace practices unlocking employee potential*, European Company Survey 2019 series. Publications Office of the European Union, Luxembourg.

Eurostat. (2019). Mental health and health related issues statistics. https://ec.europa.eu/eurostat/statistics-explained/index.php?title=Mental_health_and_related_issues_statisticsJohnson,J.V.,&

Fox, M. L., Dwyer, D. J., & Ganster, D. C. (1993). Effects of stressful job demands and control on physiological and attitudinal outcomes in a hospital setting. *Academy of Management Journal, 36*(2), 289–318.

Franca, V., & Pahor, M. (2014). Influence of management attitudes on the implementation of employee participation. *Economic and Industrial Democracy, 35*(1), 115–142.

Gini, A. (2000). *My job my self: Work and the creation of the modern individual.* Routledge.

Giordano, S., & Kostova, D. (2002). The social production of mistrust. In C. M. Hann (Ed.), *Postsocialism: Ideals, ideologies and practices in Eurasia* (pp. 74–92). Routledge.

Green, F. (2006). *Demanding work: The paradox of job quality in the affluent economy.* Princeton University Press.

Hirst, G., Yeo, G., Celestine, N., Lin, S. Y., & Richardson, A. (2020). It's not just action but also about reflection: Taking stock of agency research to develop a future research agenda. *Australian Journal of Management, 45*(3), 376–401.

Hobfoll, S. E. (1989). Conservation of resources: A new attempt at conceptualizing stress. *The American Psychologist, 44*, 513–524.

Hobfoll, S. E. (2002). Social and psychological resources and adaptation. *Review of General Psychology, 6*, 307–324.

Holland, P., Pyman, A., Cooper, B. K., & Teicher, J. (2011). Employee voice and job satisfaction in Australia: The centrality of direct voice. *Human Resource Management, 50*(1), 95–111.

Huppert, F. A. (2009). Psychological wellbeing: Evidence regarding its causes and consequences. *Applied Psychology: Health and Wellbeing, 1*(2), 137–164.

Ivlevs, A., & Veliziotis, M. (2017). What do unions do in times of economic crisis? Evidence from Central and Eastern Europe. *European Journal of Industrial Relations, 23*(1), 81–96.

Jain, A., & Leka, S. (2019). Occupation and health. In C. D. Llewellyn et al. (Eds.), *Cambridge handbook of psychology, health and medicine* (pp. 28–31). Cambridge University Press.

Johnson, J. V., & Hall, E. M. (1988). Job strain, workplace social support, and cardiovascular disease: A cross-sectional study of a random sample of the Swedish working population. *American Journal of Public Health, 78*(10), 1336–1342.

Johnstone, S., & Ackers, P. (2015). *Finding a voice at work? New perspectives on employment relations.* Oxford University Press.

Kahanec, M., & Zimmerman, K. F. (2009). *Migration in an enlarged EU: A challenging solution?* European Commission.

Karasek, R. A. (1979). Job demands, job decision latitude, and mental strain: Implications for job redesign. *Administrative Science Quarterly, 24*, 285–308.

Kohl, H. (2009). *Freedom of association, employees' rights and social dialogue in Central and Eastern Europe and the Western Balkans*. Friedrich Ebert Stiftung.

Layard, R. (2006). Happiness and public policy: A challenge to the profession. *The Economic Journal, 116*(510), C24–C33.

Marmot, M., Ryff, C. D., Bumpass, L. L., Shipley, M., & Marks, N. F. (1997). Social inequalities in health: Next questions and converging evidence. *Social Science & Medicine, 44*(6), 901–910.

Meardi, G. (2007). More voice after more exit? Unstable industrial relations in Central Eastern Europe. *Industrial Relations Journal, 38*(6), 503–523.

Meier, L. L., Semmer, N. K., Elfering, A., & Jacobshagen, N. (2008). The double meaning of control: Three-way interactions between internal resources, job control, and stressors at work. *Journal of Occupational Health Psychology, 13*(3), 244-258.

Ng, T. W., & Feldman, D. C. (2012). Employee voice behaviour: A meta-analytic test of the conservation of resources framework. *Journal of Organizational Behaviour, 33*(2), 216–234.

Nieuwenhuijsen, K., Bruinvels, D., & Frings-Dresen, M. (2010). Psychosocial work environment and stress-related disorders, a systematic review. *Occupational Medicine, 60*(4), 277–286.

Noblet, A. J., & Rodwell, J. (2010). Workplace health promotion. In S. Leka & J. Houdmont (Eds.), *Occupational health psychology* (pp. 157–193). Wiley-Blackwell.

O'Driscoll, M. P., & Brough, P. (2010). Work organisation and health. In S. Leka & J. Houdmont (Eds.), *Occupational health psychology* (pp. 57–87). Wiley-Blackwell.

Ost, D. (2005). *The defeat of solidarity. Anger and politics in postcommunist Europe*. Cornell University Press.

Pfeffer, J., & Salancik, G. (1978). *The external control of organizations: A resource dependence perspective*. Harper & Row.

Pisarczyk, Ł. (2019). The crisis of the collective bargaining system in Poland. *International Journal of Comparative Labour Law and Industrial Relations, 35*(1), 57–78.

Randall, R., & Nielsen, K. (2010). Interventions to promote well-being at work. In S. Leka & J. Houdmont (Eds.), *Occupational health psychology* (pp. 88–123). Wiley-Blackwell.

Richardson, K. M. (2017). Managing employee stress and wellness in the new millennium. *Journal of Occupational Health Psychology, 22*(3), 423–428.
Seligman, M. E. P. (2012). *Flourish: A visionary new understanding of happiness and wellbeing—And how to achieve them*. Free Press.
Seligman, M. E. P., & Csikszentmihalyi, M. (2000). Positive psychology: An introduction. *American Psychologist, 55*(1), 5–14.
Sivris, K. C., & Leka, S. (2015). Examples of holistic good practices in promoting and protecting mental health in the workplace: Current and future challenges. *Safety and Health at Work, 6*(4), 295–304.
Soulsby, A., Hollinshead, G., & Steger, T. (2017). Crisis and change in industrial relations in central and Eastern Europe. *European Journal of Industrial Relations, 23*(1), 5–15.
Sparks, K., Faragher, B., & Cooper, C. L. (2001). Well-being and occupational health in the 21st century workplace. *Journal of Occupational and Organizational Psychology, 74*(4), 489–509.
Tangirala, S., & Ramanujam, R. (2008). Employee silence on critical work issues: The cross-level effects of procedural justice climate. *Personnel Psychology, 61*, 37–68.
Virtanen, M., Kivimaki, M., Joensuu, M., Virtanen, P., & Elovainio, M. (2005). Temporary employment and health: A review. *International Journal of Epidemiology, 34*(3), 610–622.
Warr, P. (1990). The measurement of wellbeing and other aspects of mental health. *Journal of Occupational Psychology, 63*(3), 193–210.
Warr, P. (2007). *Work, happiness, and unhappiness*. Psychology Press.
Warr, P. (2013). How to think about and measure psychological wellbeing. In R. Sinclair, M. Wang, & L. E. Tetrick (Eds.), *Research methods in occupational health psychology: Measurement, design, and data analysis* (pp. 76–90). Routledge.
Wenzel, M. (2009). Związki zawodowe w badaniach CBOS 1980–2008. In J. Gardawski (Ed.), *Polacy pracujący a kryzys fordyzmu* (pp. 533–550). Wydawnictwo Naukowe Scholar.
WHO. (2006). *Constitution of the World Health Organization basic documents*. http://www.who.int/governance/eb/who_constitution_en.pdf.
WHO. (2014). *Mental health: A state of wellbeing*. World Health Organisation.
WHO. (2022). *European framework for action on mental health 2021–2025*. WHO Regional Office for Europe.
Wilkinson, A., & Barry, M. (2016). Voices from across the divide: An industrial relations perspective on employee voice. *German Journal of Human Resource Management, 30*, 338–344.

Wilkinson, A., Barry, M., & Morrison, E. (2020a). Toward an integration of research on employee voice. *Human Resource Management Review, 30*, 10–17.

Wilkinson, A., Donaghey, J., Dundon, T., & Freeman, R. (Eds.). (2020b). *The handbook of research on employee voice*. Edward Elgar Press.

Williams, C. C. (2015). Evaluating cross-national variations in envelope wage payments in East-Central Europe. *Economic and Industrial Democracy, 36*(2), 283–303.

Wright, T. A. (2010). Much more than meets the eye: The role of psychological wellbeing in job performance, employee retention and cardiovascular health. *Organizational Dynamics, 39*(1), 13–23.

Wright, T. A., & Bonett, D. G. (2007). Job satisfaction and psychological well-being as nonadditive predictors of workplace turnover. *Journal of Management, 33*(2), 141–160.

Wright, T. A., & Hobfoll, S. E. (2004). Commitment, psychological well-being, and job performance: An examination of conservation of resources (COR) theory and job burnout. *Journal of Business and Management, 9*, 389–406.

Zwetsloot, G., & Leka, S. (2010). Corporate culture, health, and wellbeing. In L. Stavroula & J. Houdmont (Eds.), *Occupational health psychology* (pp. 157–193). Wiley-Blackwell.

8

Employee Voice and Social Media: The Australian Perspective

Arlene Sale, Jonathan Sale, Al Rainnie, and John Burgess

Introduction

The purpose of this chapter is to identify the range of voice mechanisms that are available in Australia, especially in the context of the growing use and application of social media applications. The chapter discusses formal voice mechanisms that are established through workplace and industrial relations legislation; organisational mechanisms associated with HRM policies and processes; trade union mechanisms; and other mechanisms linked to institutions and processes outside of the workplace, including non-government organisations (NGOs) and political parties. The nature of voice, the mechanisms of voice, and the actors involved in the voice process have evolved with the structural development of the

---

A. Sale • J. Burgess (✉)
Torrens University, Adelaide, SA, Australia
e-mail: john.burgess@torrens.edu.au

J. Sale • A. Rainnie
University of South Australia, Adelaide, SA, Australia

T. Ajibade Adisa et al. (eds.), *Employee Voice in the Global North*,
https://doi.org/10.1007/978-3-031-31123-9_8

workforce (Barry et al., 2018; Budd et al., 2022; Holland et al., 2011); changes in working and contractual arrangements (Campbell & Burgess, 2018); changes to the process and location of work (ACTU, 2020); and changes in the institutional arrangements governing work and the workplace (Bray et al., 2018; McAndrew et al., 2018). Through time the trade union density in Australia has declined (Baird et al., 2018). Successive legislative changes have attempted to reduce trade union participation in the workplace, limit employee action such as through controls over strikes, and strengthen employer prerogative (Baird et al., 2018). The multi-layered complexity of the Australian industrial relations system (Bray et al., 2018) and the development of the digital economy (de Ruyter et al., 2019) offer an opportunity to examine the evolving nature of voice mechanisms and their effectiveness in addressing traditional industrial relations concerns such as workplace disputes, wage negotiations, and employee grievances (Walker, 2020). However, there is scope with the emergence of social media to assess the participation of new actors in the industrial relations process (Michelson et al., 2008), the development of coalitions to address issues in and beyond the workplace (Dayaram & Burgess, 2021), and for extending the domain and reach of voice and action into public policy (Holland et al., 2019). For this purpose, the chapter will examine the role of social media in supporting employees in different contexts that include non-unionised gig workers and unionised long-distance mining workers. The chapter will outline voice and voice mechanisms, then provide an overview of the Australian industrial relations system and recent developments in the system. Then follows a discussion of social media and its support for voice in different case study contexts. The chapter concludes with a reflection on how social media has impacted on voice and industrial relations in Australia.

Voice and Voice Mechanisms

Voice is about the ability or capacity to articulate one's interests or concerns in the workplace (Van Gramberg et al., 2019). A collective form of voice is associated with trade unionism. Whether voice is delivered in an individual or collective format, both forms start with the process of speaking out on specific issues to improve one's employment conditions (Barry et al., 2018; Bool-Sale & Sale, 2010; Van Gramberg et al., 2019). A worker can be voiceless and unable to speak out on concerns and issues (McMillan, 2016). A worker can be silent, wilfully suppressing information to endure and preserve oneself at work (Cullinane & Donaghey, 2020). If a workplace offers a narrow and top-down way of providing information, it demonstrates access to pseudo-voice (Bool-Sale & Sale, 2010). Voice can be activated by employees, management, the state, trade unions, and organisations external to the industrial relations system, such as NGOs. State-activated voice includes employee representation on legally imposed committees such as bargaining, Occupational, Health and Safety (OH&S) committees, and equal opportunity committees (Commonwealth of Australia, 2004). Employers may actively seek employee input into workplace conditions such as safety, policy development, performance management, and feedback for managers regarding policy effectiveness (Machin & Wood, 2005).

There are multiple voice mechanisms, different motivations for exercising voice, and differences in quality. Quality can be assessed in terms of the clarity of the communication and the effectiveness of voice in achieving the objective of the communication. Hirschman (1970) and Freeman and Medoff (1984) were pioneers in voice scholarship. Hirschman (1970) introduced employee voice and loyalty through consumers' satisfaction with product quality. Unhappy consumers either opt for exit by not patronising the product or voice by expressing dissatisfaction to improve the product (Hirschman, 1970). This concept was translated into the milieu of employment through Freeman and Medoff's (1984) voice perspective, specifically, collective bargaining, which improves the organisation's efficiency via reduced turnover and training and recruitment costs. When workers are happy, the likelihood of exit is low, and loyalty and voice are high (Hirschman, 1970; Freeman & Medoff, 1984).

Voice is meaningful when its mechanisms empower workers to improve work conditions (Barry et al., 2018). This voice is commonly referred to as participation, empowerment, and democracy at work (Budd et al., 2010; Johnstone & Ackers, 2015). Mantouvalou (2014) examined voice through labour law theory by framing participation within the construct of democracy: a right to voice grounded on the principle of equality. There is an inequality of power between employer and employee, and the need to address this incongruence to give workers an effective right to participate. According to Yeoman (2014), for voice to be realised as a shared power in decision-making, it requires individual and social agency. Individual agency pertains to expressing rational arguments to influence and persuade others, while social agency relates to a supportive legislative framework, including avenues for appeal. Liu et al. (2017) categorise voice based on the target or recipient of information. Employees *speak up* if the recipient of the information is the supervisor or *speak out* if their colleagues receive the information (Liu et al., 2017). This voice is only possible if employees have 'psychological safety' or express themselves freely without fear of negative consequences (Liu et al., 2017). Liu et al.'s (2017) speaking up is consistent with Morrison's (2014) upward voice, where employees communicate information about work to someone of higher rank in the organisation. If information is withheld, employees activate silence, denying the organisation possibly valuable information (Cullinane & Donaghey, 2020; Morrison, 2014). Employees' default behaviour is silence (Jolly & Lee, 2020). The decision to voice or challenge the status quo to improve their current affairs derives from the degree to which employees believe (1) the voice is effective and (2) they are safe from the negative consequences of voicing (Jolly & Lee, 2020). Employees' loyalty to their workplace and organisations' profitability is enhanced by voice (Bogg & Novitz, 2014).

One must contextualise a specific workplace to understand voice (Budd et al., 2022). Gans and Zhan (2022), as well as Heaphy et al. (2022), dig deeper to appreciate the 'how and why' of voice. While others focus on pro-social behaviour concerning organisational performance (Chon et al., 2021; Kim & Kiura, 2020), some evaluate collectivism, unions, representation, and consultation agencies and even connect these with perception during merger and acquisition, intention to quit, and conflict resolution (Van Gramberg et al., 2019; Nicholson et al., 2017). Budd et al. (2022) review Marchington's four decades of scholarship and contribution to employee voice, participation, and involvement. The study examined voice structures—how voice is driven by management and its informality and embeddedness in the workplace processes. Voice processes initiated by management are perceived with apprehension considering union avoidance and management controls, but the studies of Marchington in the 1980s proved this otherwise. While management-initiated voice is incomparable to union voice, employers commonly introduce informal voice mechanisms to enhance employee contribution and organisational performance. In smaller enterprises, these mechanisms allow resolution of immediate issues at the point of service or production (Budd et al., 2022). Power dynamics and reliance on management goodwill limit these informal voice mechanisms. Organisations that frequently use multiple forms of voice mechanisms have a high degree of institutional embeddedness of employee involvement and participation (Budd et al., 2022).

Despite scholarships about the benefits of speaking up, more employees remain silent as they view speaking up as hazardous to one's career well-being, rocking the boat, to say the least, or being associated with or branded as being troublemakers in the workplace. Gans and Zhan (2022) ask why workers are reluctant to exercise their voice in the workplace. Aside from workers' risk avoidance tendency, they choose silence because they are disengaged, deviant, diffident, and relational, or view speaking up as ineffectual. Contextual factors such as management style, business climate, organisational culture, and the day-to-day dynamics in the workplace also contribute to workers' choice to be silent (Gans & Zhan, 2022). Van Gramberg et al. (2019) explore the relationships among employee voices at work, dispute resolution, and intention to quit. They find that (1) employee voice has a direct negative effect on intentions to quit, (2) voice has an immediate positive impact on the resolution of the dispute, (3) dispute resolution has a mediating effect on intentions to quit, highlighting that employee voice tends to reduce intention to quit, (4) bullying and harassment and uncivil behaviour disputes were less likely to have a resolution, and (5) employees reporting disputes about employment conditions or with supervisors' decisions were more likely to intend to quit (Van Gramberg et al., 2019).

The definition of employee participation evolved from the late 1960s up until the 2010s (Gollan & Xu, 2015). During the late 1960s, employee participation was defined as a form of industrial democracy through trade unionism and collectivism. By the 1980s, employee participation focused on employer-driven human resource (HR) management approaches for organisational efficiency and productivity (Gollan & Xu, 2015). During the policies of neoliberalism in the 1990s, the orientation shifted to non-unionism and individualism, where employer prerogatives were reinforced by legislation and through processes such as privatisation, contracting out, and public-private partnerships (Sablok et al., 2013). Voice is promoted through organisational channels, controlled by management and human resource (HR) divisions while voice was prescribed via unions and employees' industrial actions (Budd et al., 2022). The literature on employee participation revolves around the meanings, forms or structures, the motives or antecedents, the implementation processes, and the effectiveness or outcomes for both employers and employees (Gollan & Xu, 2015). They find that the employer-sponsored perspective is typically less concerned with workers' voice per se and the related issues of social justice and organisational democracy and more focused on the possible business benefits of participation (Gollan & Xu, 2015).

Through time the scholarship and understanding of voice have extended beyond collective voice, grievance and pay/conditions resolutions, and formal settlement processes. As Gollan and Xu (2015) highlight, in Anglo Saxon countries where trade union densities have declined; new industries and new forms of work have emerged; new and virtual workplaces have become prominent; and the range of issues that require voice have extended beyond the workplace, new actors or stakeholders, and social media provide a voice mechanism that operates in concert with and outside of traditional workplace voice mechanisms. They open the industrial relations landscape in terms of scope, processes, issues, and participants. Social media support employee voice in situations where traditional voice mechanisms are limited. In this discussion the focus is on how social media support employee voice in situations where traditional voice mechanisms are limited. The purpose is to bring in the role of social media in giving voice, in strengthening voice, and in building coalitions that support voice.

Employee Voice and Dispute Resolution Under the Australian Industrial Relations System

Employee voice has been codified and regulated within the formal industrial relations system. Within the industrial relations system trade union voice and other employee voice mechanisms are recognised and regulated, especially around dispute management (wherein the disputants are the decision makers) and resolution (wherein a neutral third party is the decision maker) (Sale, 2005, 2016, 2021), wage bargaining, and non-wage conditions. The formal Australian Industrial Relations system is complex and fragmented. It contains elements of collective and individual bargaining, state-mediated dispute settlement processes, an enforceable safety net of minimum employment standards, and a national minimum wage. Over the course of the last 50 years, it has evolved from extensive and negotiated minimum standards that apply across sectors, known as awards, through to negotiated workplace or organisational agreements known as enterprise bargaining. After the establishment of the Australian Federation in 1901, the Federal Parliament enacted the Conciliation and Arbitration Act 1904. This piece of legislation created the Commonwealth Court of Conciliation and Arbitration, which handled compulsory conciliation and compulsory arbitration of labour disputes in Australia (Bray et al., 2018) until 1956 when this Court was split into the Commonwealth Conciliation and Arbitration Commission and the Industrial Court. The Commission was renamed Australian Conciliation and Arbitration Commission through a 1973 amendatory legislation (Conciliation and Arbitration Act 1973). From a base of unionised sectors dominated by male workers in such industries as manufacturing, construction, mining, transport, utilities, and the public sector, the process of voice was mediated through trade unions and endorsed via decisions of industrial tribunals. However, over the past 50 years the trade union density has declined, and enterprise and individual bargaining has replaced collective bargaining. Australia's voluntary collective agreement-making model, which started under the Industrial Relations Reform Act, 1993, shifted the country's industrial relations system away from the formerly dominant arbitral model and is representative of voluntary dispute management modes. There are six federal labour laws that have shaped the industrial relations system of Australia over time, and these will be briefly outlined.

1. Conciliation and Arbitration Act 1904

This law set up the federal system of compulsory conciliation and arbitration, known as the arbitral model (Bray et al., 2018), in Australia. The central institution in industrial relations was the Commonwealth Court of Conciliation and Arbitration. Through this Court, the State was comprehensively and profoundly involved in the creation and enforcement of the rules of the employment relationship (Bray et al., 2018). Under the Australian Constitution, the Federal Parliament was limited to legislating rules about 'Conciliation and arbitration for the prevention and settlement of industrial disputes extending beyond the limits of any one State' (Australian Constitution s 51). Pursuant to this 'conciliation and arbitration power' under the Constitution, the Federal Parliament delegated the authority to make rules of the employment relationship to the Court (Bray et al., 2018, pp. 100–103). That is the reason why this is called 'delegated regulation' (Bray & Stewart, 2013, p. 25). This highly centralised system was markedly collectivist in the sense that trade unions and employer associations played a large role in the industrial relations system (Bray et al., 2018). The Court performed an important and influential function as it determined the conditions of work, including wages, in Australia through 'awards and the sanctioning of collective agreements' as well as the 'structure and operations' of these collective organisations (Bray et al., 2018, pp. 100–103). Under this system, the disputing parties, that is, trade unions and employer associations, were required to undergo compulsory conciliation and if the dispute remained unsettled a Court member or panel 'could arbitrate by making a binding determination' (Bray et al., 2018, pp. 100–103).

2. Industrial Relations Act, 1988

This Act changed the Australian Conciliation and Arbitration Commission into the Australian Industrial Relations Commission (AIRC) (Industrial Relations Act, 1988). Through corporatism, the

Federal Parliament shared its rule-making powers essentially with the trade unions which meant that unions were involved in policy making while employers and their associations generally opted not to participate (Bray et al., 2018). During this time, the government and unions made joint submissions to arbitration by the AIRC, which the latter approved by and large (Bray et al., 2018).

3. Industrial Relations Reform Act, 1993

This legislation replaced centralised conciliation and arbitration with decentralised enterprise bargaining as the dominant means of handling labour disputes (Industrial Relations Reform Act, 1993). From 1993 to 1996, collective agreement-making through the enterprise bargaining model, which involved 'employers and groups of employees, the latter generally (though not necessarily) represented by trade unions', making 'the rules of the employment relationship through a process of bargaining or collective determination', played an extensive role in industrial relations (Bray & Stewart, 2013, pp. 25, 27, 30–33, 48). At the time, union collective agreements constituted around 95% of all agreements as opposed to non-union collective agreements which comprised about 5% (McCallum et al., 2012, p. 142).

4. Workplace Relations Act 1996 and Workplace Relations (Work Choices) Amendment Act 2005

From 1996 to 2007, the government adopted a neoliberal approach, which meant withdrawal of state intervention in industrial relations and fewer restrictions on the operation of market forces, and, therefore, opening of the Australian economy to international competition, privatisation of publicly owned enterprises, deregulation of previously regulated markets, and a new approach to state intervention (Bray et al., 2018, pp. 107–109). Under these two pieces of legislation, the new style of state intervention resulted in lesser power for the AIRC, creation of statutory individual contracts known as Australian Workplace Agreements (AWAs), a greater role for the Federal Parliament through direct regulation under the 'corporations power' set out in the Constitution, reduction of protection to employees and a change in the kind of protection, that is, more individual legal rights, instead of collective rights, and significant restrictions on unions and collective regulation of the employment relationship (Bray et al., 2018, pp. 107–109). Also, non-union collective agreements increased dramatically under the Workplace Relations Act 1996 and Workplace Relations (Work Choices) Amendment Act 2005, reaching more than 50% of all collective agreements from 2006 to 2008 (McCallum et al., 2012, p. 142).

5. Fair Work Act 2009

This law expanded the powers of the Fair Work Commission, which replaced the AIRC, augmented direct regulation by parliament, and set forth some support for unions and collective forms of regulation though quite decentralised at the same time (Bray et al., 2018). While AWAs are no longer recognised under the Fair Work Act, it has connections with Work Choices and neoliberalism, in many ways, and contains more individual rights rather than collective rights (Bray et al., 2018). Under the present Fair Work regime, generally collective agreement-making plays an extensive role in industrial relations (Bray & Stewart, 2013). From 2009 to 2011, union collective agreements comprised around 67% of all agreements while non-union collective agreements consisted of nearly 33% (McCallum et al., 2012, p. 142). Union membership declined (from 41% in 1992) to 12.5% in 2022 (Australian Bureau of Statistics, 2022). This decline in trade unionism is due to several factors. Government policies, privatisations, the proliferation of independent and temporary forms of work, job growth (or conversion) in weakly unionised sectors, and employer pressure to reduce labour costs accompanied by cost externalisation strategies (subcontracting, franchising, labour hire, a 'not-there workforce' model, etc.) are among the dominant factors (Bray et al., 2018; Peetz, 2019). The Labour Government's introduction of company bargaining was aimed strategically at reconnecting the trade union machine, which had been fully absorbed in the arbitration system, with local realities. This was a failure as the unions had neither the resources for local representation (delegate structures) nor the competence or the experience of direct negotiation with employers outside the arbitration system.

Behind the legislative changes in the industrial relations system, there are major structural changes to the workforce and to working arrangements that have supported individualism and reduced collective voice. The structure of the workforce has shifted away from traditional unionised sectors, such as manufacturing and construction, towards the fragmented services sector with low unionisation, such as finance, retailing, and hospitality (Bray et al., 2018). In turn these sectors have insecure employment arrangements—temporary, at call, and irregular (Campbell & Burgess, 2018). New forms of working and workplaces have emerged—mobile and distance working, at home and gig working—in general, the work is insecure and non-unionised as it is often outside the scope of the definition of employment under common law (Munton, 2022). Social media has an important role to play in a legislative and workforce setting that is very different from that which existed at the time of the development of the arbitration model. The male full-time breadwinner model is no longer relevant (Werth, 2011), manufacturing workers are a small minority of the workforce (Australian Bureau of Statistics, 2022), industrial disputes have declined (Bray et al., 2018), and trade union membership has diminished (Australian Bureau of Statistics, 2022; Bray et al., 2018). Trade union activism and voice continue to be important in the industrial and political domain since while trade union density has declined, 'union influence remains broader' through negotiations of enterprise agreements as well as submissions for awards (Forsyth & Stewart, 2016) and national minimum wage rates (Karp, 2022) that apply to workers in workplaces, industries, or the economy.

In summary, there has been a shift away from compulsory dispute management and dispute resolution mechanisms (i.e. conciliation and arbitration) to voluntary dispute management modes (i.e. union and non-union collective agreement-making), which have become the dominant approaches to labour dispute handling under Australia's industrial relations system (Baird et al., 2018; Bray et al., 2018; Sale, 2021). This paradigm shift—largely driven by a neoliberal policy programme with bi-partisan support (Cooper et al., 2009; McAndrew et al., 2018)—has been accompanied by a notable decline in indirect employee or worker voice through unions. There was ongoing decentralisation of the industrial relations system, and legislation was grounded on neoliberalism (Sablok et al., 2013). In this period, employers' strategies were also targeted at sustaining non-unionised workplaces (Cooper et al., 2009). The practice of industrial relations discipline dwindled, taken over by human resource strategies. These strategies are employer-initiated 'friendly forms of voice-substitution mechanisms' (Barnes et al., 2019). Employers packaged these mechanisms as employee participation, encouraging workers to be involved in consultation as a form of empowerment. Van Buren and Greenwood (2008) note that these mechanisms are controlled by employers, concentrated around their benefits, and can be revoked or altered anytime. The system in Australia is complex in that there are several forms of settlement of overlapping terms and conditions of employment, including company agreements, awards, national minimum terms and conditions, and other individual contractual forms. The function of regulation by arbitration remains important, but its scope has been reduced and centralised within the Fair Work Commission and by the development of a code of minimum employment conditions that apply across the workforce (Bray et al., 2018; Isaac, 2018). Albeit appointments to the Commission have been politicised of late, which may affect perceptions about its impartiality or neutrality (Peetz, 2022) and the character of employee voice mechanisms regulated through it. A recent and significant development under the present Labour Government is the Federal Parliament's enactment of the Fair Work Legislation Amendment (Secure Jobs, Better Pay) Act 2022, which aims to, among others, enhance job security and pay by setting limitations on fixed-term contracts and strengthening enterprise bargaining, including multi-enterprise bargaining (Fair Work Legislation Amendment [Secure Jobs, Better Pay] Act 2022). In the next section, we examine the extent to which the paradigm shift we have alluded to, allied to the rise of social media, have aided, or hindered union organisation and activity.

Social Media, Trade Unions, and Voice

In theory at least, social media offers voice to all employees, union, and non-union members; it opens the list of conditions to be bargained through allowing the direct input of employees into the agenda; and it allows for coalitions to emerge between employees, trade unions, and NGOs. It can also assist trade unions in traditional functions such as recruitment, informing membership, and conducting political campaigns. Social media voice can also be a catalyst for change. Employees can use 'closed groups' to create space to neutralise management power (Taylor & Dobbins, 2021). Employees can also engage collectively with other workers to share criticisms of the organisation's behaviour and policy (Thornthwaite, 2013; Walker, 2020). Social media has emerged as an unconventional voice mechanism, notably in the younger cohort of workers. Social media voice is direct and individual by nature. Unlike the traditional employee voice in the workplace, which typically operates in a tiered manner, social media voice is 'multi-directional', capable of 'flattening the organisation' by enabling anyone to voice (even anonymously) outside their manager's dominion (Holland et al., 2019). However, it is also an important tool for management in informing employees and in managing agendas around bargaining and dispute resolution.

In a managerially focussed, HRM-driven commentary generally promoting the voice-enhancing properties of social media, Holland et al. (2019, p. 84) argued that 'with the decline in union voice, not least in the younger workforce, social media is increasingly seen by forward-thinking organisations as a key aspect of voice emerging in the twenty-first century workplace. As such, we would argue that it is an area of employee communication that HR managers should become increasingly aware of and familiar with social media to harness the potential in terms of its immediacy and impact'. However, the same authors go on to comment that

> we believe social media is a resource that has the potential to flatten the organisational hierarchy of voice channels at work. Such a media gives everyone connected the opportunity to have equal input and provides the management an immediate understanding of workplace issues. The reach and immediacy of social media as a form of voice are likely to become key variables in the employment relationship in terms of the degree of genuine employee participation in organisational decisions. As such, management should look to embrace the potential of social media (smart side) in enhancing employee–employer communication rather than fear its "dark-side"

if this new voice is ignored it can become a time bomb waiting to explode (Holland et al., 2019, p. 85).

The 'time bomb' might be union organisation, but some unions have warned their members that social media might be a double-edged sword. The Australian Workers Union (AWU, n.d.), for example, have warned that employees can jeopardise their employment through electronic communications like social media such as Facebook, Twitter, Snapchat, Instagram, and more. Emphasising that members needed to know their rights around social media at their workplace, and if their employer has a social media policy, to be aware of what it says. Social media at work can be seen as part of the emergence of what Zuboff (2019) has described as 'surveillance capitalism'. Huws et al. (2020) argues that these developments have led to a new model of working that she describes as 'logged labour'. Simms et al. (2019, p. 340), on the other hand, argue that social media hold much potential for trade unions, although not yet fully realised—'a digital revolution in the [labour] movement'. Experiments like the TUC's WorkSmart app could provide a connection point with workers who have tended to evade unions, but more needs to be done to develop these. However, in a review of international experience, Carneiro and Costa (2022, pp. 44–45) suggest that experience to date points to a much more limited adoption and effect: 'digital communication technologies and social media present a significant opportunity for trade union renewal as platforms for outreach, advocacy and alliance building … however … there is still a long way to go in terms of fundamentally changing the way that they communicate … Social media behaviour is essentially a reproduction of the offline dynamics of trade unionism that persists on maintaining a vertical relationship with its ranks and restricted relationships outside labour … Effectively any social media strategy will only support trade union renewal if there are structures are in place to convert online engagement into offline mobilization'.

Forsyth (2022), in his book examining the 'Digital Picket Line', takes a detailed look at the future of the labour movement and the impact of social media. Forsyth draws on a paper prepared for the Australian Trade Union Institute (ATUI) by Moore and Walton (2020), which highlighted the imperative of unions 'bridg[ing] an ever-widening generational divide' between baby boomers and the digital natives of 'Generation Z'. Moore and Walton recommended that unions tailor specific offerings to attract younger workers who crave convenience, impact, and personalisation and 'provide a home for every worker' including the workforce engaged in insecure work. This would require a shift from 'a traditional service provider operational model' to various 'community platform operating models'. The ACTU Union Innovation Hub was set up to support unions undertaking these and other kinds of transformation through digital innovation. Forsyth pointed out that transformation was also a major theme of Coatman's (2020) report for the Trade Union Congress (TUC), examining the lessons of its WorkSmart project. WorkSmart was part of a major campaign to rebuild the UK's unions undertaken by the TUC in 2018. The TUC sought to address 'a gap in the union offer' in failing to make available 'the kind of digital experiences young people are used to', like Netflix and Spotify, contributing to the low level of membership among those aged 20–29. Through in-depth consultation with younger workers, the TUC developed the WorkSmart app, providing a personalised, mobile-first experience, with bite-size content, that's ready when workers are. Forsyth concludes with a consideration of unions exploring how they can maximise technology to reach new groups of workers: 'The future for unions is digital: in terms of what a union looks like, in the ways it communicates with and provides access to workers and in the tactics it deploys. At the same time, it must be seen that digital tools are simply new ways of forging connections between workers – connections that, in the past, were formed through union halls, workers' clubs, case del popolo and workers' education organisations like Mechanics Institutes, community and sporting groups and churches. As in the past, the next step—after workers are brought together digitally or otherwise—is the decision to take collective action together. Forsyth concludes that combining technology with the best traditions of unionism is critical to the survival of the labour movement' (Forsyth, 2022, p. 208).

In 2022 Forsyth gave an interview to the Chifley Research Centre about his book, in which he argued that 'we must demonstrate the value of collective workplace power for the vast proportion of workers who've been conditioned to believe that unions aren't relevant to their situation—and young workers who don't really know what a union is or have grown up in a very individualistic world' (Chifley Research Centre, 2022, p. 3). There are many strategies unions can adopt to overcome past legislation that restricts recruitment and action, and to address new developments in the workforce and workplace. Examples of action include digital union forms (e.g. Hospo Voice/United Workers Union (UWU), Game Workers Unite/Professionals Australia, Hair Stylists Australia/AWU) and tiered membership structures, so workers can engage in ways that suit them and what they can afford financially. Here established unions must play an 'incubator' role by investing in new membership models, like Hospo Voice, and see whether, after a few years, enough young hospitality workers have seen the benefits of collective action in fighting back against exploitation, so they move from a lower level of affiliation through an app to become full UWU members.

Hospo Voice attracted much attention as one of the first organisational attempts by a major Australian union to harness social media in attempting to reach out to workers in the hospitality sector (Petterson, 2021). Formed by the UWU in 2018 it was absorbed into the full union structure in 2022. Hospo Voice has built a set of tools largely on the Nation Builder platform which acts as the starting point in connecting with workers and potential volunteers and activists. In a report 'celebrating' the four years of Hospo Voice's existence the UWU (2022) argued that this was 'Australia's first digital union', trialling a union purpose built for hospo workers: Our quest: to turn the tables on wage theft, to ignite a powerful movement through hard-hitting digital campaigns, and to pioneer cutting-edge digital tools like Mobilise and our Fair Plate website that help workers win, no matter how big or small your workplace is. Hospo Voice was a union in your pocket, with smart digital tools to help you stand up for your rights. And we brought workers together online and with powerful campaigns to win back stolen wages across employers and change the hospitality industry for good. Over 2500 workers had joined Hospo Voice by 2022. In an interview with CallHub, early in the new union's existence, Petterson (2021), campaigns director at United Voice, claimed that the union had signed up 500 new members in the first six months. Within Hospo Voice workers have access to a suite to digital tools that allow them to report, and track pay and conditions, these include:

Fair Plate: Using this tool, hospitality workers can rate their bosses and review their workplace by sharing their experiences so that others get an inside view before they work there.

Record My Hours: Workers can record their working hours and the breaks they've taken to confirm if their pay corresponds with the hours they've put in. Pay Checker: This tool lets workers find out the right pay rate for the work they do. Harassment Diary: People can record incidents where they've been bullied and harassed so that they can act against unlawful behaviour. When a person signs up on Hospo Voice to use these tools or takes an action such as reviewing an employer, a wealth of data gets created which is used to nurture each worker through conversations and offline activities. The union then contacts its activists remotely (usually via Zoom) every week and gives them a list of contacts whom they're supposed to talk to. These activists then use peer-to-peer texting to contact the workers who have been assigned to them. Their aim here is to build relationships with workers. They engage in one-on-one conversations with them, trying to find out their workplace issues, the bad experiences they've had with their bosses, and what they'd like to change about their industry. Through these peer-to-peer conversations, these activists inform them of the steps they can take to protect their rights. They then try to get workers to sign up to be a union member and be more active in their local community by joining their local Facebook groups (UWU, 2022). Hospo Voice was not without its critics. Some member/activists argued that the introduction of the tiered membership, which was introduced at least partly to offset a budget shortfall, claiming that it would simply reinforce pre-existing inequality in the industry. The organisation was criticised for existing mostly as a source of medial releases and not very useful apps (Espejo, 2021). Hospo Voice was focussed on workers in the hospitality sector. More attention has tended to be paid to the gig economy. Forsyth (2022) provided an overview of the gig economy. He highlighted the construction by platforms globally of a narrative of freedom and flexible work, in contrast to the reality of widespread exploitation of gig workers through the imposition of presumed self-employed status. Forsyth then considered the roles increasingly being played by unions, and self-organised worker collectives, in mobilising rideshare drivers and food delivery workers to contest their precarity: 'This study has also examined the use of technology by workers and unions to contest exploitation and develop collective strength in the gig economy. The platforms have sold technology to workers as a liberating force (the flexibility, "be your own boss" trope), then utilised their apps to exercise high levels of control (algorithmic allocation of work, monitoring, customer ratings). Yet gig workers have been able to turn this automated oppression back on the platforms, using their smartphones to organise action and fight back through WhatsApp and Facebook groups' (Forsyth, 2022, p. 207). According to Chen (2019) the key to organising in the platform economy is to reclaim the platform as a political arena and organising asset. This is aided by the emergence of what has been described as 'platform antagonism'. Worker's sense of being tethered to the app, subjected to alienating and degraded work in a climate of isolation and anxiety, can become the basis of a unique form of class consciousness—platform antagonism. In the case of Uber drives, although their dependency on the app was alienating, they managed to create vibrant online communities which served as safe places for digital shoptalk and social support. 'The angst of algorithmic oppression spurs workers, quite literally, to rage against the machine. … The community of structures antagonism fosters a culture of quiet resistance, positioned not against a single employer, but a common platform' (Chen, 2019, p. 132). In the next section, we develop our analysis of organisation and activity outside of formal industrial relations structures.

Coalitions, Voice, and Political Action

An emerging trend in the publicising, analysis, and settlement of workplace issues has been that the processes have largely occurred outside of industrial relations institutions and, to a certain extent, are being driven by new actors through social media (Chifley Research Centre, 2022; Holland et al., 2019). Trade unions have a central role to play as advocates for employees and for developing the political discourse towards policy development. In the two cases that are outlined, the process unfolded as follows: first, the workplace issue/problem is identified; second, it is publicised via traditional and social media channels; third, political lobbying results in the establishment of a public inquiry into the workplace issue; fourth, the public inquiry suggests recommendations to introduce new legislation or amend existing legislation to address the workplace issue. Within this process social media is important in disseminating information, in lobbying politicians, and in organising submissions to public inquiries such as the ones that are outlined below. Since all the cases are linked to the workplace, traditional actors, employers, and trade unions are involved, but the stakeholders involved extends beyond the traditional actors to take in groups that have a direct interest or expertise in the workplace issue that is being addressed (Munton, 2022). These groups can be professionals such as health and community workers and NGOs representing families, children, and local communities. Social media supports an opening up of the public debate around workplace issues, giving voice to non-unionised workers and supporting new actors entering in the industrial relations arena.

The two cases to be discussed are as follows. The first concerns the working conditions of fly-in fly-out (FIFO) (long-distance commuting) workers in the Western Australian resources sector. The issue that emerged was the effect of the long-distance commuting, long work shifts, and hazardous work conditions of the mental health of employees. The second case was linked to the conditions of gig workers, especially in food delivery services, specifically their pay and conditions of employment, especially relative to national employment standards. Fly-in and fly-out employment (FIFO) has become the dominant employment arrangement in the Western Australian mining sector (House of Representatives, 2013). Workers fly in for set shifts at the mining sites and then return to their homes in between shifts. The commutes are typically several thousand kilometres each way. While remote working is not new, the fly-in fly-out model on the scale that it was used was new. Through time problems linked to employee and family well-being emerged as workers experienced depression as a result of isolation and loneliness; fatigue as a result of the long and demanding shifts; and family disruption as a result of absence from families and an inability to fit back in with families and communities (Albrecht & Anglim, 2018; Parker et al., 2018). Manifestations of the pressure and problems associated with FIFO work included substance and alcohol abuse, anti-social behaviour, eating disorders, and family break-down (Parker et al., 2018; Alfrey et al., 2018). Then the ultimate manifestation of employee distress, work-related suicides, began to be reported ABC News (2014). Because of the publicity and the campaigns mounted by trade unions, family and community groups, and health professionals, a public inquiry into the mental health of FIFO workers was conducted by the Western Australia legislative assembly (Jacobs, 2015). That report led to a further round of public consultations and the development of a code of practice that required resource companies to support the mental health of employees (Department of Mines, Industry Regulation, and Safety, 2019). The code was then to be linked to existing workplace occupational health and safety legislation as part of the responsibilities and duty of care of employers towards employees (Department of Mines, Industry Regulation, and Safety, 2019).

The FIFO case is instructive for several reasons. First, for its scale it was a largely untested work model. Second, the campaign was industry directed, not confined to individual companies and workplaces. Third, many stakeholders emerged in publicising the problems of FIFO work and providing evidence to the public inquiries. Fourth, coalition of interest across professions and community groups were able to highlight the breadth and depth of the issues to be addressed and remedied. In this process of publicising, understanding, and taking remedial action, social media was important for the dissemination of information, for advocacy, and for lobbying the legislators. Social media provides presence, legitimacy, and identity; it assists in coalition formation; and it overcomes the power imbalances that are present where there are individual employee grievances or grievances at a particular workplace. Direct and indirect voice is enhanced, and stakeholders who may have been excluded from the industrial relations framework are given voice through public inquiries to exercise professional advice or to give voice to those impacted upon by FIFO working arrangements such as families and local communities where FIFO work takes place or FIFO workers live (House of Reps, 2013; Jacobs, 2015).

The second case involves gig work, a form of work associated with ICT developments and the online economy (Ayentimi et al., 2022). As a technologically mediated form of work, it is new, but in terms of its conditions of work—unregulated, self-employed, non-unionised, irregular—it draws on a long traditional of informal, at call, and unprotected employment arrangements (Stanford, 2017). Since it is outside of formal regulatory arrangements and mediated by online platforms, it is difficult to track. There are two forms of gig work: first, the online work such as data entry, data analysis, freelancing, crowdsourcing; second, physical gig work that is mediated through a platform in such activities as food delivery, taxi services, and household garden services (Ayentimi et al., 2022). It is difficult to estimate the number of gig workers, but the evidence suggest that it is growing in Australia, the conditions and pay of employment do not meet minimum standards, and there are personal risk factors associated with physical gig work from traffic accidents to assaults (Industrial Relations Victoria, 2020). Research in advanced economies has highlighted how gig work has eroded employment conditions, undermined employment regulatory norms, and removed voice mechanisms from workers through classifying them as self-employed contractors (de Stefano, 2016; de Ruyter et al., 2019; Stewart & Stanford, 2017). There has also been push back by workers who feel that gig work takes their jobs and undermines their conditions—such as in the case of the taxi industry protests (Reuters News, 2018).

Once again, the innovation and rapid development of the gig industry has highlighted the inadequacies of the labour regulatory system to deal with workers whose status is ambiguous, whose workplace is not fixed, who are not unionised or employed under an industrial agreement, and whose employer is also ambiguous (de Ruyter et al., 2019). A similar path of publicity and exposure developed as in the previous case. Important catalysts included the death of delivery workers in traffic accidents, assaults, underpayment, and unrealistic timetables that contributed to stress and accidents (Goods et al., 2019; Kaine & Josserand, 2019). Coalitions of trade unions and NGOs emerged to lobby for and negotiate for improved conditions and for recognition of employee status and access to minimum employment standards. Again, public inquiries into gig work followed that highlighted the precarious and exploitative nature of gig wok arrangements and the absence of minimum employment standards (Industrial Relations Victoria, 2020). Social media has been important in organising gig workers, disseminating their stories, lobbying, providing input to public inquiries, and developing coalitions among unions. Ironically, the ICT processes that support gig work also support gig workers in exchanging information, lobbying, and mobilising and generating voice (Corporaal, 2017; Johnston & Land-Kazlauskas, 2018; Ford & Honan, 2019). Employee voice and collective action are supported by social media and community networks (Ford & Honan, 2019). Social networking platforms both support information sharing, coalition development, union recruitment, and community action (Ayentimi et al., 2022; Wood et al., 2018). There was a public inquiry into online working in the state of Victoria (Industrial Relations Victoria, 2020). That inquiry received submissions from platform owners, gig workers, trade unions, and NGOs. Of note were submissions from collectives of gig workers in the food delivery services sector (Industrial Relations Victoria, 2020). The inquiry recommended that the status of gig workers be regularised, that their protections be increased, and that formal support and dispute resolution mechanisms be put in place. Overall, there were 20 recommendations, all of which were accepted by the Victorian Government. Federal and state occupational and health legislation has been strengthened to provide for a duty of care by employers to protect gig workers of unsafe conditions in the performance of their work (Safe Work Australia, 2021). Subsequently the federal government has indicated that it will amend national industrial relations legislation to improve and protect the employment conditions of gig workers (Ziffer, 2022).

With these cases and others such as the enforced working from home arrangements associated with the COVID-19 lockdown (ACTU, 2020; Dayaram & Burgess, 2021), there have been significant changes in working arrangements that do not fit within a regulatory model based on regular employee-based employment and presumed employment model supported by conditions that are being undermined by a combination of ICT, employer labour use strategies, the weakening position of organised labour, and the eroded system of labour regulation. Managing crisis has meant that governments have been forced to accommodate these changes and to impose remedial labour regulations to in part modernise labour regulations as the gaps in the existing regulations become apparent.

Conclusion

The Australian industrial relations system is complex and has undergone significant changes with the context of a neoliberal policy agenda that has supported workplace and individual bargaining, limited the ability of trade unions to organise and take industrial action, and strengthened employer prerogatives (Baird et al., 2018; McAndrew et al., 2018). While trade union voice has been diminished as manifested by a declining union density and by regulations over union activity, new technology and social media provides an avenue for trade unions to organise, recruit, and form coalitions of interest to address emerging workplace challenges (Carneiro & Costa, 2022). Social media gives voice to the non-unionised, the invisible, and those without bargaining power the potential to collectivise, organise, and be heard (Anwar & Graham, 2020). Coalition building and political activism are enhanced and supported through social media campaigns that encompass the workplace but can be extended to address wider issues such as sustainability and social justice, such as in the case of the Rana Plaza building collapse in Bangladesh and the subsequent activism for an improvement in the employment and safety conditions of garment workers (ILO, 2015). The case studies identified highlight how social media through the congruence of interests across different stakeholders can influence public opinion and eventually result in legislative change. In the cases presented here the process was activated by the failure of the regulatory system to protect workers, provide mechanisms for voice, or support minimum employment standards.

References

ABC News. (2014). *Nine FIFO suicides in 12 months leads to call for investigation*. Ultimo, New South Wales. Australian Broadcasting Corporation (ABC). http://www.abc.net.au/7.30/content/2014/s4070542.htm

Albrecht, S., & Anglim, J. (2018). Employee engagement and emotional exhaustion of fly-in-fly-out workers: A diary study. *Australian Journal of Psychology, 70*(1), 66–75.

Alfrey, K.-L., Vandelanotte, C., Gardner, B., & Rebar, A. (2018). Mental health and well-being concerns of fly-in fly-out workers and their partners in Australia: A qualitative study. *BMJ Open*. https://doi.org/10.1136/bmjopen-2017-019516

Anwar, M. A., & Graham, M. (2020). Hidden transcripts of the gig economy: Labour agency and the new art of resistance among African gig workers. *EPA: Economy and Space, 52*(7), 1269–1291.

Australian Bureau of Statistics. (2022). Trade union membership [Data set]. https://www.abs.gov.au/statistics/labour/earnings-and-working-conditions/trade-union-membership/latest-release

Australian Constitution s 51

Australian Council of Trade Unions (ACTU). (2020). *Working from home report*. ACTU, Melbourne.

Australian Workers Union (AWU). (n.d.). *Social media in the workplace*. https://www.awu.net.au/campaigns

Ayentimi, D. T., Abadi, H. A., & Burgess, J. (2022). Decent gig work in Sub Sahara Africa? *Journal of Industrial Relations*. https://doi.org/10.1177/00221856221111693

Baird, M., Westcott, M., & Constantin, V. (2018). Changing terrain: Defining the contemporary workplace and workforce in Australia. In J. Parker & M. Baird (Eds.), *The big issues in employment, HR management, and employment relations in Australasia* (2nd ed., pp. 23–50). Wolters Kluwer.

Barnes, A., Balnave, N., Thornthwaite, L., & Manning, B. (2019). Social media: Union communication and member voice. In P. Holland, J. Teicher, & J. Donaghey (Eds.), *Employee voice at work* (pp. 91–111). Springer.

Barry, M., Dundon, T., & Wilkinson, A. (2018). Employee voice: Conceptualisations, meanings, limitations, and possible integration. In A. Wilkinson, T. Dundon, J. Donaghey, & A. J. S. Convin (Eds.), *The Routledge companion to employment relations* (pp. 251–256). Routledge.

Bogg, A., & Novitz, T. A. (2014). The purposes and techniques of voice: Prospects for continuity and change. In *Voices at Work: Continuity and change in the common law world* (pp. 3–31). Oxford University Press.

Bool-Sale, A., & Sale, J. (2010). Turnover and voice in Philippine call centres. *Philippine Journal of Labour and Industrial Relations, 30*(1–2), 1–17.

Bray, M., & Stewart, A. (2013). What is distinctive about the Fair Work regime? *Australian Journal of Labour Law, 26*(1), 20–49.

Bray, M., Waring, P., Cooper, R., & Macneil, J. (2018). *Employment relations: Theory and practice* (4th ed.). McGraw-Hill Education.

Budd, J. W., Gollan, P. J., & Wilkinson, A. (2010). New approaches to employee voice and participation in organisations. *Human Relations, 63*(3), 303–310.

Budd, J. W., Johnstone, S., & Lamare, J. R. (2022). Never 'one-size-fits-all': Mick Marchington's unique voice on voice, from micro-level informality to macro-level turbulence. *Human Resource Management Journal.* https://doi.org/10.1111/1748-8583.12451

Campbell, I., & Burgess, J. (2018). Patchy progress? Two decades of research on precariousness and precarious work in Australia. *Labour and Industry, 28*(1), 48–67.

Carneiro, B., & Costa, B. (2022). Digital unionism as a renewal strategy? *Journal of Industrial Relations, 64*(1), 26–51.

Chen, M. (2019). A new world of workers. In L. Panitch & G. Albo (Eds.), *Socialist Register 2020.* Merlin Press.

Chifley Research Centre. (2022). The digital picket line. Chifley.org.au.

Chon, M. G., Kim, J. N., & Kim, C. S. (2021). Conceptualizing allegiant communication behaviour: A cross-national study of employees' self-orchestration of voice and silence. *Public Relations Review, 47*(4), 102093.

Commonwealth of Australia. (2004). *Occupational, Health, and Safety Act.* Canberra. Conciliation and Arbitration Act 1973.

Cooper, R., Ellem, B., Briggs, C., & Van Den Broek, D. (2009). Anti-unionism, employer strategy, and the Australian state, 1996–2005. *Labour Studies Journal, 34*(3), 339–362.

Corporaal, G. F. (2017, April 18) Organising freelancers in the platform economy: Part one, *OpenDemocracy.* https://www.opendemocracy.net/beyond-slavery/greetje-gretta-f-corporaal/gig/organising-freelancers-in-platform-economy-part-one

Cullinane, N., & Donaghey, J. (2020). Employee silence. In A. Wilkinson, J. Donaghey, T. Dundon, & R. B. Freeman (Eds.), *Handbook of research on employee voice* (pp. 474–485). Edward Elgar Publishing.

Dayaram, K., & Burgess, J. (2021). Regulatory challenges facing remote working in Australia. In D. Wheatley, I. Hardill, & S. Buglass (Eds.), *Handbook of research on remote work and worker well-being in the post-COVID-19 era* (pp. 202–219). IGI Global.

De Ruyter, A., Browne, M., & Burgess, J. (2019). Gig work and the Fourth Industrial Revolution: Conceptual and regulatory challenges. *Journal of International Affairs, 72*(1), 37–50.

De Stefano, V. (2016). The rise of the just-in-time workforce: On demand work, crowdwork and labour protection in the gig-economy. *Comparative Labour Law & Policy Journal, 37*, 471–504.

Department of Mines, Industry Regulation and Safety. (2019). *Mentally healthy workplaces for fly-in fly-out (FIFO) workers in the resources and construction sectors*. WA Government, Perth.

Sablok, G., Bartram, T., Stanton, P., Burgess, J., & McDonnell, A. (2013). The impact of union presence and strategic human resource management on employee voice in multinational enterprises in Australia. *Journal of Industrial Relations, 55*(4), 621–639.

Thornthwaite, L. (2013). Social media, unfair dismissal and the regulation of employees' conduct outside work. *Australian Journal of Labour Law, 26*(2), 164–184.

Fair Work Legislation Amendment (Secure Jobs, Better Pay) Act 2022

Espejo, D. (2021). *Hospitality workers petition against tiered union membership*. Honi Soit July 7 2021.

Ford, M., & Honan, V. (2019). The limits of mutual aid: Emerging forms of collectively among app-based transport workers in Indonesia. *Journal of Industrial Relations, 61*(4), 528–548.

Forsyth, A. (2022). *The future of unions and worker representation*. Hart Publishing.

Forsyth, A., & Stewart, A. (2016). Swimming against the tide: New challenges for unions under Australian labour law. *Comparative Labour Law and Policy Journal, 38*(1), 99–121.

Freeman, R. B., & Medoff, J. L. (1984). Trade unions and productivity: Some new evidence on an old issue. *The Annals of the American Academy of Political and Social Science, 473*(1), 149–164.

Gans, R., & Zhan, M. (2022). A story about speaking up: Mediation effects of narrative. Persuasion on organizational voice intentions. *International Journal of Business Communication*. 23294884221091275.

Gollan, P. J., & Xu, Y. (2015). Re-engagement with the employee participation debate: Beyond the case of contested and captured terrain. *Work, Employment and Society, 29*(2), NP1–NP13.

Goods, C., Veen, A., & Barratt, T. (2019). "Is your gig any good?" Analysing job quality in the Australian platform-based food-delivery sector. *Journal of Industrial Relations, 61*(4), 502–527.

Heaphy, E., Lilius, J., & Feldman, E. (2022). Moved to speak up: How prosocial emotions influence the employee voice process. *Human Relations, 75*(6), 1113–1139.

Hirschman, A. (1970). *Exit, voice, and loyalty: Responses to decline in firms, organisations, and states.* Harvard University Press.

Holland, P., Pyman, A., Cooper, B. K., & Teicher, J. (2011). Employee voice and job satisfaction in Australia: The centrality of direct voice. *Human Resource Management, 50*(1), 95–111.

Holland, P., Cooper, B., & Hecker, R. (2019). Social media at work: A new form of employee voice? In *Employee voice at work* (pp. 73–89). Springer.

House of Representatives Standing Committee on Regional Australia. (2013). *Cancer of the bush or salvation for our cities?* Parliament of the Commonwealth of Australia, Canberra.

Huws, U., Spencer, N., & Syrdal, D. (2020). Online, on call: The spread of digitally inclusive leadership. *Journal of Hospitality and Tourism Research, 45*(6), 1092–1113.

Industrial Relations Act. (1988).

Industrial Relations Reform Act. (1993).

Industrial Relations Victoria. (2020). *Report of the inquiry into the on-demand workforce.* Victorian Government, Melbourne.

International Labour Organization. (2015). Bangladesh Rana Plaza compensation scheme: Technical report on the scheme design and operationalisation, and lessons learnt. www.ilo.org/wcmsp5/groups/public/%2D%2D-ed_protect/%2D%2D-soc_sec/documents/ publication/wcms_431795.pdf.

Isaac, J. (2018). Why are Australian wages lagging and what can be done about it? *The Australian Economic Review, 51*(2), 175–190.

Jacobs, G. G. (2015). *The impact of FIFO work practices on mental health: Final report.* Education and Health Standing Committee [ESHC]. Perth, Western Australia Legislative Assembly Parliament of Western Australia.

Johnston, H., & Land-Kazlauskas, C. (2018). *Organising on-demand: Representation, voice, and collective bargaining in the gig economy.* Conditions of Work and Employment Series No 94. International Labour Office.

Johnstone, S., & Ackers, P. (2015). *Finding a voice at work?: New perspectives on employment relations.* OUP Oxford.

Jolly, P. M., & Lee, L. (2020). Silence is not golden: Motivating employee voice through inclusive leadership. *Journal of Hospitality & Tourism Research, 45*(6), 1092–1113.

Kaine, S., & Josserand, E. (2019). The organisation and experience of work in the gig economy. *Journal of Industrial Relations, 61*(4), 479–501.

Karp, P. (2022, March 31). Australia's minimum wage should be raised by 5% to counter inflation and living costs, unions say. *The Guardian*. https://www.theguardian.com/australia-news/2022/mar/31/australias-minimum-wage-should-be-raised-by-5-to-counter-inflation-and-living-costs-unions-say

Kim, H., & Kiura, M. (2020). The influences of social status and organizational justice on employee voice: A case of customer care workers. *International Journal of Business Communication*. https://doi.org/10.1177/2329488420969776

Liu, W., Song, Z., Li, X., & Liao, Z. (2017). Why and when leaders' affective states influence employee upward voice. *Academy of Management Journal, 60*(1), 238–263.

Machin, S., & Wood, S. (2005). Human resource management as a substitute for trade unions in British workplaces. *Industrial and Labour Relations Review, 58*(2), 201–218.

Mantouvalou, V. (2014). Democratic theory and voices at work. In A. Bogg & T. Novitz (Eds.), *Voices at work: Continuity and change in the common law world* (pp. 214–231). Oxford University Press.

McAndrew, I., Edgar, F., & Jerrard, M. (2018). Human resource management and employee relations paradigms in Australia and New Zealand. In J. Parker & M. Baird (Eds.), *The big issues in employment, HR management, and employment relations in Australasia* (2nd ed., pp. 1–19). Wolters Kluwer.

McCallum, R., Moore, M., & Edwards, J. (2012). *Towards more productive and equitable workplaces: An evaluation of the fair work legislation*. Department of Employment and Workplace Relations. https://www.dewr.gov.au/workplace-relations-australia/resources/towards-more-productive-and-equitable-workplaces-evaluation-fair-work-legislation-final-report

McMillan, K. (2016). Politics of change: The discourses that inform organisational change and their capacity to silence. *Nursing Inquiry, 23*(3), 223–231.

Michelson, G., Jamieson, S., & Burgess, J. (2008). *New employment actors: Developments from Australia*. Peter Lang.

Moore, B., & Walton, C. (2020). *Rise! Empowering Australian workers through the collective spirit and collaborative energy of unions*. ACTU/Strategic Membership Solutions.

Morrison, E. W. (2014). Employee voice and silence. *The Annual Review of Organizational Psychology and Organizational Behavior, 1*, 173–197.

Munton, J. R. (2022). The participants. In J. Fleming (Ed.), *A new work relations architecture—The AIER model for the future of work* (pp. 168–182). Hardie Grant Books.

Nicholson, D., Pekarek, A., & Gahan, P. (2017). Unions and collective bargaining in Australia in 2016. *Journal of Industrial Relations, 59*(3), 305–322.

Parker, S., Fruhen, L., Burton, C., McQuade, S., Loveny, J., Griffin, M., Page, A., Chikritzhs, T., Crock, S., Jorritsma, K., & Esmond, J. (2018). Impact of FIFO work arrangements on the mental health and wellbeing of FIFO workers. School of Psychological Science Social Work School of Allied Health UWA Business School, Office of DVC Research.

Peetz, D. (2019). *The realities and futures of work*. ANU Press.

Peetz, D. (2022). Administrative reform and the institutional framework. In J. Fleming (Ed.), *A new work relations architecture—The AIER model for the future of work* (pp. 32–51). Hardie Grant Books.

Petterson, T. (2021). Case study: HospoVoice. https://callhub.io.hospo-voice

Reuters News. (2018). Taxi drivers protest against Uber 'invasion' in Greece, March 6. https://www.reuters.com/...protests...uber/taxi-drivers-protest-against-uber-invasion-in-gr...

Safe Work Australia. (2021). Managing risks of food delivery riders. https://www.safeworkaustralia.gov.au/sites/default/files/2021-12/Gig%20Riders%20%20Riders%20fact%20sheet_Dec21_0.pdf

Sale, J. (2005). Labour dispute settlement and decision making. *Philippine Journal of Labour and Industrial Relations, 25*(1&2), 13–43.

Sale, J. (2016). Labour dispute management and resolution. In V. Binghay (Ed.), *Labour and industrial relations in The Philippines: A reader* (pp. 77–107). University of the Philippines.

Sale, J. (2021). *Harmonisation of ASEAN labour laws on disputes settlement: The Philippines and Malaysia as case studies* [PhD thesis, The University of Newcastle]. NOVA open access repository. http://hdl.handle.net/1959.13/1430275

Simms, M., Holgate, J., & Roper, C. (2019). The TUC 150 years on. *Employee Relations, 41*(2), 331–343.

Stanford, J. (2017). The resurgence of gig work: Historical and theoretical perspectives. *The Economic and Labour Relations Review, 28*(3), 382–401.

Stewart, A., & Stanford, J. (2017). Regulating work in the gig economy: What are the options? *The Economic and Labour Relations Review, 28*(3), 420–437.

Taylor, C., & Dobbins, T. (2021). Social media: A (new) contested terrain between sousveillance and surveillance in the digital workplace. *New Technology, Work and Employment, 36*(3), 263–284.

UWU. (2022). *Goodbye HospoVoice. Hello UWU hospitality.* United Workers Union.

Van Buren, H. J., & Greenwood, M. (2008). Enhancing employee voice: Are voluntary employer–employee partnerships enough? *Journal of Business Ethics, 81*(1), 209–221.

Van Gramberg, B. V., Teicher, J., Bamber, G. J., & Cooper, B. (2019). Employee voice, intention to quit, and conflict resolution: Evidence from Australia. *ILR Review, 73*(2), 393–410.

Walker, M. (2020). Successful social media resistance: Implications for employee voice. *Labour and Industry, 30*(2), 174–184.

Werth, S. (2011). Survival of the male breadwinner. *Hecate, 37*(1), 145–156.

Wood, A. J., Lehdonvirta, V., & Graham, M. (2018). Workers of the Internet unite? Online freelancer organisation among remote gig economy workers in six Asian and African countries. *New Technology, Work and Employment, 33*(2), 95–112.

Yeoman, R. (2014). *Meaningful work and workplace democracy: A philosophy of work and a politics of meaningfulness.* Palgrave Macmillan.

Ziffer, D. (2022). Gig economy and 'Uberisation' overhaul as Albanese government preps laws to change employment. *ABC News.* https://www.abc.net.au/news/2022-09-19/gig-economy-set-for-shake-up-in-employment-laws/101448664

Zuboff, S. (2019). *The age of surveillance capitalism.* Profile Books.

Index

T. Ajibade Adisa et al. (eds.), *Employee Voice in the Global North*,
https://doi.org/10.1007/978-3-031-31123-9

The manufacturer's authorised representative in the EU is Springer Nature Customer Service Centre GmbH, Europaplatz 3, 69115 Heidelberg, Germany. If you have any concerns regarding our products, please contact ProductSafety@springernature.com

Printed and bound by CPI Group (UK) Ltd, Croydon, CR0 4YY
01/10/2026
02225834-0001